YES, MR BRONSON

MEMOIRS OF A BUM ACTOR

Second Edition

MICHAEL SHEARD

SUMMERSDALE

First published 1997
Second edition published 1997

Summersdale Publishers
46 West Street
Chichester
West Sussex
PO19 1RP
UK

A CIP Catalogue Record for this book is available from the British Library.

Printed and bound in Great Britain.

ISBN 1 84024 007 5

Cover photo courtesy of BBC Picture Library.

Photos from *The Empire Strikes Back* and *Indiana Jones and the Last Crusade* courtesy of George Lucas and Lucasfilm.

These jottings are dedicated of course to Ros Sheard - 'Dearly Beloved' - for being my missis and for always being there. I couldn't have done it without her.

I'd also like to thank my chum Roger Moore for writing me such a smashing Foreword.

M.J. Trow (Mei), Alf Paice, Chris Gardner, and everyone at Summersdale Publishers, particularly my editor, Robert Bircher, for all their help and encouragement.

Indeed, everybody I've met and worked with for helping to make it such a fantastically great first thirty years.

Foreword

I once congratulated Noël Coward on his ability to speak almost non-stop for nearly twenty-four hours, without repeating himself. He said that it was very simple when one spoke about oneself, a subject which one should know, of course.

There is more to it than that, however. I once started writing about myself, but after fifteen thousand words I was still only sixteen. Then the diskette, which was in my hand baggage, was stolen at Geneva airport and I have not had the heart to go back to the keyboard.

Michael Sheard has gone further than sixteen, I'm pleased to say. He's taken the subject he knows best and written THE BOOK with warmth and humour, and given us an enthralling insight into the nuts and bolts of the Business. Bravo, Michael: now let's have THE NOVEL. Oh, by the way, do ask for me on your next film!

Roger Moore
24th January 1997

Postscript for the Second Edition

Congratulations on reaching your second edition before the first has hit the shops. Even Noël didn't do that!

19th June 1997

Prologue

I was interviewed by the press again the other day. This rather strange lady arranged to meet me for lunch and no sooner had we sat down with the menus than she looked me straight in the eye and said, 'I was told you're famous; are you?' Before I could even begin to reply she continued, 'Oh dear, oh dear. Why I'm sent on these fools' errands I'll never know. Such a stupid waste of time. You don't even dress like an actor.'

I'd had enough. If she didn't want to interview me, fine, but my time was valuable too. I pointed out that I had, in fact, appeared in hundreds of television productions and over thirty-five feature films with more famous people than I could remember. Stars like Larry Olivier, Stef Powers, Rog Moore, and Peg Ashcroft - OK, I was showing off, but these people were my friends and I used their usual, affectionate names. Peggy Ashcroft, dammit, had insisted that everyone called her Peg, rather than Dame Peggy, or Ma'am.

But the lady reporter picked up on it straight away. 'Oh no,' she said, 'not Larry and Peg. I don't believe it.' Then she added with a deal of disgust and scorn, 'I never watch the minor media, of course, television or films, you obviously do things differently there. Who am I to judge?'

Who indeed! But the damage had been done. When the article came out the dear lady had hung the whole thing on 'Larry and Peg' and completely missed the point that the actor is really no different from anyone else. He's lucky in that he works in a profession he loves, one in which all thespians (another great word the lady hated), be they big names or small are equal. 'When it's your turn to fill the screen, son, you are the star.' That was said to me by John - Duke - Wayne, by the way.

So lady reporter, please take note that the following pages are full of 'lovely' people, 'great' chums, and even 'super' thesps.

There are lots of Tonys, a number of Dons, an Ernie or two, a smattering of Kennys, and even a Telly. I call people by whatever handle I choose, and I'll only call someone a shit if they were in my opinion of that ilk. OK?

My Dearly Beloved is sure to tell me that I'm protesting too much but just for once I don't care. I'm not going to have my wonderful profession sneered at, particularly by a lady reporter who doesn't even watch telly or go to the movies, and who is bound to be called Cub or, perish the thought, even Ace by her friends.

She may not read this book. I hope and trust that you enjoy it.

Michael Sheard.
Ryde. Isle of Wight.

I

It was Lord Laurence Olivier no less who was kind enough to class us all as bums and vagabonds, so I always had a title for my book. But it wasn't until I changed agents recently and my new agent classed me as a known face with no name and urged me to put pen to paper - or rather floppy disc to word processor - that I thought I might finally have a go.

Before, however, I talk about all the great and famous people I've met and worked with, I think I should spend a little time telling you how I began in this super, crazy, wonderful, sometimes heartbreaking, business of ours.

And my starting point is...*The Wooden Horse*. I was a wee lad in Aberdeen when this, one of the very early World War Two escape films, was released in 1950 and I was completely poleaxed by it. During the week it played Aberdeen I saw it five times - on two occasions I saw it round twice! Now, I'm not sure if it's a very good film or just a medium good one. I think it's very, very good but of course I'm biased. Whatever, it's a spendid yarn, there's no doubt, and what is more important, to me at least, is that it bit me with the acting bug. From the very first moment that I saw the very first frame of *The Wooden Horse* I knew that there was only one thing I wanted to do with my life. I wanted to be an actor.

Years later I worked with one of the cast from *The Wooden Horse*, gentle Michael Goodliffe. I told him the above and I'm delighted to report that they all enjoyed making the film and Michael was very pleased that it had inspired me to join them on the slippery slope!

I also worked with Leo Genn, one of 'The Horse's' stars, on a TV something or other towards the end of his career. But my memories of him, I'm afraid, are rather sad. He'd have been about sixty-five by then and he was still vigorously chasing the girls. So much so, in fact, that the make-up lady asked me to act as chaperon and sit and chat to them both in the location caravan whilst she very carefully blacked in Leo's pronounced bald patch, about which he was very concerned. Leo was also constantly worried that, having been nominated, he had failed to win an Oscar for *Quo Vadis* way back in 1951. He wasn't in the least consoled when I told him he should have got one for *The Wooden Horse*. He felt that the industry had betrayed him.

I was sorry for Leo and his bald patch and I thought *The Wooden Horse* was magic.

School. I must mention School. I got my taste for thesping from *The Wooden Horse* right enough, but it was at school that I had the opportunity to find out if I had 'it' in me - and a few other things besides!

My Dad, Donald Marriott Perkins (Sheard comes from Mum), was a minister of the kirk in Aberdeen and he was a very wise man. When I was a weeny little lad, long before I saw 'The Horse', he used to put on plays he'd written, in his church hall. His main purpose was to keep the children of his parish off the streets, but he always seemed to find a spot in these extravaganzas for his tiny son, who was really far too young to be included, but who loved it. I didn't realise it at the time, and for me *The Wooden Horse* is still very much my starting point, but those small totters must also have helped to set me on the right road and I'll say a wee thank you to Dad when I next see him. Not yet a while though! Well into his eighties, he sailed off to the big Church in the sky a couple of years ago.

But why was my Dad so very wise? Well, I'm sure he had other ideas, like my getting a good all round education, but I think he was wise because, after I'd seen *The Wooden Horse*, he realised that there was no hope for me. I do tend to blether, particularly when my enthusiasm is fired by something, and he must have realised that I was hooked on the business, and that I'd better go South for the last years of my schooling. Why South? I'll talk of this in more detail later, but the move certainly helped to start my transformation into a Sassenach. For it was then that I began to lose my Scottish accent.

And by heck, when I did arrive in England I found that Dad had not only sent me to a school which had a very good drama department, but by heck again, it was a mixed school. Real live girls to play the female parts. Girls who had bumps in all the right places and were...OH! Well, I was a good strong chap going past puberty after all. My Dad really had hit that old nail right where a young man most needed it.

Let me tell you about *Henry IV Part One*, and Ann. Ann was my first love and I couldn't believe that life could be so wonderful. She used to live in Sutton, Surrey. Telephone number: Vigilant 1436 - I remember the number because the first time I met Ann's mother she said with a laugh that their number was Ann's age, 14, and hers, 36.

Ann truly was the most beautiful, gorgeous, wonderful creature I had ever seen. And W...W... OOW!

My first leading role in the school dramatic society was that of Falstaff in the above-mentioned play and Ann played Mistress Quickly. A very aptly named part for, by Shakespeare, did we have to do things quickly at times!

Ann and I learnt a lot together, everything in fact, and even today I dream about her - about twice a year on average. She's been married for many years to a nice chap I met once at a reunion, but during 'Henry' and the other great plays I cut my amateur teeth on - *King Lear*, *To Live in Peace*, *Thunder Rock*, *A Sleep of Prisoners* - she was mine and I was hers and we loved each other passionately.

Ann never appeared in a production after 'Henry'. I suppose, in truth, it was because she didn't want to do any more plays, but I like to think and remember that the real reason was because she was my 'Mistress' Quickly and could more easily be waiting for me after the curtain came down - we used to do at least seven performances of each play - in the little copse at the back of the theatre/school hall. There's a lot of adrenalin builds up during a thespian's performance and oh, but those meetings after the show were wonderful. The fumblings, the straps, the suspenders, the stocking-tops, the young, white, eager flesh...OH!

Ann and I split up during our GCEs and went on to conquests new. But I thank you, Ann, with all my heart, for being the first. I thank you for all those long, lazy, summer Sunday walks in the country and I thank you for breaking my heart. For you did you know, for just a little while after we parted. At least until I met...I don't know, I honestly can't remember.

Until you find your life-long Dearly Beloved you only really remember your first love, don't you agree? It may sound chauvinistic - it's not meant to I assure you - but after Ann, I scraped through my exams and met lots of lovely ladies, but I don't remember a single one with any clarity.

Then I went to drama college. The Royal Academy of Dramatic Art in London to be exact. It's now part of London University - so there you are, Mum and Dad, I did go to university after all, I know you'll be pleased! Actually I only did half the RADA course to begin with, because I was far too eager to get started. If I'd taken a year off after leaving school and not gone straight to Dramabum College, National Service might have been abolished by the time I'd finished the course. As it was I was one of the very last to be called up. And because no one could be quite sure when conscription would end, the principal of RADA, John Fernald, suggested that I did not apply for deferment, but that I break the RADA course, as lots of others had done before me, and do my National Service in the middle. Then I could come back, complete my training, and be able to go straight into the profession without the worry that I still might be called up.

What a bore. Here was I, the only person I know who has been accepted into RADA three terms before he is due to leave school and, moreover, even after restricting himself to doing two Shakespeare speeches at the audition, silly fool! That's something never heard of before or since. The recognised form has always been one ancient and one modern piece, but I was all starry-eyed ambition in those days with no sense at all.

Then, after my first year, this wonderful new world I found myself in had to be held in abeyance for the next two, whilst I became Aircraftsman Second Class, Number 5050481 - it's true, you never do forget your forces number.

II

Now, I'd never have admitted it then, certainly not at the beginning, but after I'd got rid of the resentment I felt at being yanked away from the life I loved, I really enjoyed my two years in the Royal Air Force. I matured too, so I've got a heck of a lot to be thankful for.

Snippets of memories come fluttering back...The drill corporal giving us instruction on how to salute, shortly after we arrived. 'And I don't care if 'e's 'angin' by 'is balls from the flagpole. If 'e's han hofficer and 'e's wearing 'is cap you salute 'im. Right?' What an actor!

When I was being 'suited' for a job, the sergeant looked at my records and said, 'Hm, so you're one of those nancy-boy actors are you? Let me hear you speak.' I said very loud and clear that there were no more nancies in the acting profession than there were in any other, particularly the RAF, and that anyway, I certainly wasn't one of them. The sergeant looked at me nonplussed. 'Oh well,' he said. 'At least you talk posh, you'd better be a telephonist'!

Having completed our square-bashing, we were just on the point of leaving RAF Bridgenorth when I caught Asian flu, along with many others. There was an epidemic. I was in sick-bay for over a week and got 'back flighted'. Being back flighted meant that the lads who had started square-bashing with me overtook me, so to speak, and passed out! By the time I returned from sick-bay they'd marched past some high-ranking officer, saluted, and had dispersed to start their trade training in other camps. I had to wait until another lot caught up with me, and I was put into what they called Pool Flight. Pool Flight was the waiting flight and contained all sorts. Some like me who'd had the flu and were waiting, some who were to be discharged the service on longer-lasting medical grounds, and some, even, who were awaiting an appearance in court. And our object in life was to do all the odd jobs around the place, of which there were many. I don't mean jankers, peeling potatoes and the like, I mean general duties, like helping in the office, or taking the station commander's pet labrador to the vet.

I was very lucky. I got to guard a whole airfield! Not quite on my own, there were two others like myself from Pool Flight, and a couple of corporal drill instructors. All the DIs were given this two-week stint, in rotation, as a relaxation from training erks, like what we had just been!

We had a grand time, the five of us. This huge airfield, surplus to requirement, was empty, and it was our job to guard it from the 'enemy'. We lived like kings in what had been the officers' mess, doing our own cooking and mostly drinking and watching the telly. Every two hours however, day or night, one of us, drill instuctor corporals included, had to walk around the camp, with a loaded rifle would you believe. Not a job for the faint-hearted, particularly at two in the morning when the wind is howling eerily around the empty hangars. Suppose the Martians had landed!

My main reason for taking you down this little diversion is to ask if anyone can help me. The airfield we guarded was called Halfpenny Green and had been a very active station during the last war. In 1945 one of my favourite films was made, namely, *The Way to the Stars*, with John Mills, Rosamund John and Michael Redgrave. The airfield which was featured in that film was called Halfpenny Field. Is it possible that they were one and the same, does anyone know? Every time I see the film I sort of hope so.

Later on, after I'd done my training as a telephonist, and after I'd become a senior aircraftsman/acting corporal in charge of the telephone exchange at RAF Chivenor, North Devon (actually, I was having a very hot affair at the time with a girl who lived in Kent - I'd asked to be posted there!), I was invited to play squash by the admin officer, Squadron Leader Desdemoni (his real name). I'd never played squash before, and after explaining the rudiments, the squadron leader suggested that we might just as well have a game, as this was a better way to learn. It was! Almost the first ball I hit for real went straight into the squadron leader's eye. He was poleaxed and developed the biggest, brightest, shiner I've ever seen.

The education officer at Chivenor was a long, thin gentleman who really didn't want to be in the forces at all but had been virtually forced into signing on because Daddy had been a Group Captain. He and I formed a drama society, The Chivenor Amateur Dramatic Society, or The CADS. Our first production was that old Whitehall favourite *Dry Rot*, which I, because I was a half trained RADAbum, was persuaded to direct. Our first job, however, was to find somewhere to stage this mammoth production. So we went to see my old mate the admin officer. Dessie's eye was improving by this time.

Bearing in mind that this was the early 1960s and a decent wage then was something like twenty quid a week, this is what Squadron Leader Desdemoni said in reply to our request: 'I think our old cinema would suit you very well. Let's see though, it hasn't been used for a bit, it'll need refurbishing. You'll also want money for scenery and things won't you? How about £450 to start with? I think the RAF can afford that.' £450...it was more than either of us had ever seen. Heavens, I only got £80 for a whole term's maintenance at RADA! (It wasn't enough of course, I had to find paid work in the holidays to make ends meet.)

I will never know what made the squadron leader so generous. It might have been because his daughter was playing the female lead in our production, it might have been my expert presentation, or it might have been his way of encouraging something outside his rather restricted, regimental life. After all, he'd shown me, a mere telephonist, how to play squash. Even though I'd given him that black eye we played many more games and I became quite good. But perhaps the real reason he helped us was simply that the squadron leader with the daft name was a very, very nice man.

So I had a good life in the RAF. The March of the Royal Air Force is still one of my favourite tunes and I'll always feel proud when I hear it. But I was of course delighted when my two years were up and I could get back to business.

III

There are a huge number of would-be actors, alas, who go through training at the many and various drama schools and colleges throughout the country and are never heard of again. RADA is no exception. Even though it is supposed to be the top of the tree and there is no production - theatre, film, or television - anywhere in the land which does not have, at the very least, two ex-students in its cast.

Shortly before I began, RADA had turned out the likes of Susannah York and Albert Finney. But of the twenty odd classmates who started with me, before I went into the RAF, I cannot think of one who is still in the business. (I tell a lie, but he is no longer an actor. Hugh Whitemore is now a very respected scriptwriter and author.) Of those I joined after I returned from the forces, however, there are quite a few who are still hopping around and making a crust. Journeyman actorbums such as Geoffrey Whitehead, Bridget Forsyth, John F. Landry, Geoffrey Hinsliffe, Ian Thompson, and Phillip Voss spring to mind. And three, particularly, who have got a very long way up the slippery slope, Sarah Miles, Tom Courteney, and John Thaw.

We lived an idyllically charmed existence at RADA's headquarters in Gower Street, protected as we were from the cold outside world and of course we were all going to be fabulously famous. Came the day though when the end of training was almost upon us and we were rehearsing like mad for our final productions. The ones which all the agents and casting directors come to see. You hope!

I actually did quite well. I didn't win the gold or silver cups, they went to the likes of Tom, or John, or Sarah, who were already up and running before most of us had got started. But I did win the coveted Tennant's Contract, awarded for all-round ability. This entitled me to go straight to work in London's West End, in one of the theatres owned by H.M. Tennant. I was very proud and I turned it down. I'd discovered that I'd mostly be required to understudy, or work backstage on props or something, and that there would not be much opportunity to practice my art. Oh I might be given a walk-on part now and then, but I wanted, desperately, to play big important roles.

There was only one place where this was possible and that was in Repertory Theatre, and it so happened that as well as the Tennant's Contract, I'd been invited to join not one, but two reps. I was spoilt for choice. In the end I sought advice from John Fernald again. He accepted that I wanted to act rather than piddle about backstage in London, and anyway he thought that I might be able to pick up my prize later on, after I'd had some rep experience. (That didn't work out in fact. When I eventually returned to London, Tennants were very nice, but they didn't want to know. They said that the offer should have been taken up straight away on leaving RADA. But perhaps they did me a favour, for it was then that I decided to try television and films!)

But back to my talk with Mr Fernald. I'd turned down Tennants for the time being at least and I was left with the two choices, Farnham and Perth Reps. John Fernald said that of course Farnham was much nearer London and I could get all sorts of people to come and see me work, but on balance he preferred Perth and said that he could think of no better place for me to start my career.

Neither of us knew how grateful I was to be to him, for apart from anything else, 'twas there that I also met Dearly Beloved!

Ah but they were braw days. Working like mad from ten in the morning till midnight. Rehearsals for next week's play during the day, performances of the current week's play in the evenings, then back to the digs to learn the next lot of lines, hundreds of them. All for the princely sum of £7 10s a week. And Fernald had been right, Perth was damn good. For a start it was a fortnightly rep, not weekly, so we had a little more time to work on a role, and we did everything from Shaw and Sheridan, to Pinter and Panto.

A wee word about that £7 10s. I'm not sure if two can in fact live as cheaply as one, but back then, if you added £7 10s to £6 10s and thus made £14, it certainly began to look like quite a lot of money.

There was this rather fetching LASM (Lady Assistant Stage Manager) in the company, with the most wonderful calf muscles I'd ever seen. She and I decided to pool our wages in the manner described above, and we rented a tiny cottage with a certain Donald Sutherland. (A super trouper by the way. He broke his toe on the first night of the first production but carried on regardless.) We, the LASM and I, had the upstairs, Don and his (then) missis had the down.

I have a good claim, incidentally, to being the catalyst which set D. Sutherland on the road to mega stardom. Later on in that season at Perth we did a production of Ibsen's *Ghosts*. Don desperately wanted to play the lead part of Oswald, but they gave it to me. As a result Don left Perth Rep in a huff and walked straight into a starbumming film career, starting with Hammer Horrors and followed very shortly by *The Dirty Dozen*, and so on and on and on!

And that lady ASM with the exquisite calf muscles? We are still pooling our shillings 30 years and three kids later!

IV

And so we returned to London, Dearly Beloved and I. No agent, no contacts, no cash, no job, nothing. Now we can really get started!

But one quick word first. Because so much has happened over the years, and water flowed under bridges, I might not always be absolutely accurate chronologically. I'm going to start at the beginning, of course, and work forwards, but I can't promise that A will necessarily always come before B. That is the only area, however, where I might stray a little. Everything else is completely and utterly the truth.

Right. I finally acquired an agent of sorts - the fun is about to begin.

The very first part I ever played on film or TV was so tiny that I wouldn't mention it, except that it's the one time Dearly Beloved and I worked together on the screen. Dearly B. decided soon after this that family should come before career, but we did do this one TV show together.

We were part of a Wild West bar-room scene in *The Country and Western Show*. We played cowboys and girls and sang, yes sang, 'They Call the Wind Maria', whilst Shani Wallis, the lady who was going to give a wonderful Nancy in the film of *Oliver* a few years later, danced all over the place. I tried once to get a copy of this show as a memento, but alas, I was told that the tape had been destroyed.

My first actual featured part on TV should have a quick mention because it gave me the key to the technique I needed to start me on my fascinating journey down tele/film lane. There was this series called *Moonstrike* which was about the resistance movement in the last war, and the pilots who flew agents across the channel in their flimsy aeroplanes. I played a German interrogator who was trying to get information out of a captured agent. It was a very small scene. All I had to do was tell him that I was going to get the information I required, then take my lighted cigarette and stub it out on the guy's face. Not quite, of course. Just as I start to close in on the poor chap, glowing cigarette to the fore, we cut to another scene. So there were never any grizzly bits!

End of my first television speaking part. But in that one tiny shot - cigarette from mouth to hand, then cigarette turned and pushed towards the man's face - I learnt the first and most basic rule of acting in front of a camera. It's simple really when you think about it. I'd just come from rep, and on the stage your audience is sitting some distance from you and therefore everything you do has to be just a little larger than life, otherwise it would never be seen. The cigarette would have to be taken slowly from the mouth, and then even more gradually and with great menace it would be pushed towards the chap's face. For television and film, where you could be virtually sitting in your audience's lap, particularly if it's shot in close-up, the above would come over as gigantic. I realised very quickly that, fag taken out of the mouth and simply and without fuss moved towards the face, was more than enough.

I've been using it as my key ever since. 'Little is good, less is better,' is how Jack Lemmon described the secret of film acting. Ringo Starr even sang a song about it - 'Act Naturally'. I'm very glad I learnt that lesson early on.

My first feature film was *Nobody Runs Forever*, with Christopher Plummer, Rod Taylor, and Lillie Palmer starbumming. Rod of course had starred in masses of films, such as *The Birds* for Alfred Hitchcock. I too worked for Mr Hitchcock - more of that later! You can imagine what I felt like on the first morning's filming for 'Nobody Runs'. It really was my very first feature film. I'd done a few television shows, so I knew one end of a camera from the other, but that's all. I played a reporter, a tiddly, teeny, little part, in a scene where Chris is coming down a long, wide, imposing staircase.

The stairs were in fact in the Royal Academy of Arts, Piccadilly. I was made up in a room somewhere on the other side of the road, and then sat waiting and worrying because no one came anywhere near me for ages. I thought they'd forgotten all about me. But in the end of course they came - 'Sorry you've been kept waiting, this place has been a bitch to light.'

We had a script conference actually on the set at the bottom of those stairs. There were a goodly number of us and only a very few chairs, so I was surprised when the director, Ralph Thomas, seemed to be waving me towards one of them. Me? I was nothing. 'Sit, sit down,' he kept saying. So I did. 'No, no, not you!' Then I discovered that Chris Plummer had been standing right behind me, waiting for me to get out of the way. I felt awful. But Chris just smiled and insisted that I stay put. Everybody else smiled too, Rod Taylor included. He was not in the scene, but happened to be visiting the set that day with one of the other stars, lovely, eternally young Lilli Palmer. I was so embarrassed. Imagine thinking that the director was signalling me to take one of the very few seats available. Oh dear, I shudder even now at the memory. But it kind of broke the ice. We did a good day's work and I was introduced to the casting director for the film, whom I'd not met before. Very important person as far as bums are concerned, the casting director, and I'm glad to say that Weston (Budge) Drury Jr. used me many times in the future. My only other thought about 'Nobody Runs' is that I learnt how very quietly the actors spoke their lines in feature films, exactly like we talk to each other. Another important lesson that. Anyway nice first picture, nice Christopher Plummer, Rod Taylor, Lillie Palmer, et al.

Chris always said that he had a career, then there was a thing called *The Sound of Music*, and then he had a career. I know what he means, but I have to say that there are a hell of a lot of us bums who'd love to have had a career like that bum. I saw *The Sound of Music* again the other night and I thought it and he were super. Indeed a lot of us could be jealous of Mr Plummer's careers, any one of them, but of course we're not...I should coco!

But you know, there is a very odd side to our business. Of course we get a wee bit envious if someone lands a part that we know we could play - far better than they ever could! But it doesn't seem to matter. It doesn't alter people or friendships. I went to meet a director for a part recently and there, waiting to go in to meet him for the same part, was an actor I'd known for ages. We said the usual hellos, how are yous, etc., and he said he'd wait for me after his interview and we could go for a jar and a natter. When I'd finished, we went to a pub round the corner, bought our drinks, and sat down to talk over old times. And I found myself thinking, here we are, two chums who've known each other for years, having a right old blether, each hoping like mad that the other does not get the part. Funny old business...By the way, I have to admit that I got the part. That's why I'm glad that I paid for the drinks!

Now, picture if you will a car park at the bottom of Kensington Church Street. *Madigan* had come to London. It was the first day of filming, and four or five of us were standing about in the cold. George Cole was there and he was well up the slippery slope, a Star Characterbum no less. But we were all waiting outside this huge location caravan to be called for a script conference with the tip top superstar of *Madigan*, one Richard Widmark. I don't know about the others (certainly not George because he'd seen it all before), but as I'd only recently started in what is called the 'commercial' side of the business, I was apprehensive to say the least. Virtually brown-trousered as my youngest son would say. Here was I, a nobody for goodness sake, about to play a good scene with a screen legend.

We were finally summoned and we dutifully filed into this vast trailer, and there was nobody there. At least I couldn't see anyone. Only a large desk right at the far end. We waited and shuffled, George said something funny and then...Have you seen *Kiss of Death*, Widmark's first film, made in 1947? Apart from a great performance it was his distinctive laugh which made the film and Widmark's career. Well here it was again, that laugh, coming from behind the desk, from this tiny, weeny, little man. So small, in fact, that we'd simply not seen him. But R. Widmark had been there all the time . . 'Oh, hell,' he said. 'It's damn cold out there, let them share my van when we've done these lines and give them a drink, for Christ's sake, and turn that heater up.'!

He was a lovely, lovely man and a great time was had by all. I didn't 'fluff' my lines and Richard directed the traffic in Piccadilly superbly. How did he come to do that? Well at the end of the piece, George Cole has been demoted to traffic cop for helping Madigan. He gets the traffic in

Piccadilly in an awful mess and Madigan sorts it out for him. Trouble was that the film company couldn't get permission to film in Piccadilly. But this was nothing to Mr Widmark. 'Hell,' he said, 'get your cameras in position, get me to Piccadilly [actually, I think it was finally filmed in Knightsbridge, but no matter], and leave it to me.' They did and Richard got out of his car, calmly walked to the middle of the traffic and whilst the cameras rolled, proceeded to direct the astonished drivers to great effect! See the film, and you'll see. As I say, a super, lovely man.

I've mentioned that I had a good scene with Richard and George. I played an analytical chemist and I was supposed to be in the process of investigating this large jar of piddle, don't ask me why. Anyway, this jar, filled to the brim with something that looked just like yellow whatsit, was sitting there on the set when we were called for rehearsal. Richard walked in, picked it up and drank. 'Ah, that's better,' he said. 'Nice glass of cider!'

V

By the way, I'm not going to take you through every blessed thing I've ever done. Good God no, it would take for ever, thank goodness - thank goodness that I've done so much work! No, I'm going to pick up the odd engagement along the way which was particularly enjoyable or interesting, either because of the actors involved, or for other equally fascinating reasons. For example, I don't think that anyone would dare to call Stephen Spielberg a bum, not that is if they wanted to work again...And you're not a bum, Stephen, far from it. I'll be including the Indiana Jones films later and telling them what a nice and wonderful and talented guy you are!

Now I want to say a word about a lovely sweet man with whom I worked a lot at the start of my TV/film career, because he was doing a television series at the time and I was always being asked back to do more episodes. Who am I talking about? Well, if I tell you that the series was *Dixon of Dock Green*, then it can only be Jack Warner.

Dear Jack has been dead for a lot of years now and for many years prior to that he had suffered very badly with his legs. But I never saw him as anything but the true professional. We'd be filming in the snow and he'd be there in the thick of it. Literally, there were no star caravans on these occasions. This was a little TV production with no special privileges.

I can remember, honestly as though it were yesterday, sitting in one of the cars we were using for the filming, going over the lines with Jack. Then we did the scene. It wasn't very long, but it involved a girl being thrown through a car's windscreen. We did the dialogue part of the scene without any problems, but then we came to the part where the car stops sharply and the girl goes through the windscreen.

And here is one reason why things sometimes take a long time to film - the special effects. Well they can't just take a girl and chuck her through a windscreen, because they're not really supposed to hurt us! What normally happens with this kind of shot is that they turn the camera upside down and film the action backwards. The girl slowly raises her head from a resting position on the already busted windscreen and sits back into her seat. When they run the film, quickly, the right way up, it looks as if she's going forward fast. They then put a previously filmed long shot of the car stopping, on the front of the upside down bit, and a close up of the girl's face covered in blood on the end. A bang, a crunch, the screech of brakes and glass shattering is added to the soundtrack, together with the odd scream or five, and there you have it, girl going through a car's windscreen. Simple!

On this occasion, however, the crew discovered a camera problem and they couldn't get it right, so we had to do the backwards shot again and again and we had to wait and wait. Trouble was that it was two o'clock on a bloody cold November morning and the poor girl was dressed in a thin party frock. She was turning blue before our eyes, but she stayed where she was because she was a professional. And Jack Warner, as well as being a professional, was also a gentleman. It really was very, very cold, but Jack, without a murmur, took off his costume police tunic and put it round the girl while we waited. I was gob-smacked. Dammit, apart from anything else, the man was in his seventies. It was one of the very nicest, truest, kindest, gestures I've seen in all my thirty-odd years in the business and I've seen a few, I can...no, I *will* tell you!

VI

'And I've got billing for you, too,' said my agent. I could hardly believe it. A lovely film, a challenging part, my first trip abroad to work, and billing! Not above the title, of course, that's for stars, for 'bankable' bums, but a supporting credit just under the title. Wheee! For a few minutes I allowed myself to think that I'd really arrived and that next week I'd be a star. Then I remembered that my next part would probably be a taxi driver or some such, with two lines. It also occurred to me for the first time that I actually rather enjoyed being what I was, a pretty darn good, supporting actor, a journeyman vagabondbum. Of course it was wonderful to have a featured credit in a big feature film, but it was also nice to know that afterwards I'd be off playing something else equally enjoyable and interesting though maybe not quite so prestigious. Helmut Griem and I talked it over at dinner in the hotel when we started this movie some two months later.

The McKenzie Break is a great film. It still turns up on television and if you haven't seen it I urge you so to do. Apart from Helmut Griem, there was Brian Keith - what a great performance - and poor Ian Hendry, who died far too young, in the leading roles and of course me just under the title! Together, it must be said, with some others of equal note including: Jack Watson, Patrick O'Connell and sweet Mary Larkin. I mentioned that my part in 'McKenzie' was challenging, so before I go any further I'd better explain why. The story concerns a German prison camp in Scotland during the last war. It was filmed in Ireland (hence my first job abroad), and to play the Germans they'd got the very best *German* actors from *Germany*, and me. My whole part was in German, my character couldn't even speak English! I do just about speak German, but that's very different from spouting a lot of technical stuff at great speed, hunched double in the roof void of a hut where I, the engineer in charge of building the tunnel, have stored all the earth. On top of everything, we did all the roof of the hut scenes in the first two weeks of filming, just Helmut and I, and as the star of a film is usually eased in gently, Helmut had about one line to every fifty of mine. Yes, I was most definitely nervous for this one, too. It's certainly not all 'one take and up to the bar' in this business.

However, the first couple of days, when everyone is apprehensive, crew included, went rather well. I'd got most of my long speeches behind me, and the director, a lovely man called Lamont (Monty) Johnson, said that the rushes (the daily peep at what's been filmed the previous day), were some of the best he'd seen. We all started to relax. And Helmut and I had dinner in the hotel that evening and talked about the differing types of actor.

Helmut is a great chap, indeed all the actors from Germany became chums of mine - Horst Janson, for example, I've worked with a couple of times since - but

Helmut is, well he's very Germanic. 'Now, Michael,' he said. 'You have a good part in this picture, what do you do now? You will become a famous film star, yes?' And I, flushed with the success I'd just had - why the director had said that the rushes were the very best rushes he'd ever seen (he didn't actually say 'very' but I'm sure he meant to) - said, no, I didn't want to be a star. 'Explain,' Helmut demanded. Well, how do you explain a thing like that? It's a frisson. It's the tingly feeling that another big chance could always be just around the corner - the phone might ring any minute. It's also knowing that there are some interesting small parts I might want to play and couldn't, because, if I were a star, I'd be much too far up the old slippery slope and it would be beneath me. And it's the knowledge, I'll be honest, that if this film is a flop it's you, Helmut, who'll carry the can, not I. I'm not worried about the money or the loss of prestige, it's the possibility of all the lovely opportunities I'd miss if I'm out of favour because, as the star of the picture, I've failed to make the film a success at the box office. I told Helmut this and I think he understood. I'd like, too, to think that he was glad, knowing he'd probably never be troubled in the Star stakes by such a talented and nice supporting bum as I!

I never saw Helmut again after the picture finished. I nearly did. He was going to be in a super movie I made with Michael York, Simon MacCorkindale and Alan Badel, but he felt that the part was not large enough to live up to his image. See what I mean?

One other little anecdote from 'McKenzie' which is worth recording. Helmut played the baddie, and he and his men escape from the prison camp when he collapses the above-mentioned earth-laden roof on top of the rest of us. My character discovers him in the act and he kills me by smashing my head in with a spanner, just before the roof caves in and buries me. This sequence couldn't be shot, of course, until the very end of the schedule because the hut was still needed. I'd completed all my other scenes, so I spent three weeks doing nothing whilst I waited, except explore the countryside and play golf and cards. Nice enough, but frustrating after a while.

Then came the day - I discovered baddie, Helmut, he socked me with a rubber spanner, I screamed, then tons and tons and tons of Fullers Earth and gallons and gallons of water were tipped on top of me. It was all very carefully controlled, but I, who didn't know quite what to expect, thought the end of the world had arrived. And to top everything...the camera jammed and we had to do it again!

I'm glad I said what I did about coming down to earth and playing two lines, because I didn't even appear in my next picture. I'd been doing tellies, happily lots of them, and all nice varied parts, then along came Roger Moore's first outing as James Bond - *Live and Let Die*. I shall be writing about Roger and the other film we did together, later on, but on *Live and Let Die* I only saw him once, from the back, when I came to the the studio to meet the director. Roger was dressed in black and was stalking through a studio jungle. I remember the scene in the film.

There was going to be a prologue, or pre-title sequence for *Live and Let Die*. I was to be a secret agent sitting in a garden, waiting for James Bond. He arrives and I give him the secret message which I have concealed inside my contact lenses - I practised with a borrowed pair from my local optician, agony! Suddenly we hear someone approaching and we leap over the garden wall in order to escape. Or rather I do. James Bond just manages to stop himself from jumping. He had to, otherwise there'd have been no *Live and Let Die*. Because, in reality, we were in a roof garden right at the top of a very tall skyscraper and you were going to see me come sailing through the air and land, splat, on the sidewalk.

They made a dummy of me to do the fall. They even had a standby dummy in case the leading dummy got it wrong! They were both immaculately dressed in exact duplicates of the clothes I was going to wear. The costume designer and I shopped at Austin Reed in Regent Street, and when we'd found what we wanted - excellent (and expensive) light fawn cavalry twill trousers, superb (and expensive) bottle green corduroy jacket, beautifully expensive brown brogue shoes - the designer turned to the Austin Reed assistant and said, 'I want three of each, of course.'! OK for me, yes, and just about yes for dummy number one, but to spend that sort of money on a standby dummy! When I asked the costume lady why they couldn't take the clothes off dummy one, if he got it wrong, and put them on dummy two, she laughed. 'You've not been in feature films very long have you,' she said. 'They can afford it. And they'd lose far more time and money if things did go wrong with the first dummy and they had to take the clothes from the ground floor all the way up to the top of the skyscraper. Anyway, you wouldn't want a dummy, looking the image of you, lying naked in the street, would you?' I should also mention that both my look-alikes had very costly toupees made for them which matched my hair exactly - what there was of it, I was balding nicely even then.

But the sequence was never filmed. When the rest of the film was finished they decided that a prologue was not needed after all, or they did something else, I can't honestly remember. Pity really. I got paid, but I'd have liked to do a Bond film. Ah well. As I say, I did a marvellous film with Roger called *Escape to Athena* about five years later, and Guy Hamilton, the director of *Live and Let Die*, used me in the sequel to *The Guns of Navarone*, *Force 10 From Navarone*. More about that later, too.

One remembrance helps me to remember others. I did another prologue/pre-title sequence which never made the screen and this time we actually shot it. It was for *Hitler - The Last Ten Days*, with Alec Guinness as 'is nibs. Freddy Jones, Peter Sallis, yours truly and a few others did an opening scene about financing the Third Reich. I think the feeling was that it didn't really fit the picture. Anyway it was left on the cutting room floor. I feel sure Sir Alec rather wished that the whole film had been consigned to the dustbin. He wasn't at all happy.

I also worked with another former James Bond at around this time. A very sad George Lazenby. He'd made a complete and utter ass of himself whilst playing Bond in *On Her Majesty's Secret Service* - fast cars, girls, enormous ego, shouting his mouth off etc., etc. - not a nice bum at all. When he lost the part of Bond, he and Cy Enfield put together a little film called *Universal Soldier*. (Not to be confused with the Jean-Claud Van Damme film of the same title which was made much later.) Cy was a very well respected American film director who, after settling in the UK, had made such films as *Zulu* and *Hell Drivers*. He had also directed the very successful 'Big Fry' TV adverts which featured George. Indeed it's said that it was chocolate which got George the part of Bond.

Universal Soldier worked rather well, in spite of George. As producer, as well as star, Mr Lazenby felt that he could make suggestions as to how we other actors should play our parts. Oh dear! I had a couple of lines or ten as a passport official at London Airport and I happened to share a car with George out to Heathrow. As we trundled along he started pontificating. 'Now, Michael, this is a very important part you're playing in my movie and I want you to feel you are this passport official, right down to your balls'!

Amongst the tellies I was doing then was one about a hospital which guest starred two great names from days of yore, Jean Kent, and Richard Greene, who'd been the original TV Robin Hood. Richard had great difficulty remembering his lines and Jean, who was sitting at the side of the rehearsal room with her knitting, rather like Mme. La Tricoteuse at the Guillotine, was heard to bitch: 'Well, dear, it's no wonder is it? He's not really done much acting lately has he? He's been playing at being a farmer or something!'

When I was a lad, Aberdeen had more cinemas than any other city in the country, thank goodness. In the school holidays and at weekends I sometimes saw three films in a day. I'd see anything on a screen, but the films I liked more than any other - *The Wooden Horse* excepted - were the swashbucklers, with their sword fights, bows and arrows, and deeds of derring do. There was Errol Flynn of course. His *Robin Hood* was magic, as indeed was Richard Todd's version in the early 1950s. Then there was Louis Hayward as *The Man in the Iron Mask* and *The Son of Monte Christo* and...well there were hundreds of them and if you like that kind of escapism you'll have your own favourites.

But I must mention one more buckle swasher, because I worked with him. Do you remember a film called *The Black Shield of Falworth*? Its star was a very young man with a quiff of dark hair in the middle of his forehead. He married his leading lady, the delectable Janet Leigh, and he did not say in the film, as rumour has it, 'Yonda is the Cassle of my Faddah', in a Brooklyn accent. He went on to become one of the biggest stars in Hollywood...Of course, I mean Tony Curtis.

There was this TV film series made in England called *The Persuaders*, and Tony Curtis came over from America to star in it. By this time he'd been right to the top of the slippery slope and had made some really great films. Do you remember *The Sweet Smell of Success* with Burt Lancaster and *Some Like it Hot*, for example? He was now perhaps a little on the way down, though you'd never have noticed it. He still had all the aura of Great Stardom.

But at the same time he was also a damn nice guy and a caring person. Let me tell you a little story. My character has been killed and shoved down a well outside this cottage in the country. Along comes Mr Curtis to get some water from the well. He turns the handle to bring up the bucket, and up pops my corpse. The time came to film the bit where I appear. It was a fake well, made up in the studio, so I had to crouch down out of sight and then emerge as Tony turned the handle. I don't know why, but these scenes always seem to be filmed in winter, when it's cold, and I also had to be drenched with with water, of course, because I'd been down a well. Anyway, we got ready, make-ups were checked, wardrobe was happy, and just before the director said, 'action', a little prop man came trundling along carrying two very large buckets of water with which to douse me. And Tony Curtis stopped everything. 'This water's freezing cold,' he said, 'you can't pour freezing cold water over Michael, he'll catch pneumonia. I'm not going to film this scene until you've got some warm water and Michael and I have tested it.' Nice one, Tony. Thanks.

And the next gem is *The Saga of the Six Black Virgins.* What a title!

I went to meet the director, a guy called Green, Guy Green. (He'd been a brilliant lighting cameraman - *Great Expectations* and *Oliver Twist* et al. - before he became a director.) Again, I remember my meeting with Guy as though it were yesterday. Irene Lamb, the lovely casting director (remember how important I said they were to us bums?), said to me as I was waiting, 'Michael, don't forget that you've only got about three minutes in there [the interview room] to make an impression. Make sure you do.' I have never forgotten that excellent advice, Irene.

I got the job. A lovely part in what was I believe a trueish story of the Second World War: the Madame of a brothel in Paris hears Winston Churchill say on the radio that everyone must do their bit, and the brothel spends the rest of the war enticing Germans into its beds and killing them.

You'd have thought that the production company would have had no problem raising the money to make this film, but they did. They had hoped to get Angela Lansbury to play the Madame of the brothel, but they couldn't. And in the end they sold the story to the Boulting Twins who re-titled it Soft *Beds, Hard Battles*, and turned it into a vehicle for Peter Sellers.

They tried to emulate the great *Kind Hearts and Coronets* - you know, fifty-three parts all played by one man - but this time it didn't work. Oh dear, it was a terrible film. Mind you I still had a part, oh yes, you can't keep a good bum down. I played the Military Governor of Paris who finally accepts the surrender of the city - can you believe this - from the Madame of the brothel!

I have to admit that I don't particularly like 'technical' actors, those who show us how they achieve a performance and you can almost see the wheels going round. Larry Olivier was one of these, God bless him, albeit a very good one, and Sellers' performances in *Soft Beds, Hard Battles* were fine but very technical. It wasn't his fault that the film was a flop. Well yes, of course it was to some extent, he was the starbum for goodness sake, but John and Roy Boulting are the ones I really blame. I'd enjoyed their movies up till then. The films they made with Ian Carmichael were great. (Worked with him too, I have, on *Peter Wimsey*.)

I enjoy a damn good fart too. But trying to make a joke out of giving a lot of Germans something in their goulash which makes them desperately want to go to the loo as they run for the plane that will take them back to Germany demands great subtlety. Sorry, Twins, the film might have worked if it had been better scripted, thought out, and directed.

I did get to work with Curt Jurgens though (*The Enemy Below*, *Inn of the Sixth Happiness*, *Ferry to Hong Kong*, etc.), and that was a very great pleasure. Mind you, I think he was as embarrassed as I. More so, because he was one of the stars. After our one scene together - the fart scene mentioned above - Curt had finished on the picture and he left like that old bat out of Hades. He was back home in Germany almost before we'd completed the day's work, or rather night's work - farting around at night seemed to make it even worse.

Another actor playing a wee part in this film was Windsor Davies, later to go on to such triumphs as *It Ain't 'arf Hot Mum*. If that sounds patronising it's not meant to, Windsor. The rest of us bums should be so lucky!

VII

England Made Me, starring Peter Finch, Michael York, Hildegard Neil, Michael Hordern, Joss Ackland and...me.

Not a lot of people know this, but this wonderful film was started without all the money in place, or a distribution deal. If you've seen it you can't help but remember the sequence where Michael York rows Hildegard across the lake to the big house - the sunlight dapples through the trees and glistens on the water...It has almost nothing to do with the fine Graham Greene story and the great performances given by all concerned, but it's pictorially very beautiful. And it was the very first scene to be shot on the lovely lake at Bled in what used to be Yugoslavia. The rushes were rushed back to London and the rest of the cash was on the next plane out, together with a signed contract for a cinema release. Thank heavens!

I've enjoyed all my engagements over the years. I really have. Even when I've been 'shufflin' through shit' and doing a tele-part just to pay the bills, I can honestly say that I've always found something to lift my spirits. I've been enormously lucky too, of course, helped perhaps by just a smidgin of talent! And I've also done some really smashing things, and *England Made Me* was the smashingest so far. Apart from Michael and Hildegard (I worked later with Hildy's husband, Brian Blessed, also in Yugoslavia - what a small world!), and Michael H. and Joss (Joss and I shared a gigantic suite of rooms in the hotel) there was for my money one of the best starbums of them all, dear and very, very sadly missed Peter Finch. (Apart from anything else we're back to *The Wooden Horse* again. Do you remember the Australian who helped Leo Genn when he was in hospital? It was one of Peter's first film parts in Britain. He then went on very quickly to play the Sheriff in *Robin Hood*, and D'Oyly Carte in *The Story of Gilbert and Sullivan*, and was soon the biggest Star around.)

We were doing this scene in *England Made Me*. Peter is in a rather sleazy nightclub, watching Michael and Hildegard dancing. In comes yours truly. I want a word with Peter and he invites me to sit at his table. (I should explain that I was playing a poor little Jew, the story is set in, just, pre-war Germany, and I'd come to Peter, who was playing a very important financier, in the hope that he could help me to find my son.)

We filmed the master - the whole scene in mid shot - lots of chat, mostly me, and when we'd finished the very first take, the director, the crew, and above all, Peter were suddenly slapping me on the back, telling me how excellent I was and making me feel very humble and delighted.

But oh dear, never count your takes before the sound man's had his say. Basil Fenton-Smith was a nice man. Very posh and a wee bit stuck up perhaps, well you'd have to be with that name, wouldn't you? Sorry, Basil. Actually the poor man's been dead for a number of years, so I don't suppose he cares. He was nice, he even bought me a drink later, but at this moment, as everyone was saying how wonderful I was, he was not so nice. In fact he was horrid.

Please appreciate that to do a very important master in a very big movie in one take is virtually unheard of. Everyone was delighted and we were about to go on to the next set-up when Basil shouted - or rather spoke loudly, you can't shout with a name like that - from his little corner. (Sound men always find themselves a little corner. They seem to take a delight in hiding and having people forget all about them until, as Basil did now, they stop the show.) 'Sorry, no good for sound,' he loudly spoke. And he continued, 'Michael scraped his chair when he sat down, noise went right over the dialogue. We'll have to go again.'

Now, a sound man can, indeed he must, say when a take is no good for him. Heavens, I've heard enough bad soundtrack, or rather not heard it, I'm sure you have. But sometimes he may be, well, a little over-zealous, and on this occasion you could have heard a pin drop. Until that is P. Finch moved. In a second he was over in Basil's corner. 'Let me hear it,' he said. Basil gave Peter the earphones and Peter listened to the dialogue of the master we'd just shot. When he'd finished he quietly handed the phones back to Basil, turned to the director and said, 'There's nothing wrong with the sound and I'm not going to do the shot again. Can we please move on. Michael was brilliant and I want to see if I can match him in the close-ups.'...Michael was brilliant!

And that's not the only happy memory I have from *England Made Me*. There are many, and they include: the bells; my meeting with George Sanders; Peter playing cards; Ken Coles the camera operator; me causing a re-take in the scene with the naked ladies; my smack in the mouth from Joss; and Peter Duffell the director, who gave me some super parts in future productions, including *Caught On a Train* which won the 1981 BAFTA award, the television Oscar, for the best TV play.

I must quickly eat a couple of mouthfuls of humble pie before I tell you about the bells. Basil Fenton-Smith was quite right to say what he did about the sound in the nightclub scene even if he was wrong - which he was. But he certainly bore me no grudge. In fact we became good friends. I've already mentioned that he bought me a drink, well, on the following sunny Sunday morning, Basil, and his boom operator Terry - the guy who holds the long pole with the mike on the end of it - asked me if I'd like to join them to record some 'sound overs' for that scene on the lake where Michael rows the boat. The one that enabled Jack Levin, the producer, to get the distribution deal.

We were all living in this large hotel right on the edge of the lake at Bled. Goebbels had built it as his Summer Palace during the war and the Yugoslavs had taken great delight in turning it into a hostelry. We actually shot quite a chunk of the film in the hotel, particularly in its huge reception rooms and entrance hall.

One sequence was filmed in what had been Goebbels' very own private retreat, which was situated some sixty yards from the main building. An extraordinary structure, consisting of one very large room, plus kitchen and bathroom, it was balanced on two gigantic columns at least fifty feet up in the air above the lake. The only entrance was from the top of the cliff, where a small bridge was attached, and there was an enormous ninety foot balcony running the whole length of its lakeside frontage.

Although it was understood that he had never occupied it, Marshal Tito had taken this beautifully furnished ex-Goebbels hideaway for himself, and only a very few, very privileged, members of our film unit were allowed to enter - having first taken off their shoes.

I was now one of these, for it was from here that Basil was going to do his recordings. And standing on that balcony, looking out over the huge lake to the little church on the island, was complete and absolute magic. I really don't think I've ever been so thrilled or moved. The sun shimmering on the water and the lilting song of the church bells rippling across the waves. This was the sound that Basil wanted for that scene. We spent the whole morning making recordings, and all three of us found it difficult to leave the peace and the beauty...Ah!

My George Sanders memory is in fact rather sad and had absolutely nothing to do with *England Made Me*. But I must mention our meeting, even though some of my illusions were shattered that day. I happened to travel out to Yugoslavia with the *England Made Me* Costume Designer, John Furniss, and we were sitting at London Airport waiting for our flight to be called when who should stride up but George Sanders. I'd always thought that he was one of the greatest film actors ever. I've been told that it all came very easily to him and that sometimes he didn't even try to understand the script or care what was going on, he just said the lines. But no matter - it worked. He'd very richly deserved his Oscar for *All About Eve*, and from his huge list of credits I cannot think of one performance that I wouldn't want to see again. He must also have been worth a lot more than a couple of bob, yet instead of greeting John warmly that day, or, dammit, even courteously, and asking whither we were bound and what we were filming, there was George Sanders, in the middle of Heathrow Airport, asking rather testily why he'd not been sent a pair of shoes that John had bought for him to wear on a film they'd done together some months previously - 'After all, old boy, you did promise.' I couldn't believe it. Nothing else interested the man and he didn't care that his voice was rising the more his passion heated. John Furniss was completely bewildered, but promised to cable his assistant the moment we reached our destination. 'But can't you do it now? They might sell them!'

I've wondered since if Mr Sanders was actually travelling somewhere and just happened to bump into John, or if he'd heard that John was leaving the country and had gone to the airport on purpose to accost him. Out of boredom, perhaps? I'm sorry, but I'm inclined to think it was the latter.

Nevertheless, I'm pleased to say that I did get a moment to shake hands and to tell George Sanders how much I'd enjoyed his work. All actorbums look on praise from their fellows as being of the ultimate, but this guy didn't seem to care. Perhaps the truth is just that he really didn't give a damn.

George Sanders always said that he'd finish at sixty-four when he got bored, and within a matter of months after our meeting he'd killed himself. He was just sixty-six years old.

Ach well. Enough of trying to fathom sad events that seem to make no sense. Back to *England Made Me*.

Peter Finch playing cards. Well actually Peter couldn't play cards and that's the point. In the evenings, after a damn good hotel dinner, about four of us, or six, used to play the odd hand of poker - to be honest there wasn't very much else one could do - and Peter often joined us. We weren't much good, but he was hopeless. He'd sit down, put his cash on the table, wait till his hand was dealt and then show it to us and ask if it was worth playing! He was so insistent that he wanted to play that we let him win every so often to keep things even. And when the cry, 'It's yours, Peter,' went up, usually from Ken Coles the camera operater, Peter would eagerly gather in his winnings - easily as much as fifty pence - as though it were a king's ransom. 'There you are,' he'd say, 'told you I could play this piddley game.' Happy evenings were had by all.

What else did I say I'd report? Of course, Old King Ken, mentioned above. Ken was, is, a great chum and damn good at his job. He's got offspring following him now, too. One of his sons is assistant to a lighting cameraman called Alec Mills. (Alec was the camera operator on duty when the camera jammed on *The McKenzie Break* and I had to get soaked a second time. Small world eh?)

Actually, apart from adding that he's a good egg, I'm not sure that I'm going to tell you anything more about Ken. He knows what I mean, and he, and most certainly I, have absolutely nothing to be ashamed of, have we, Ken?! Well, I'll say this much and decide if I'll tell you the whole story later. Some time after we finished *England Made Me*, Ken was invited to produce a movie and he asked me if I would be a guest star. Yes, a GUEST STAR-BUM with GUEST STARBUM BILLING! Ken's film was titled after a very big, expensive, and important movie which was going the rounds at the time called *The Towering Inferno*. Can you name it?

What's next? Ah yes, naked ladies. How apt! In order to tell you this anecdote I must first explain something about the film camera. I'm not a photographer so I don't know about these things, but I understand that that which is true for a film camera is equally true of a Box Brownie. Namely that if you want to keep light out of the camera lens you shade it. You could even use your hand, but on the film camera they try to be slightly more sophisticated and they have pieces of flat black metal called flags which can be attached to the side of the camera. On this occasion the camera was positioned at the top of a hill, on a path which led up to the big house. At the bottom of the hill was the lake and a landing stage, and as the camera was looking down the hill it could see everything - or rather it could once the the area had been lit. Yep, it was two in the morning again! Three huge arc lamps were set up behind the camera. They shone down the hill, and to prevent any residue of light from shining directly into the lens, a large flag was fixed to each side of the camera.

OK. The camera is ready. Set the scene. A big pre-war German party is in progress in the house and has overflowed into the garden. It's the sort of do where everything gets out of control. The Third Reich is getting ready to rule the world. Debauchery is everywhere, and down at the bottom of the hill around the landing stage by the lake, a dozen girls are dancing in the nude, watched by drunken German soldiers. One of the naked girls - in fact she is wearing a pair of officer's jackboots - goose-steps drunkenly to the end of the landing stage and falls into the lake. This Yugoslav extra got more money for doing that because the water was near freezing.

Into all this comes a little Jew called Erik Fromm, played of course by guess who! He's coming to the big house to try and find P. Finch again, to see if Peter has any news of his son.

Once all the background action had been sorted out it was really quite a simple scene to shoot. Just me coming up the path, looking from side to side, completely bewildered and rather frightened. So off we go. We all wanted to get the scene in the can as quickly as possible, because of the cold and those poor naked girls. Or did we? I swear it was not my fault, I really am far too professional to be so easily distracted. But...everything was going well, I wandered up the path, giving a superb performance, and just as I was about to pass the camera the girl fell off the landing stage. Now, because it was so cold, this was the one part of the scene we hadn't rehearsed - her falling in the water. Nobody was to know that the water was not in fact near freezing, it was several degrees below. And the girl screamed and screamed and screamed. It would have been fine, indeed I believe some of her screams are still in the final film, but we had to shoot the whole scene again because I walked into one of the flags! All the aforementioned extras had to be debauched all over again. The naked girls had to dance, and yes, the girl even agreed to fall into the water again, after she'd agreed another fee. But it took ages to set it up. And all because I'd turned too sharply on hearing the girl scream and walked straight into that damn flag, which in turn had jogged the camera. Everyone was very understanding. The girl in the water was pleased because of her extra money. But I got my leg pulled like mad for many a day. Apparently everyone thought that I'd done it on purpose because I wanted a second look!

Gob-smacked by Joss. Although we did this scene fully three weeks after the above, if you see the film, you'll notice that my meeting with Joss comes directly after I've walked up the path and seen the girls. Such is the way of movie making. I finally arrive at the big house and ask for Peter, but it is Joss who comes to the door. He doesn't want his boss disturbed. I plead the urgency of my case, he gets irritated and bashes me up. There's a lot of blood and I'm eventually thrown under a car. Bang smack and goodbye, the end of poor little Erik Fromm.

And we did the whole thing ourselves. The cameras were really too close to use stuntmen effectively. But to be honest, it wasn't that difficult or dangerous. Even for a non-expert, straightforward throws are quite easy. Relaxation is the key and it's one of the things you learn at drama college. When you are thrown you must go completely limp. If you do that you won't get hurt, well nine times out of eleven you won't, not much anyway.

Full-bloodied fisticuff battles are a bit different and it's better to have a stunt double do the long shots for you, particularly if it's a complicated fight. After all, that's what they're paid for and they are damn good at their job. But I don't know, when you're out there on the set and the stunt arranger explains that it's nothing, a piece of cake, well, you'd feel a bit of a sissy if you said no you didn't want to do it. So on this occasion, as I'd done countless times before, I said that of course I'd do it myself and the director said splendid he'd get some nice close-ups, which he couldn't have done if a stunt-man had been used. So it was worth it - everyone would see me being brave!

Actually a simple single punch (or three) should also be quite safe, provided you trust the man who's doing the throwing. Try it yourself. Position a chum, facing you, with his back to a full-length mirror. Then make a fist and extend your arm so that the fist is about four inches from your friend's face. Now, making quite sure that you don't lean forward because then you'll really hit him, swing your fisted arm across the front of his face and at the same time get your chum to jerk his head backwards. When you've perfected this sequence, watch what happens in the mirror and you'll see what a camera would see: You giving your friend an almighty crack across the face. When you become proficient you can even turn the camera, as it were, and show the whole thing to the camera - your fist hitting his face. Your chum will be looking in the mirror then of course. And although you in fact never hit anything, it looks as though you do. Simple! Well fairly simple, I have seen things go wrong on the odd occasion and nearly always it's been due to over zealousness.

On *England Made Me* two cameras were used, one on Joss and one on me. I filled my mouth with blood pellets, which I bit into with increasing vigour as the battle progressed, and away we went. Once it was all cut together it looked very convincing - Joss's face as he raises his fist, my face in horrified anticipation, Joss's fist swinging down on me, my head jerking back, my face with blood starting to ooze from my mouth, my broken glasses, etc., etc. There was a private showing of the film at the Odeon, Leicester Square, just before it was released, and when, after the above fight, Joss drags poor me to my feet and hurls me against a car, the whole audience went 'Ah...!'

England Made Me was one of the best. I could go on for hours - Joss and I hiring a car in Bled and getting lost in the mountains. I think we visited at least three other Communist countries that day. Waiting a week for my booked telephone call home was not so nice.

I said too that I'd mention our director, Peter Duffell, and the super parts he gave me later on, particularly in the BAFTA award-winning TV film *Caught on a Train*. But if you don't mind I'll wait till they come up chronologically.

VIII

Speaking of television, I'm feeling a little guilty. I've been a lucky enough bum, or reliable, or talented, or perhaps a wee bit of all three, to have done a goodly number of feature films in my time and it's in movies that I've tended to meet the stars. But the bulk of a working actor's life is spent in the theatre or in television. I've done no theatre at all since I came back from Perth Rep and went to see H.M. Tennant's about the award I'd won at RADA and they said hard luck. I haven't missed it, it's just the way things have gone. But I have done (as I mentioned in the Introduction), around 750 wonderful television productions. So I'm going to concentrate on TV for a while.

The Dick Emery Show. Dick was a very nice, very talented and I think a very insecure man. And I loved doing his show. Over several series I played everything from a Man from the Ministry to a barman. Dick always had a heck of a lot of lines to learn and I'm happy to say that he asked me to do some very nice duologues with him because he thought I was so solid on my lines, and of course talented!

So did Johnny Mills - sorry, Sir John! I did a super *Tales of the Unexpected* with John, called 'The Umbrella Man'. Here was another very big star name from my childhood - *We Dive At Dawn*, *I was Monty's Double*, *Tunes of Glory*, *Scott of the Antarctic*, etc., etc., etc., and etc. - what a filmography. When I turned up for the first day's rehearsal I was completely starstruck. But what a lovely person John turned out to be. No airs, no harking back to his days of super stardom. We rehearsed in an army barracks in the

Kings Road, Chelsea, and every lunchtime we'd repair to the local wine bar. We'd dive back to the rehearsal room, oh, about two hours later, and John would always say, 'For God's sake don't tell Mary where we had lunch, she'd kill me!' It seems we are all slaves to our better halves!

Later, John did a comedy series with Dandy Nichols and asked that I should be in it, again because I was solid on my lines, and, I am happy to say, because we got on so well. I was all set to go round to his house to do some pre-rehearsal line work, when it was discovered that the series would run longer than I had time free - I was already contracted for another show - and very reluctantly I had to bow out. Of course I was terribly disappointed but... C'est la vie!

Now we're back to buckle and swash. Do you remember a film called *The Moonraker*? No not James Bond, that one was called simply *Moonraker. The Moonraker* was about the Roundheads and the Cavaliers. Wasn't half bad as a matter of fact. Apart from the Star I'm about to mention it had: a chart topper theme song - 'Oh come with me my turtle dove, Oh come with me and be my love'- sung by Ronnie Hilton; Sylvia Syms - I played her boyfriend in an episode of *Paul Temple* later; Peter Arne as the baddie; Marius Goring - I played a judge in his TV series *The Expert*; and a lovely actor called Paul Whitson-Jones, who alas died many years ago, but not before, I'm delighted to say, I had the very great pleasure of doing an episode of *Softly, Softly* with him.

The Star of *The Moonraker* was a chap I'd first seen playing a small part in 'The Damn Busters', name of George Baker. After George's all too brief feature film career foundered, he concentrated on the small screen and found his forte, as we all know. One of his very early leading roles for telly was in a sitcom called *Bowler*, made by London Weekend Television. I can't remember much about it now except that George played the name part, and I was a mad doctor, who wore a ghastly red wig and was chased by a very 'big' girl. George was a sweety. He'd also got hundreds of kids and was a fantastic cook.

Space 1999 was to have been a very big tele-break for me, but the American stars, Martin Landau and his wife Barbara Pain - sorry, Bain - felt that there were too many regulars taking up too much of their screen time, so a number of us were axed. We were all blown up at the end of the first episode! For some reason I made a return visit some fifteen episodes later, don't ask me why. I know it now has a cult following - it's out on video and we're all still making money from it - but it was a terrible series.

One fun thing I do remember, however, is a lady member of the production staff going round the studio with a roll of sticking plaster and a pair of scissors. All the women - and I mean all, extrabums and starbums alike, there were no exceptions - had to stand to attention with their chests thrust out. And if there was the slightest outline of a nipple showing through their futuristic woollen costumes, as there invariably was, they were led by the hand round the back of the set and the sticking plaster was used to good effect. The only lady who didn't need the sticking plaster treatment was Mrs Landau - Miss Bain. The suggestion being that she was far too professional!

I did my first stint in *Coronation Street* at around this time. I don't remember much about it, except my admiration for the cast. Some, like Bill Kenwright, moved on to pastures new - Bill's now one of the most successful theatrical impresarios in London's West End - but others stayed on. I can remember joking with Eileen Derbyshire (Emily), that I'd return one day and play her boyfriend. And blow me, something like twenty years later I did. I came back into 'The Street' for a while and played a chap called Arthur Dabner, who courted Emily but who turned out to be married, the dastardly chap. Eileen was still there of course, doing the same professional job she'd been doing all those years before. I think 'The Street' cast, indeed the casts in all the long-running series, and I've done guest spots in most of them over the years, are probably the best bums of all. They may earn a regular wage, but they don't fly off to exotic locations or have the challenge and excitement of playing different and varied parts. Year in, year out, they rehearse, film exteriors, and record two or three episodes every week. That's one or one and a half hours of television viewing, for goodness sake. I think it's absolutely bloody marvellous. The professionalism and dedication shown by all is second to none.

Now, what can I say about dear Kenny More? Apart from anything else of course, he starred, or rather Starbummed (he'd have liked that word) in some wonderful films. *Reach for the Sky* is one of my most favourite movies ever, and did you know that Richard Burton turned down the part of Douglas Bader? Thank you, Richard!

I was really too late to work with Kenny in features. For some stupid reason the film people had all but forsaken him by the time I came on the scene. I worked with him in television, on a grand series called *Father Brown*. Sir Alec Guinness, with dear P. Finch as the baddie, had made a film version earlier, but for my money, the TV series with Kenneth More was the best. He had G. K. Chesterton's kindly character to a tee.

There was a lot of kindness in Kenny, you know. Little things, like buying coffee for a table of eight at lunchtime and giving a poor bum (guess who) a lift to the station at the end of a very long day's filming. Oh dear, why is it that those actors who finish their contracts down here early and go off to take up engagements in that Great Theatre or Studio in the sky are some of the nicest?

I won't dwell long on this because it makes me sad, but apart from Kenny, those actors I've worked with who have subsequently died, and I'm afraid there have been many, include: Peter Finch, Jack Warner, Robert Urquhart, Dick Emery, Curt Jurgens, Peter Sellers, Leo Genn, Ian Hendry, Michael Goodliffe, Paul Whitson-Jones, and Allan Cuthbertson.

Neil McCarthy - we shared the same agent at one time; Anthony Sagar - we shared the same agent early on, and I got a part which he wasn't free to do; dear Ronald Lacey - I knew him for years and he was in both the Indiana Jones films I did (isn't his daughter damn good by the way?); Percy Herbert - he and I shared the same agent at one time; Michael Bilton - although Mike suffered dreadfully from arthritis, he was always cheerful and a wonderful piss taker.

William (Billy) Hartnell and Patrick Troughton - I've worked with more Dr Whos than any other actor who played, like me, a different part each time; Patrick Newell - everybody's favourite 'mother' in *The Avengers*; Nigel Stock - he taught me at RADA, and you know that scene in *The Great Escape* where Nigel comes into his room and, unaware that most of the bed boards have been removed by Steve McQueen, jumps into his top bunk and crashes through it? Well he broke his arm, but he did it in one take. He told me all about it when we did a series together called *Knights of God*. Absolutely wonder-bloody-ful.

Alan Badel; dear Dame Peggy Ashcroft; Robert Shaw; Richard Burton; Lee Marvin; Kenneth Connor; Peter Arne; Hilda Baker; dear, lovely David Niven...of them, who wouldn't say to me today: 'I've been offered this super part, Michael, and I can't play it now, so you do it. Go on, you'll be great. And while we're at it, my agent will be looking for a new client, I'll have a word'...Bums are very generous, kind, loving, wonderful people and I love 'em to bits.

On to other things. Still television, and we have Lord Peter Wimsey, alias Ian Carmichael.

Being a Scot, I've played many a number of characters from my homeland and one fine day I was asked to play Inspector MacPherson in the BBC's production of Dorothy L. Sayers' *Lord Peter Wimsey - The Five Red Herrings*, the last in the Ian Carmichael series of Lord Peters. My first memory of Ian was in *The Colditz Story*, another of my most favourite films. Ian was smashing in an early supporting part. John Mills as star again, too.

I enjoyed *The Five Red Herrings* very much. Dearly B. thinks I was particularly excellent, even if I did look like a little Homepride flour grader in my little bowler hat! Ian worked extremely hard, was always very exact in what he did, and I think the finished product is superb.

There's an odd wee postscript to this memory. We filmed 'Herrings' in lovely Galloway in Scotland, in the county of Kirkcudbrightshire - indeed where possible in exactly the locations Miss Sayers had chosen for her book - and we stayed in Kirkcudbright town. Some years later I did a television play which was also filmed in Galloway, and we stayed at the same hotel. Nothing too unusual in that. But without my asking, to be given the very same room? And it happened again. I'll be telling you about two more films I did in Yugoslavia, *Force 10 from Navarone* and *High Road to China*. These were made at least five years apart, but we were in the same hotel the second time around and I was given the same bedroom. And then *again*, on Rhodes: *Escape to Athena* and *The Dark Side of the Sun*. Eerie!

IX

OK. Enough tellies for the moment. On to...Oh God, *Frenzy*, and Sir Ars'ole Hitchcock. I've been putting off telling you about *Frenzy*. I've been reluctant to talk about it because, along with many others, I couldn't stand Sir Alfred. I'm sure that some people loved that fat, debauched, uncaring, old-fashioned (fancy building Covent Garden in the studio when the real thing is just down the road), self-opinionated, tricksy, voyeur. It's been said thousands of times that he treated actors like cattle. Well, yes he did, but that's all right, we bums can get on with anybody. But on top of everything, he didn't even watch the scenes whilst they were being shot and I find that incomprehensibly complacent. I said to Barry Foster just before the first assistant director was about to shout 'action', 'Where the hell is Hitchcock?' Barry just smiled and said that he'd be round the back somewhere and that I'd get used to it!

I don't want you, please, to misunderstand me. I've watched Hitchcock's films over the years and I think most of them are great. But to me they are also definitely flawed, mainly because of his continued aversion to location filming. (See the backdrop with its painted ship, and the mock houses that so obviously have no backs to them, in the studio street in *Marnie* for example.)

I'd been looking forward to working with 'The Master'. But dear me no, I'd never get used to that way of working. More's the pity probably. What a fart.

X

Let's change the subject. And the next offering is...Billy Graham no less. Yes, Billy Graham the evangelist. *The Hiding Place* is a spanking good story about a wonderful Dutch family during the last war who helped Jews to escape the Nazis. And the film was produced by Billy Graham's own film company, World Wide Pictures.

I think it's great when people such as he feel that a story like this should be told. It does of course have a religious content. The heroine, Corrie Ten Boom, was an exceptional lady who did what she did with love and faith. But I also feel sure that Mr Graham was pleased when, as well as being the most successful offering ever at his conventions, the film turned out to be so good that it also played the commercial cinema circuits, standing on its own feet as it were.

I played the Kapitan who arrested, among others, lovely Julie Harris (remember her in *East of Eden* with James Dean?), and Arthur O'Connell, who'd done more films than almost any of us have had those old hot dinners - *Picnic*, *Anatomy of a Murder*, *The Poseidon Adventure*, et al. (He should have been on my list by the way, he died alas, only five years after this picture was made.)

We filmed in the Amsterdam district of Haarlem, where the story actually happened. And people remembered. When we broke for lunch we had to walk up the street to a restaurant, where the meal had been laid on by our caterers, and I found that the local populace were looking at me, and pointing and whispering. Apparently I looked, in my Nazi uniform, very like the actual guy who'd been in charge of the district during the war!

It was fascinating to visit the very house where the events took place and see the room which had been shortened to make the Hiding Place behind a wardrobe. What courage those people must have had. Thank God for the English Channel.

We couldn't in fact film in the house itself because it was now a museum and open to the public. And anyway, everything was so cramped there would have been hellish location and camera difficulties. So the production team rented another house, not far away, at the top of a small T-junction, and they 'dressed' this to look like the real 'Ten Boom - Watchmakers and Jewellers', for that is what the family had been. This new house was far better for our purposes. The camera could move with comparative ease, and because the house faced down the street, which was the upright of the T as it were, the director could get lovely shots of me, and others, driving towards it, and soldiers marching. He could also, if he wished, show cars sweeping round the corner, and he could of course turn his cameras to look either way along the horizontal of the T. All in all an excellent substitute for the real thing. Except...

Nobody knew this at the time of the negotiations, but the street down which I and my staff car were going to hurtle was the one street in Haarlem where the ladies who were members of the oldest profession plied their trade, and the house at the T junction, our house, was owned by their pimps. Without realising it we'd landed up in one of Amsterdam's satellite red light districts! Every morning before we started work the production staff had to go down the street and buy off the ladies for the whole day. This was very expensive! And when the contract for using the pimp-owned house ran out, the renewal premium demanded was so high that it was decided to build a replica of the front of the house back in the studios in England, plus the bits of street either side. This is indeed what happened, and it still cost the company a bomb.

I've never heard what, if any, comment Billy Graham made when he was told of this balls-up. Imagine, his movie at the mercy of whores! As Executive Producer I'm sure he'd have been aggrieved at the extra expense, but I feel quite certain that he'd also have had a damn good laugh.

I'm delighted to have had the opportunity to appear in this film, even if my staff car - an actual VW survivor from the war - had lost its exhaust and the fumes were almost suffocating, and I must tell you one more little fond remembrance.

Billy Graham did not interfere in any way in the day to day making of the film. Indeed, he only visited the set on a very few occasions. He first put in an appearance not long after we'd started. We were having lunch in the restaurant I mentioned and he sat down to eat with us. He was a very handsome man, still is as far as I know, tanned and tall. The sort of chap who really does stand out in a crowd. At the end of the meal he was asked to say a few words, and with the right amount of humility he stood up and started to speak: 'Before we pray for the success of this picture, I would like to tell you of my arrival here in beautiful Holland. Nobody knew I was coming. Nobody. And when I arrived at the grand Hilton hotel I went straight up to my room. As I opened the door I surprised the maid, who was cleaning up and was about to make the bed. 'Oh, you're Billy Graham aren't you?' she said. 'Nobody told me but I'd know you anywhere. Why...why have you come?' I explained that we were making this movie. 'Oh, Mr Graham, please could we pray for the success of your film?' I replied that of course we could. And we did. We knelt down right where we were in my hotel room and we prayed for the success of our film.'

Now I don't know what I think about this sort of high-powered, high-profile, American preaching. But what I can say is that the above speech was delivered with more expertise than could have been achieved by many an actor. It was quite a performance. And I'm pleased to report too that Billy Graham laughed with the rest of us when, after he'd said a short prayer and had sat down, a little no-nonsense props man named Alf called out from the back of the cafe 'That's all very nice, mate, but did she make your flippin' bed?'

Although perhaps we were not about to join him at Wembley, there were many in the company who liked Mr Billy Graham. I certainly did.

XI

Telling you how I was mistaken for the German who was in charge in wartime Haarlem, reminds me of the tele-film *To Encourage the Others* - the true story of the Craig/Bentley murder case. I, with my head shaved, played Police Sergeant

Fairfax, who had become one of the most hated men in the country because of the evidence he had given at the trial. When we did a hunk of night filming on the roof of the actual sweet factory in Croydon (since demolished) where the robbery and the killing of P.C. Miles took place, we went to a nearby pub for a warmer. Suddenly the locals were all pointing accusing fingers at me. 'That's him,' they said. 'That's Fairfax. Let's get the bastard.' And until they learnt that it was only me, they most certainly were not joking. At times it can be a good deal more than a little worrying to look so like the factual people I've played!

Around this time I did a film called *Holiday on the Buses*. I'd done the last of the TV series playing the Depot Manager and I played him in the movie, same as all the regulars, who played their TV roles.

A double-decker bus, open-topped, was hired for the film. I wasn't involved in the sequence, but in one shot it had to be driven onto the beach, and it accidentally got stuck in the sand. No great problem, arrangements were made to have it pulled out by tractors the following morning. Trouble was though, that the tide came in that evening and started to engulf the bus. Nothing daunted, the director got everybody, crew and actorbums alike, out of the hotel and down on the beach. Then he improvised a scene, which is still in the final film, of bus and passengers getting stuck. (The bus was rescued the next day, albeit a little the worse for wet!)

Nice film in the 'Carry On' mould. Nice series, nice people. But you don't want to hear about the nice director, who was very large, appearing after lunch one day wearing the most ridiculous pair of enormous shorts I've ever seen, do you?

So I'll move on...*In Sickness and in Health*. I'm putting this one in because it included the most nervous afternoon I have ever spent in our rather nervous profession. Oh yes, every bum must have a good number of butterflies hopping around before he can give of his best. Even David Niven, with all his experience, once said to me just before a take, 'My God, Michael, it doesn't get any easier. I'll never get used to it.'

Euston Films, they who made *Minder* and *The Sweeney* amongst many, did a few pilots which didn't make it into series. Nobody's fault, it just happened that some subjects didn't click, and *In Sickness and in Health* was one of these. It told the story of a hard-pressed young doctor who worked in a seedy part of London. Patrick Mower played the doctor and I played his Bank Manager (the idea was that he was very short of money so he'd be visiting me all the way through the series!) And a very young lady - five years old to be exact - had a very, very important part. Her name?...Susannah Sheard! The casting director had said to me: 'Michael, you've got a young daughter haven't you? We need a little girl to play one of Pat's patients. I'll tell you what, we could arrange for one of your scenes to be done next Tuesday morning and do your daughter's scene in the afternoon. Then you could bring her with you and you'd be free to chaperon her when you've finished.' Well, it was nobody's fault but mine. Susannah was really super. She played beautifully with Pat, showing him her pretend badly-cut knee, but I was so full of nerves I shudder even now when I think of it. My scene in the morning had just the required number of tummy butterflies. It had been a piece of cake!

Susannah, by the way, is herself a Doctor of Medicine now and no, her ambitions had nothing to do with this piece. Her abiding memory of that day she spent on *In Sickness and in Health*, is having lunch. We had another double-decker bus as our location restaurant, and Susannah had her first course downstairs and her pudding up top!

Hitler. He looks like me too! I've played Hitler four, almost five times. The almost was going to be in *The Winds of War*, but they took so long to decide dates, I wasn't free. One of the times I actually played him was in a children's telly for the old Thames TV company - Hitler turned out to have been deep frozen by a very young Nicholas Lyndhurst, and was really a green blob from outer space - more about two of the other times I gave my Adolf H. later, *Rogue Male* now.

Based on the novel by Geoffrey Household, Peter O'Toole played an Englishman who went off to Germany just before the war and almost shot Der Fuhrer - actually had him in his gun sights. It was fiction, of course, but a good yarn, and what if it had been true?! This was my first crack at the H. role and it came off pretty well, though I say it as shouldn't. O'Toole was charming and wouldn't sit next to me at lunch because he said I looked too much like the real thing. A compliment to me, I think!

I've just remembered, there could have been a sixth Adolf for me. This time I would most certainly have been the star of the picture, but I turned down *The Sex Life of Adolf Hitler*.

There was a little tiddler of a comedy series called *The Top Secret Life of Edgar Briggs*, made by London Weekend TV. In charge was a guy named Bryan Izzard, one of the real personalities of our business. He was the very large director who had shown such initiative on the *Holiday on the Buses* film when the bus got stuck. I've got a lot of time for Brian, and until he went on to make tapes of operas and things for his own company we worked together a lot.

'Edgar Briggs' did quite well I believe, but it didn't create any records either and it wasn't retained for another series. The star was an unknown, rather short, comedy actor. About six months after we'd finished, I happened to be walking down Regent Street, when I was hailed by this guy. We had a coffee and he told me how terrible things had been for him. He'd done nothing. 'Not a bloody thing, Michael. Absolutely f'all.' It was all rather depressing, particularly as I'd been doing rather well. Anyway, very soon after our meeting he got a smallish part with Ronnie Barker in *Porridge*, and the rest as they say is history...More 'Porridges' followed, and *Open All Hours*. Then he went on to star in *Only Fools and Horses* and *The Darling Buds of May*, in which I also served, and - well you can name them. David Jason is a smashing chap and probably the best comedy actorbum this country has produced since...Oh, off the top of my head, Ronnie Barker.

XII

There was an airport strike, and I was doing a TV play in my homeland, when I was asked if I'd like to pop down to London to meet Guy Hamilton again. He was going to direct a movie called *Force 10 from Navarone* in Yugoslavia, starring Harrison Ford, Robert Shaw, Edward Fox, Barbara Bach (Ringo Starr's wife), Franco Nero, and Alan Badel. But the strike meant that, because of my work commitments in Glasgow, there was no way I could get to London and back in the little free time I had - the train would have taken too long.

I asked my agent to explain to Mr Hamilton and the casting director the reasons why I couldn't make it, to say that I'd love to play the part, that perhaps they could see from my CV how experienced I was, and that Mr Hamilton had of course cast me before, for *Live and Let Die*. I told the agent to add that I fully understood that they wouldn't normally offer a good part such as this without first meeting the actor, but perhaps just this once...I'm sure you understand, all the usual flannel!

My agent, I may tell you, was not happy. (Not the agent I've talked of previously by the way, this was an earlier version.) She said that I simply couldn't treat people this way and that I should come to London whatever the problems. Completely overlooking the fact that I would be breaking my Scottish contract and holding up production on a very important project, one which she had got for me in the first place. I said that there was no way I was going to London and that she must tell them what I'd said. 'All right. But that'll be it,' she replied. 'They won't offer you the part now.'

But they did. Somebody somewhere, I think it was probably Guy or the casting lady - it was lovely Irene Lamb again - or both, decided to convince the American money men that there was no need to meet such an important bum as me before offering me the job, and that they would be very lucky to get me to play Sergeant Bauer. And so they were!

What a damn good film it turned out to be, still very regularly appearing on television. And what a plethora of memories come flooding back. I've already mentioned how I stayed in the same hotel, in Ljubljana, and had the same room I would occupy later on *High Road to China*. Well the breakfasts never changed either, in spite of all my efforts.

Do you remember a huge seven-foot-tall giant of an American actor called Richard Kiel? He played Jaws in a couple of Bond films. Well Richard was also in 'Force 10', and on the first morning after we arrived he asked me to show him a typical traditional English breakfast. So without any foreboding I led the way through the vast reception area to the dining room. The dining room was also enormous, with a very long table running right down the middle, on which the starters were laid - cereals, fruit juices, etc.

As we were being traditional, we helped ourselves to corn flakes and sat down at one of the little tables at the side of the room which overlooked the sea. When we'd finished our flakes, the waiter came over to take our main order. And then the fun began. I can't remember exactly how long I was in Yugoslavia on 'Force 10', but together with the time I spent on the later film it certainly ran into a good few months. And during all that time I never managed to order tea with cold milk, and above all else, ordinary, simple, bacon and eggs. Richard and I seemed to rise at about the same time and we often had breakfast together. And he, and his lovely, petite wife when she joined him, took great delight in my frustration. Oh we'd get the tea right on occasion - when I pinched some of the cold milk set aside for the cereals - but I never did manage the bacon. We'd get loads of pork. Ham and eggs seemed to be a speciality of the house. I was even invited into the kitchens to explain to them what bacon was, but to no avail. We had a bonus of six eggs each on one occasion to compensate, but bacon, never.

I also made a fool of myself on this movie. As you now know I hadn't met the director before the start of the film. A good few years before I'd met him, yes. But then it was only very briefly, because my part in *Live and Let Die* had never happened. And when I arrived at the 'Force 10' location hotel with the rest of the bums, Guy Hamilton was already out scouting the locations, so I didn't meet him then either.

On the first evening I wandered into the hotel bar. It was full of the film crew, all either getting to know each other or renewing old acquaintances. There were a good few I knew too and before long I was happily chatting to some old chums. And some new ones as well! There was this nice, rather tall chap, wearing a light-coloured trilby. I asked him if he'd been in the business long, if he liked it and if he had much to do on this film. You know the sort of thing. He replied that he did enjoy his work and that yes, his was quite a heavy responsibility. But he didn't say exactly what he did and I don't know, I felt it was a bit rude to ask. But then he was smiling at me. 'You haven't a clue who I am, have you?' he said. 'But I know you, you wouldn't be here but for me. I'm your director, Guy Hamilton.' I felt very, very small and I'm sure I was blushing very crimson!

Guy was absolutely fabulous. And so he should have been. Some thirty years earlier he'd been the assistant director on *The Third Man*, another of my favourite films.

Did you know that a film company can get insurance against the rain? And heavens, did it rain on this picture. The only trouble is that if, as we were, you are filming at night, you have to hang around until two in the morning, I think it is, before you are entitled to the money and everyone can go back to the hotel and their lovely warm beds. Imagine therefore a huge marquee, at least half way up a mountain in deepest Yugoslavia. The rain is belting down outside and it is anything from eight in the evening to two in the the morning. The place is packed with film crew, hot mugs of tea in hand, all singing at the top of their voices. Led, in such evergreens as 'Underneath the Spreading Chestnut Tree', by that master of the chorus, Mr Guy Hamilton!

The only one not there I'm afraid was Robert Shaw. He would spend his nights of rain, and there were many of them, in his caravan. He was writing a book, but I'm afraid he was also at times very much the worse for wear. There is a scene in the film which we shot around this time - yes the rain did stop eventually - in which Robert, Harrison and Franco are supposedly forcing me, at gunpoint, across the Chetnik camp towards the armoury. But dammit, Robert was so pissed that night that he had to be held up by Harrison and Franco, and in order to make it look real, Harrison had to direct operations under his breath - 'Slow down a bit, Michael. Alright, you can move a little faster now' Look for yourself the next time the film is shown on TV, you can just see that all is not quite what it should be if you know what you're looking for.

And it didn't end there. When we returned to England to do the interiors at Shepperton Studios, Guy came to me one day and said that poor Robert was unable to do the scene which had been scheduled because he was 'unwell' again, but that if they didn't at least do my close-up, with dialogue, they'd get so far behind they'd never be able to catch up. Did I think I could do my part of the scene without Robert, with the continuity lady reading in his lines? I defy anybody to say whether Robert was there or not - of course he wasn't. It's all in the eyes, if I see a non-existent Robert, then it's OK.

I'll be talking in detail later about using bits of sticking plaster for an eyeline, when the person you are doing the scene with can't be in their place, and although this method is usually used for close work, it can be adapted for wider shots. It's a little more difficult, because you can see the rest of the room, or whatever, but provided you concentrate like mad, and it looks as though you are seeing what you should be seeing, even though it isn't there, you'll be fine.

I liked Robert Shaw a lot. He was a super actor, all the way from his early days in *The Dam Busters*, to *Jaws*, *The Sting* and, yes certainly, *Force 10 from Navarone*. And he was great fun to be with. Very competitive, always eager to join in any sort of game. Mind you, he did like to win.

Franco Nero is a very nice Italian actorbum. Loves his food, especially pasta. It does seem, however, that they have a rather different way of making films in Italy. Nothing, absolutely nothing, must stop the camera from rolling.

I've just told you how Harrison, Robert, Franco and I crossed the camp to the armoury. Well, after we get there and they have forced me to let them in, all hell breaks loose and most of us are killed. The few that remain, our heroes - Franco included - rush out of the armoury, jump into a truck that happens to be nearby and drive off at high speed. Trouble was that when they came to film the scene, Franco, the driver, couldn't get the vehicle to start. But his training in Italian pictures came to his rescue. With great panache, and to the astonishment of those present, he suddenly grasped the steering wheel and started making lorry noises. 'Vroom, vroom...vroom, vroom.'

'Cut!' Guy Hamilton shouted. 'Franco what are you doing?' Franco turned towards the assembled crowd. 'In Italy we never stop,' he said, 'you put the sound of the car on afterwards.'

'Perhaps we could do that,' Guy said, 'but we also want to see the lorry moving in this shot.'

'Then you push,' the Italian replied!

Harrison Ford is also a very nice chap and a damn fine thespian who did as many of his own stunts as they'd let him. No fuss, no pretensions. Until he got his big break in movies, he'd waited patiently, working as a master carpenter. I've sort of left Harrison till last because it will lead me neatly on to the next time I worked with him, in that great cricketing film, 'The Umpire Strikes Back'!

XIII

Actually *The Empire Strikes Back* of course. The big break Harrison had waited for had come with the original *Star Wars* movie some three years previously, and this was the first sequel. And by heck hasn't he gone on and on. He's done some wonderful, smashing work. What a very great starbum.

I played Admiral Ozzel in 'Empire', the commander of Darth Vader's space ship, and I had a little souvenir model made of me to be sold with all the other models of all the other characters. Darth Vader finally got cross with me and although he was supposedly miles away at the time, simply looked into the television link-up we had between us, and I choked, coughed and died.

I had a wonderful time. And when I later worked on the Indiana Jones films, the first thing that George Lucas said to me was that he remembered how well I'd choked in 'Empire'!

Now I've got myself into a muddle again. *Escape to Athena* came before *The Empire Strikes Back*, and I haven't written about the Ken Coles film either and that came a good bit before both of them. Not to worry. But if I'm going to relate the saga of the Coles film - something I've never spoken of before - then I'd better do it now. I'll go straight on to 'Athena' after that.

Right. Now then. You remember that Old King Ken asked me to be a Guest Starbum in a film he was producing, and that the film took its title from *The Towering Inferno*? Well Ken's film was called *The Erotic Inferno*. Actually a very clever title. No! Sheard did not do a porno film - don't even think it!

In fact, I couldn't really blame you. When my youngest son was at university, some of his fellow undergrads got hold of a copy of this film and thought that they'd have a laugh at his expense by showing it. I'm pleased to report that my son was not in the least fazed, and after the screening, which showed no more of me than usual, quietly asked if he could have the video, as his dad had been trying to get hold of a copy of the film for ages to add to his library.

It is quite simply just a film, made as well as it could possibly be made on a lowish budget. It has a proper British Board of Film Censor Certificate and it ran longer in the West End than any film I know - albeit in a little cinema in Brewer Street. Yes OK, it's a soft porn, bare everything movie, and there are lots of naughty bits and even simulated sex (the whole of the movie world it seems is make-believe), but it's as good a film as Ken could make it, and he did have me as his Guest Starbum! If you have a Guest Star credit on a film such as this, incidentally, it means that you are the class in the picture and that you never take anything off. Or indeed do anything that you wouldn't want your own mother to see. Heavens, I didn't even catch sight of so much as a shapely ankle on the days I was filming.

Really, the story is almost Shakespearean - King Learish: a father wants to know which of his three sons loves him the most so he pretends to be dead. He gets his solicitor (me) to call the boys to his large house in the country to await the reading of his will. The three lads bring their girlfriends with them and...so on! (It's always advisable to have a large house or some such as your main location on a movie like this, as far as possible removed from inquisitive neigbours and peeping Toms.)

As one of our most durable TV quizmasters has said on many occasions, 'I've started so I'll finish.' I'm going to admit more! I've always been interested in the possibility of us, the bums, and them, the technicians, making our own films and television programmes. (I'll be mentioning this off and on throughout, and indeed even as I write there is the possibility of something coming up involving a producer, a writer and me.) Anyway, after *The Erotic Inferno* was completed, Ken was asked to make a series of movies of similar type and he suggested that I might be interested in becoming his associate.

I love what I am. An actor first and foremost, who can sometimes have the odd toe-dip into the fascinating world of the moguls in the front office. I didn't really see myself as exclusively a producer, particularly long term. So I suppose I have to admit that I'm pleased I wasn't free to accept Ken's offer because I was already contracted to do several tellies and a movie. But I was very flattered that he should ask me and we promised to try and get something off the ground later.

I did help Ken to prepare his next production however, and although in the end the series of films never happened, because the money man - Ken's Executive Producer - lost his distribution deal with the American drive-in movie circuit, let me tell you about *Long Distance Love*. My suggested title.

And a damn good title it is too. It tells you exactly what will happen, once you've accepted that it's a naughty film and that the 'Long Distance' refers to lorries - driving, fighting, chasing and copulating; or thrills, spills and frills! We had a director, quite a well-known and respected television name, and we began to get a pretty good script together.

My main job was to find things which cost nothing, and Ford Motors offered me the free use of one of its new continental trucks which had a bed behind the driver's seat! The only stipulation was that we would guarantee that its logo would be in shot, somewhere in the film, for a minimun of five seconds. (When you're enquiring about the loan of things such as lorries, you don't necessarily tell the company into which category your film will fall.)

Then we started casting, and this was both a nightmare and an eye-opener. Because it was my neck of the woods, it was suggested by the Executive Producer that I should set up a casting session. 'I think next Wednesday would be good. That's three days from now. OK?' Only three days. Where do I start!

I rang an old buddy at Spotlight, the actor's directory, because I hadn't a clue where to find girls who would be prepared to show a bit more than a leg, go a bit further than a kiss and a cuddle, and perhaps be able to act as well. The first thing that Carey Ellison did was to congratulate us on getting a film off the ground, any film, it didn't matter about the content. Then he gave me the names of a couple of agents who would have girls on their books happy to do this kind of picture, told me not to forget to have an Equity chaperon at the casting session, and wished us luck.

The casting session was hilarious - we were far more embarrassed than the girls, at least I know I was. The thing is you see, there's no point having a casting session and finding a girl who'd be great for the lead, only to discover on the first day of filming that she's got a huge birthmark on her bulges, or an ugly appendix scar. These girls expect to have to take their clothes off at a casting interview, hence the need for an Equity chaperon. They don't mind, in fact they're so used to it that a lot of them arrived dressed only in a tracksuit, with nothing on underneath. And whether they were right for the parts or not one thing is certain, they were highly amused by our embarrassment!

Hey ho. I mentioned that *The Erotic Inferno* ran forever in London. Well I'm lucky enough to have stood in Piccadilly Circus and been able to see two West End cinemas at which there is a big budget film playing that features me - with my credit just below the title. Two at the same time. That's a truly wonderful feeling for any actorbum. But so is knowing that you've got guest star billing in a little film playing round the corner which has run for longer than anything else. Even if you don't talk about it!

XIV

I meant everything I said just now, and what I said to Helmut Griem that far off day when we were making *The McKenzie Break*. I love being a working vagabond, a journeyman bum actor, and I'm very proud of the things I've done. So as I've just been talking about my guest star role in a movie, I thought I might lump together two two-handers. These were half hour plays I did for telly and both were made in Scotland, but for different companies.

The first was an in-depth study of a playwright and the woman he is interviewing for the lead in his play. She in fact turns the tables on him half-way through and they both end up in emotional shreds. My leading lady was the beautiful and very talented Wanda Ventham, whom I'd first seen in a 'Carry On' film, I think it was. (What I do remember, Wanda, is that you were dressed in bra, pants and stockings only, all gleaming white, and with your lovely golden hair you looked...absolutely fabulous!) We only had one week to get this duologue play in the can and we worked like stink. We hardly had a moment to eat or sleep and it was one of the most stimulating weeks of my life. The script ran to about seventy pages, mostly dialogue, and when it came time to record, four cameras were used. And we videoed the whole thing with just one break, and that was for a camera move!

The play was called *If the Face Fits* and it was made by BBC Scotland for their Scottish Playbill slot. It was one of only three plays in that series which was shown south of the border on network television, and the national press loved it and us. The *Times* in particular was very nice.

The second two-hander was called *Thieves*. This one was made by Scottish TV and was never shown in England, but it did win an award in America - best short play or something.

The story this time concerned two strangers who have been picked up for suspected shoplifting in a large department store and left in a small office to await the arrival of the police. The two come from very differing backgrounds. He - me - is a professional older man who would never do such a thing as steal, it is all a mistake. She is a street urchin, played by a very talented newcomer (and to my shame, darling, I can't recall your name, I'm very sorry), who has been thieving all her young life. After a half-hour's talk they are both much more understanding of each other and indeed very protective.

We had a few breaks in the taping of this play because of the different methods used by the two directors - the Beeb guy liked to tape in one go, STV in bits - but *Thieves*, too, was most enjoyable. And I understand that my framed photo is still hanging in one of the hallways at Scottish Television as testament to our winning that USA award.

A word or six dozen now about my Island! There are surely times when we all like to get away from the hustle and recharge the batteries. I suppose my Island of Peace should be in Scotland, in the Outer Hebrides probably. But it's not, that would be far too far off the beaten track to be in time for any studio call, let alone an early morning one for 5.30am! No, my Island is the Isle of Wight, and it's not second best, it is the tops. I really can't think of a better place to live and rest.

When I was a wee lad, not long after I was that tiny wee tot in Aberdeen, my Grandma lived on the Island and my parents and I used to spend part of the summer holidays with her.

There was some excellent sea fishing to be had then off the end of Sandown Pier (alas it's far from good now), and there were steam trains on the Island too. Little puffers that would take you almost anywhere you could wish - over hill and down dale to Ventnor in the South; round Newport corner to Cowes, where the world-famous sailing week is held every year, and before 1952 you could even puff all the way to Freshwater, via Yarmouth. I was just in time for that run. Most of the trains have gone now. You can still travel down Ryde Pier and on to Shanklin in a former Piccadilly line tube, courtesy of London Transport Underground, and some rail enthusiasts have bought the piece of track which connects Smallbrook to Wootton and run the very successful Isle of Wight Steam Railway, but it's not the same.

These are only little niggles you understand, the Island is still a simply super place to live. Even the fact that the cinema in Shanklin has closed is sad, but it makes no difference. (It's now boarded up and looks like a vast coffin and someone has written R.I.P. on its side.)

When my Grandmama died, the Island and I sort of lost touch with each other until, that is, I had three young 'uns of my own who didn't feel they'd had a proper holiday unless they had actually crossed water to get there. It didn't matter that I had, at the time, to be near a phone and within easy reach of the studios. We also had a dog we wouldn't leave in kennels.

I thought of my happy times on the Isle of Wight. Dearly B. and I popped our family tent on the top of the car and ourselves and the kids inside, and a super time was had by all. And I even travelled back to London in the middle of our stay to do a couple of days filming - on *The Squad*, a series for Thames TV about police cadets - and returned to complete the holiday when I'd finished.

That set the seed I'm sure. We had several further splendid Isle of Wight holidays under canvas in different parts of the Island, then we bought a holiday flat in Sandown and finally, when the children had flown the nest, Dearly Beloved and I sold our place in Surrey and moved into a wee house in Ryde, overlooking the Solent. And we love it. I can get to the studios in next to no time, and when I'm not required I can take sandwiches and a bottle of vino and fish for those non-existent mackerel for as long as I like!

I always knew that there is an intangible common bond that unites all of us who have the privilege of working in this super business and you can find it in the oddest of places.

The moment Dearly Beloved and I moved to our Island hideaway, we felt that there was an empathy between us and the man who owns the local pet shop. I was in his shop buying food for our moggies and hound and we got into conversation. I casually happened to mention that I was thinking of writing these delights. 'Can I be in your book?' he asked suddenly, 'I'm an old pro...No, no, not one of them! I was in the business for years.' Then he added with pride, 'I was a magician and I was damned bloody good.' (See my answer to George Cosmatos in the next but one remembrance. We're all the same.)

And 'The South's Leading Mentalist', as he was called, Terry Delgado - he pinched the name from Roger Delgado who played The Master, Dr Who's arch enemy - was bloody good, many people have told me so. And not all of them have been related to Terry!

Why did he decide to give it all up and become a Pet Shop Boy?

I don't honestly know and it doesn't matter a jot. The point is I knew that he and I were kindred spirits the moment we first met, and we've been taking the mickey out of each other ever since. Once a bum always a bum. I was able to give his shop a plug when I was interviewed on local radio recently, and because he's lived in our neck of the country all his life he knows everybody, and has thus been very useful to us. Terry's been able to put me in touch with the right expert for every single thing I could ever need...Thanks Terry. I'm bound to say in fact that there is one exception to these 'right expert' introductions. I shall come back to accountants later!

Can you imagine a movie, the script for which has been written, first in Italian, it's then been translated into French, before finally being reworked in English? No wonder the title ended up as *Escort Service*! No, we are not back to naughties, this film was about espionage. I played the head of MI5, and I was finally shot dead on Tooting Common.

It was quite gory in fact, and rather well done. First you see me walking along with not a care in the world, umbrella a-swing, newspaper tucked under my arm. It's a lovely spring day and I sit down on a park bench to read my newspaper. The villain, who has been watching me all the while, then raises his gun, aims very carefully, and fires. We quickly cut to a shot over my shoulder, looking at the newspaper I've been reading, and we see my brains suddenly splatter on to the page, the headline of which reads something like, 'MI5 fear new attack'. Behind the camera the while has been a chap with a large barrelled airgun, which has just fired. This gun has been filled with an unusual charge - bits of string, loads of pretend blood, and masses of other bits and pieces which together look like the inside of a man's head.

The leading player was an Italian who couldn't speak one word of English and he was playing one of my English operatives, for goodness sake! Actually I felt quite sorry for the guy, particularly when the Italian director, who also spoke no word of our language, except 'Actioni', insisted that a new English script should be written for one of the scenes. Just twenty short minutes later the scene had been rewritten and this poor Latin thespian was expected to have learnt it.

I'm still trying to discover what happened to this extraordinary multinational co-production, but so far I've had no luck. If anyone has even the remotest idea where I might lay my hands on a copy, please let me know. I'm not very optimistic on this occasion, but I have found many times that a film which has been made under the most difficult of conditions can turn out to be one of the best!

XV

Escape to Athena. Starbumming: Roger Moore, David Niven, Stefanie Powers, Elliott Gould, Richard Roundtree, Sony Bono, Telly Savalas, Claudia Cardinale, and...Me. Oh yes, and Tony Valentine, we shared the screen for our featured credit.

It all started when I went to meet the director, George Pan Cosmatos, or Georgie as he came to be known. All the Star actors had been signed and in place for ages. It was one hell of an expensive film and their names had been needed to raise the money. Think about it. Stefanie explained it to me like this: she was there to catch the TV audiences and the younger men; Richard Roundtree to bring in the black moviegoers; Niv for the older generation; Rog 'cos he was handsome, and a very, very big Star, particularly after the Bond films; Claudia was there to catch the older roving eyes; Elliott, because, as he said, he was under contract; Sonny already owned most of Las Vagas but still desperately wanted to be an actor; and Telly...well, nobody quite knew why he was there except that the film was set in Greece.

But George Pan had one part left! Not important enough to tempt a starbum and so help with raising money, but a grand part for a featured bum like me. 'Are you a good actor?' Georgie asked me. I'd hardly had time to get into the room let alone sit down. So - 'Of course I bloody am. Why the hell else do you think I'm here,' I replied, thinking that this one was a waste of time. 'OK then. I want you to play the part of Sergeant Mann, Roger Moore's assistant. We will be making the whole film on Rhodes and we will be there for five months. You won't need to be with us for quite that long, perhaps four and a half.' It's strange but true. Ninety-nine times out of a hundred the best parts just plop into your lap.

My memories of 'Athena' are happy and numerous.

Stefanie Powers is one of those lovely people who likes everyone and whom everyone likes. She is a no-nonsense professional trouper, and just happens to be a bloody good actress as well. I had only one difficulty with Stef - she is a fitness fanatic!

The hotel at which we were staying was about two miles outside the town of Rhodes, along the coast road. One day I'd had the afternoon off and I'd been into town to look around and ET - phone home! (Never make long distance calls from the hotel, of course, they put masses on to the bill. Make your calls home from the local post office, that way you'll get value for money.) When I'd finished, I was waiting for the bus to take me back to the hotel, when along comes Stefanie. 'Oh, you don't want to take the bus,' she said. 'Come on, I'll race you.' I mentioned something about not wanting to take advantage of a lady and she looked at me rather mischievously. 'I'll tell you what,' she said. 'If you beat me I'll buy dinner, and if I beat you, you buy it. And to make it quite fair I should tell you that my Bill is going to be ringing me in just over ten minutes, so I'll have to hurry. Let's go.' Stef was in time for her call. I trundled in a good fifteen minutes later. And yes, we had a very enjoyable meal in the taverna adjoining the hotel, which I paid for.

The Bill she'd mentioned, by the way, was her long standing companion, William Holden, one of Hollywood's greatest stars. Do you remember a film called *Stalag 17*? Bill Holden won an Oscar for his performance. It was of course set in a German prison camp during the last war. Our film, 'Athena', was also set in a prison camp, and when later on Bill came over to visit Stef, the production popped him into American army gear and got him to lean against one of the huts with a cigar, his calling card in *Stalag 17*, wedged between his teeth, just as I come trundling past, leading Elliott to see the Commandant, Roger. Elliott stops and says to Bill, 'Are you still here?' To which Bill replies,

'Why not? It's not a bad life.' I look at them somewhat puzzled and then on Elliott and I trudge. Bit of an 'in' joke I know, but fun, and it works well. It's still in the film, have a look next time it's on the box. But don't blink or you'll miss it!

Stefanie was super. I almost worked with her again a few years later when she came to England to do some episodes of *Hart to Hart*, but to my great sorrow I wasn't free. I wonder why the producers asked for me...?! (Actually I know why and I wrote and thanked Stef for suggesting me.)

As far as I know there has never been the slightest sign of any sort of racial prejudice in our business, and colour makes no difference whatsoever. We're all bums, remember. But Richard Roundtree on 'Athena' did seem to be unhappy. He was nice enough and he was good to work with - he and I had two or three good little scenes together. But he didn't mix in the evenings with the rest of us. He kept his distance and always seemed to be rushing off on his own to play golf or something. OK, you may well think it was because he was black and that he felt unwanted, but it's not. I know what it was because I asked him.

My description of the striptease scene, which really made the film for me, and my performance, comes a little later, but at the end of it I have a few moments with Richard, when his character, Judson, invites me, Sgt. Mann, up on to the stage. Whilst we were waiting for things to be readied, I asked Richard if he was enjoying the film and if not why. And he gave me the sort of answer I would only really have expected from the likes of Helmut Griem - remember *The McKenzie Break*? Richard said that he wished he'd never accepted the part in 'Athena' as it was not nearly good enough for him. He'd recently made an enormous impression as 'Shaft', and his part here was nothing. He wanted only starring roles, with himself as the only star.

In other words, he was bored, and felt frustrated and humiliated. Poor man. Perhaps he should have turned the part down.

Now I'll tell you about the dances in 'Athena'. One, the striptease mentioned above, and the other, well I suppose you'd call it a victory dance. I'll deal with the victory dance first, because Telly Savalas and Claudia Cardinale made so little of it there's virtually nothing to tell. Mr Savalas and Miss Cardinale had known when this dance was coming up weeks before it was filmed. There was a dance instructor on hand to help them with the choreography and time was allotted for rehearsal. And they did nothing. It seemed that they simply didn't care. When the scene was shot, they just walked out into the square, lifted their arms and busked it. Dearly B. says that they were not supposed to be professional dancers. True, but they were meant to be native Greeks, and the Greeks are always dancing. And I think their lack of expertise damn well shows on the screen and that's unforgivable.

Now contrast that if you will with the striptease dance as performed by Stefanie Powers and Elliott Gould. Elliott if you remember was only doing the film because he was under contract, so he probably didn't care about the outcome any more than did Telly Savalas, but the difference between them was vast. Elliott is a 'trouper' Starbum and always gave of his best, whereas Telly was an 'I don't give a fuck' Starbum. The evening before our first day's shooting, he and his entourage still hadn't arrived at the hotel. When they finally showed up, very late, one of his underlings asked for a script, the suggestion being that his master hadn't even read it.

For ten days before Stefanie and Elliott were due to film their dance they rehearsed it every evening in the hotel. We could hear them. It wasn't really a striptease, it was a spoof, but we, the audience, were supposed to think that Stef would take off all her clothes. Little Sergeant Mann (me) had a wonderful time collecting all the discarded articles, but Stef never in fact showed a thing. It was superbly done by the two of them and their rehearsals were most certainly worthwhile. They were so good that it made my part shine even more brightly. They quite unselfishly all but gave the scene to me.

When we filmed the scene, I was sitting in the audience front row, next to Roger. Elliott starts the music and I become more and more excited as Stef goes through her routine. At the end I'm invited up on to the stage by Richard, he magics my gun from its holster and fires a shot. This is the signal for Niv and Savalas to take over the camp.

The end of the scene took no time at all to shoot, and if I remember correctly we did it first. The dance took longer, as it had to be shot from many different angles. To begin with there was a wide shot of the whole dance. Then close-ups of Stef, and close-ups of Elliott. Next there were several wide shots from behind the two of them looking at us, the audience, then a two-shot of Roger and me, and finally there were individual close-ups of the two of us. These were both done at the same time, one camera on me and one on Rog. So that's, let's see, at least eight set-ups, which took something like two days. And Stef and Elliott did the dance every blessed time we did a take. Even when they were not in shot they went through the whole routine, just so that we could react to it; a bit different from Robert Shaw on *Force 10 From Navarone*, eh?

Stef and Elliott are an example to all, especially those big-headed Starbums who think that it is beneath them to perform unless the camera is on them, preferably in close-up.

Now then, I think this is an opportune moment to talk about two filming techniques which were used to very great effect on *Escape to Athena*: the helicopter shot and the Steadycam.

But before that I must give mention to the man who made such excellent use of them, our super lighting cameraman Gilbert (Gil) Taylor. Almost every time I watch a favourite movie on the box, this mans's credit as Cinematographer (to give him his full title), comes up. Gil started in 1929 and that in itself has to be some sort of record. It's a hell of a long time ago! Heavens, he'd have been very well into his sixties when we made 'Athena'.

Gilbert Taylor photographed such evergreens as *The Guinea Pig*, with a very young Richard Attenborough. (Although he was not quite as young as he was playing. Richard was twenty-six at the time, and was very convincing as a thirteen year-old school boy. I know Gil would have had a lot to do with making that believable, in his choice of camera angles for example.) *Seven Days to Noon*, one of the very best British thrillers, was another of Gil's; *Ice Cold in Alex*, with lovely John Mills; *Dr Strangelove*, *The Omen*,...*Star Wars*, even. The list really is very nearly endless. Gil is a smashing guy. Always encouraging and always suggesting possible alternatives. He obviously still greatly loved his work, even after all those years. (And he was the first in the queue, and full of congratulations for my performance, when Roger and I had the cameras turned on us during Stef and Elliott's dance. Read on!)

But first - helicopter shots and the Steadycam.

Everyone who has seen *The Sound of Music* will remember the opening helicopter shot. Ted McCord, the lighting supremo on this occasion, received an Oscar nomination for his work. We seem to fly through the Austrian mountains, and finally end in close-up on a joyous Julie Andrews singing 'The Hills are Alive', etc. Magic sequence - super film all through, actually.

Now let me make it quite clear, there is certainly no copycat criticism intended when I say that Gil Taylor used a similar opening shot for *Escape to Athena* - not the

Austrian mountains of course, but the idea, the helicopter. In fact I think that this time the helicopter shot is used to even greater effect. We glide into Greece and into our story. Across the shimmering sea, over the rooftops, and end on a group of civilians who have been lined up against a wall by the Germans. But no...we suddenly soar away and only finally come to rest as a rifle shot rings out and the dialogue and main story begins. If *The Sound of Music* opening is magic, then the *Escape to Athena* opening is magic plus. And I honestly don't mean that simply because I get a wonderful featured credit as the camera sweeps in over the blue Aegean and the theme music suddenly bursts forth!

Dearly Beloved and I watched *The Guns of Navarone* again last evening and it surely is a superly great movie, one of the very best ever. Lots better than *Force 10 from Navarone*, a damn good film in its own right. But the opening of 'Guns of N.' - oh dear! Bear in mind that both 'The Guns' and *Escape to Athena* were made on the Island of Rhodes, so the same shots were available to both cameramen. Then, when you can, compare Gil Taylor's opening helicopter shot for 'Athena', against the usual cut from fixed angle to fixed angle used on 'The Guns of N.' Don't misunderstand me, 'The Guns' has to be the better movie, but the opening of 'Athena' knocks the other opening into mediocrity.

Steadycam. Gil Taylor used the Steadycam throughout 'Athena', particularly in the Stefanie/Elliott dance scene. Normally when you're filming a tracking shot in a movie it is simply that, a camera which follows you as you walk down a road or whatever. It takes a hell of a time for the camera crew to lay the rails or boards on which the camera will run, and forever if the ground is anything but completely level, because they have to wedge it here and dig the earth out there. A tracking shot can also be very restricting for the actors. If you deviate an inch from the given line, the camera will be unable to accommodate you and you'll be out of shot.

Then this guy came up with the idea of counterbalancing a camera using weights and gyros, so that the camera operator could actually wear the camera. By simply walking backwards in front of you, he could now obtain perfectly 'steady' pictures every time even if he stumbled, and allow you the luxury of moving a little. You can't use the Steadycam in every situation of course and tracks still have their place, but the Steadycam is a marvellous addition to the cameraman's armoury.

It does have one big drawback though - cost. When we were doing 'Athena', there were only two chaps in Europe who were trained to operate the Steadycam, and indeed strong enough to carry its enormous weight. They were, they are, very much in demand, and the hire cost is therefore extremely high. What tends to happen is this: a director and his lighting cameraman decide that a particular shot, or even complete scene, should be done with a Steadycam, they convince the producer, and the producer then hires it, and the operator, for that shot or scene only.

As I say, it's hellishly expensive, particularly if you're flying them out from the UK, but the final result has to be worth it, and it most certainly does save time. When you next see *Escape to Athena*, look especially at the roof top sequences during, and Sonny's entrance over the small hill at the end of, the Stef/Elliott striptease dance. They are Steadycam shots and I think they're flipping wonderful.

I want now to tell you a few little snippets about a very big Starbum who is most certainly a Super Trouper. When he'd finished his close-ups, he even insisted on reading his lines off camera so that I could react to them. And in our first scene in the picture, I didn't even have to speak.

Very much earlier in these pages I said I'd be talking later about Roger Moore. Well...now is the time!

I've just been telling you about the striptease, and that the last shot, in the dance section of the scene, was the simultaneous reverse close-ups of Roger and me. One camera on Rog, one on me. Stef and Elliott again went through the whole routine behind the camera so that Roger and I could react.

Now I report this with the greatest humility! At the end of the take, when George Pan said 'cut,' the whole crew, director George, camera personnel, sound, make-up, wardrobe, Stef and Elliott, everybody, came rushing over to me to say how wonderful I'd been with my grabbing of the undies, and my lascivious gruntings. If you recall, I was sitting next to Roger and I happened to glance in his direction ...and not one person was taking a blind bit of notice of him. I'm sure he sensed that I might be rather embarrassed at receiving all this adulation while he was left out in the cold, and he quietly leant over and whispered in my ear: 'Congratulations, Michael. And don't worry, they're paying me more than they are you.'

On another occasion we were watching rushes - when you're away from home base and the film has had to be sent back to London for processing and then returned, you're actually looking at stuff you shot two weeks ago, so the word 'rush' seems just a smidgin inappropriate. Anyway, after one set of takes, in a scene between Rog and Stef, Roger asked me what I thought. I replied that it was damn good, as indeed it was. 'Oh no,' he said. 'For God's sake don't say that. I've got to think of the image. Please say it was nothing out of the ordinary.' Everyone who knows him knows that Roger is an excellently good film actor. He'd never have lasted as long as he has if he wasn't. But he loves trying to preserve the image that he's only adequate. It certainly isn't insecurity that makes him do it. I think it's impishness. Well, Roger, I'm one of very many who says that you're fooling absolutely no one.

Behind our hotel there was a winding path that led up and up to the top of a cliff. There was then a sort of plateau which stretched on for miles, right into the middle of the Island. Sometimes on a Sunday morning, a couple of the stuntmen and I would take a walk up the cliff and over the top, and Roger's six year-old son, Christian, would join us. When Christian first asked if he could come along, I of course said that we must ask his parents - you have to remember that Roger was a very, very big star, a prime target perhaps for kidnap, who knows? But Christian's mum and dad just told the lad to be careful, to remember that Michael was in charge and to have a nice time. And we did, we used to play football up there, and we found an enormous collection of beehives which filled one complete hillside. I was a little nervous at this, I admit. Suppose a swarm had taken it into their heads to attack Christian? But then, I'm sure that Rog and Luisa, having made certain he was alright, would just have told their son that he must be more careful next time.

For some reason Roger and I seemed to meet quite often in the hotel lift. These occasions were reserved for enquiring after each other's health, with much mock solemnity: 'And how is your poor Achilles heel today, my good Sir?'

You must have realised by now that I have a great deal of affection for Mr Roger Moore, Star Actorbum. I could go on for ages telling you nice things about him - his loyalty for example. He'd had the same hairdresser and the same stand-in (he who looks something like the star and 'stands-in' the set for him whilst they are lighting and fiddling around) with him on the payroll for years. And he always insisted that Paul Engelen did the make-up on his movies.

Paul, and Mike the hairdresser, were both great, and totally different. As well as being the make-up supremo, and thus responsible for overseeing the work of his two assistants, Paul of course did Roger's make-up himself. Paul had his lovely wife with him, and she was almost on the point of making him a daddy. We were all on tenterhooks. The champagne had been on order for weeks, long before the infant was due! In fact we'd finished and returned home before the great day, and I'd done another super movie, courtesy of a very special gentle man I'll be introducing in a page or two, before I was introduced to the Engelen's super daughter and heir. On the set of *Les Miserables* it was, version 290 odd!

Mike was a sort of maverick. Indeed a more unlikely hairdresser I'm sure I'll never meet. I know he won't mind if I get the details slightly wrong, but as far as I can remember, Mike had been married four times, and he was certainly always on the lookout for conquests new! I remember one day I was coming down from the hotel's roof top bar with Paul Weston, one of the stuntmen, and there was Mike, pissed to high heaven, (it was a weekend so there was no filming), sitting on the floor of the landing strumming a guitar. And strumming exceedingly well I must add. In a flash he'd started a calypso which began, 'Michael he is an actor. Damn good he is too-oo. I cut his hair for him. Nice for me to do-oo!' And it was very nice for me to have Mike as my barber. He was a brilliant hairdresser and everyone was after him to cut their hair, even the ladies. Roger, I'm pleased to say but not surprised, was very happy to let us use his own personal hair man. And no, Mr Moore does not wear a wig. His predecessor James Bond had many, but not Roger, no way!

I must also say a wee word about John, Roger's stand-in. I'll be talking in more detail about stand-ins, stuntmen and extras a bit later, so for the moment let it suffice that John, who also had his wife with him, was a kind, nice man. I think he felt that I might be in some sort of no man's land, with all those big name bums around and then little me all on my own. There was of course never a them-and-us problem on 'Athena' (excepting perhaps earnings-wise!), far from it. They were all such super people. But John didn't know this, particularly when we first arrived, and he and his missis used to hire a car and invite me to join them on trips to all the places of interest on the Island, such as the butterfly gardens where thousands of butterflies nest (or is it roost?...gather, perhaps?!) I believe it's something to do with the aroma from the particular type of tree which grows there.

I've just remembered. I can't name the film, but John did once play an actual part in a Roger Moore movie - he played Roger's father. John told me that he didn't have much thesping to do (the thought of doing any more frightened him almost to death!), because he was playing a very old man who just sat there most of the time and said very little. And his scenes had to be shot outside the UK, because he had no Equity card. John very happily admitted that he enjoyed his usual life as Roger's stand-in. But what a nice gesture for Rog to give him a named part in one of his films, with all the extra lovely lolly it attracted.

In the meantime: talking about 'Athena'...!

There's Elliott lending me his tie so that I would be allowed into the Casino in Rhodes town. It worked like this: nobody is allowed into the Casino without a tie, except very famous people. I am not very famous and I have no tie, Elliott is very famous and he does. So Elliott undoes his tie and gives it to me, I put it on and in we both go.

(I ran out of chips one evening whilst playing Blackjack at the same table as Roger. Roger insisted that I take a £100 worth of his chips. I then won £150 and paid him back.)

There's my honorary membership of the Stunt Artists' fraternity. If you've seen the film you'll know that it contains masses of mind-blowing stunts. These were performed by a smashing band of chaps, led by Vic Armstrong, who is now a film director in his own right. If I was free when they went to practice the stunts, I used to go with them as often as not and I'd help to carry the equipment. We had some great times, and for my carrying abilities I was made an honorary member of the Stunt Artists' Association and was given the T-shirt. I'm very proud of that.

You could hire a sort of motorised mountain bike at the hotel, and sometimes when I had a day off, I'd get one of these and go off exploring. Over the top of the Island was best, all unmade roads - dirt tracks if you like - and not a soul to be seen. And no crash helmet I'm afraid. So, bloody daft really, but very exhilarating.

The producers. David Niven Jr. and Jack Wiener. I'll be telling you more about Jack and his kindness later. Niv Jr. was a chip off the old block, and always had time for a jar and a chat. When his dad died only five short years after we finished 'Athena', I wrote to Niv Jr., as I know did thousands of others, and I did not expect a reply. But he wrote me a super letter which I very much appreciated.

And so I come to the best of a very great bunch. A man who could light up the whole darn place with his smile. When David Niven Senior started telling stories about his early years in the business, it didn't matter a hoot that you'd read them before in his books, it was simply a very great privilege and joy to be hearing them from the man himself.

Something that has never occurred to me before. Is it possible that my decision to embark on my memoirs was in fact subliminally prompted by my reading David Niven's two autobiographies: *The Moon's a Balloon*, and *Bring on the Empty Horses*? I do hope so.

I was lucky enough to spend many very enjoyable evenings having dinner with David and listening to his stories of Hollywood - or Hollywoodland as it was called when he first arrived. In 1935 a poor British actress named Peg Entwhistle jumped off the Hollywoodland sign and killed herself. The 'land' part of the sign was finally removed in 1949.

David really enjoyed his grub and thus our plates were filled with as many wonderful things as you can imagine. Stuffed Eggplant, Mezedes, Souvlaki, Gyros, Dolmades - don't ask me to describe them all, for as often as not I didn't even know what they were, except that they were delicious. Fish I knew and liked enormously, and fish David liked too. And that leads me on to a particularly precious David N. memory.

If you've seen *Escape to Athena* (if you haven't you should be made to see it by tomorrow at the latest!), you'll remember that at the very beginning of the film I have a scene with David in which I arrest him for having escaped. Actually I hit him with the butt of my revolver because he's been very rude to me - Sgt. Mann was a rounded character alright! Now, it's simply the way a film location schedule can go sometimes and normally I'd be perfectly happy because I'd be on the payroll for longer, but this time I'd finished all my work on 'Athena' except for this one scene, it wasn't due to be shot until a fortnight next Thursday, and I'd been offered another film which was starting next Monday! As time was getting so short, the company on this other movie had of course got someone standing by to play the part, but they were still waiting in the hope that I might be free. That was very gratifying, but it was already Tuesday and it really did look as though I was going to have to miss this other film. I know - 'Oh dear, what a pity, never mind. Think of that other poor bum who is waiting and hoping that you wont make it. At least he'd be happy.' And I didn't mind. Well, not a lot. But I was pondering, when Niv happened to pass by. He asked why I was looking so unaccustomedly glum and I told him what was up.

That evening I was in the hotel bar, not drowning my sorrows by any means, but having a wee dram and thinking how super it would have been to go from a wonderful movie in Greece, straight on to a wonderful movie which was going to be made in Holland and Germany, when suddenly up strides David Niven. 'Come on, Michael, hurry up. You're on for a fish dinner tonight aren't you? Good. Oh, and by the way, I've have some news for you.' (It's strange. I suppose it must be because he had such a distinctive voice, but each time I quote David I really do hear him saying the words. See if you can too. Close your eyes and imagine him saying something like the above. It's quite uncanny.)

David wouldn't tell me what he had to say that evening until we were sat at our table, in a superb sawdust-on-the-floor restaurant in Rhodes harbour. (I wish I could remember its name, the film crew used it a lot.) After we'd finished our seafood salad and were waiting for the swordfish, he finally came to the point. 'I take it you're packed?' he said.

'Packed?'

'That's right. They've changed the shooting schedule and we'll be doing our scene the day after tomorrow. Our production manager has already spoken to the people on your next movie and they're delighted you'll be free to join them. And you won't have to wait here for a rushes report on our scene either. I've told George Pan that we'll be so good that everything is bound to be OK. If it's not, if there's a scratch on the negative, or there was a hair in the gate, or something, you can always fly back from Holland at the weekend and we'll re-do it...'

I know I've said a good few times that so-and-so was lovely. I've said too that nearly every bum in our business is a super bum. Well David Niven was the superest bum of all. The trouble he must have gone to to sort things out for me is only one of very many kindnesses he showed to us all. We did another film later on (*Rough Cut*, with Burt Reynolds), but not together, if you see what I mean. We didn't work on the same days. But there was a message of best wishes from David waiting for me when I arrived.

I miss you David Niven. And so do you, and you, and you...and you...

XVI

And the film that he made possible for me? I flew home from Rhodes and *Escape to Athena* on the Friday, and flew out to Holland two days later on the Sunday, to start work on *The Riddle of the Sands*, with Michael York, Jenny Agutter, Simon MacCorkindale and Alan Badel. Heaven again!

Apart from anything else I knew almost everyone. Michael - *England Made Me*; Alan - *Force 10 from Navarone*; and Simon I'd worked with in the TV play which made him a Star - *Three Weeks*.

We had a wonderful time on 'Riddle'. The first half of the film schedule was spent in Holland, the second half, right at the top of Germany. Unlike 'Athena', this film did not have a huge budget. It had very big ideas, it expected to do great things (and did), but lots of money for its making it did not have. And the whole experience was completely magical. We had a joyously warm feeling that this was what filming was really all about - one man pointing a camera at another man and filming a movie. We felt like hugging the happiness we were so excited.

And 'Riddle' was full of talent on both sides of the camera. I've already mentioned the thespians, but the crew was also brim full. I've recently talked about Gil Taylor. The only other Cinematographer who can come anywhere near him in my opinion, is Christopher Challis. Some people indeed might say that he is even superior to Gilbert. But whatever, this is not a contest, and we were exceedingly fortunate to have Chris - *The Small Back Room*, *Genevieve*, *Ill Met By Moonlight*, *Those Magnificent Men in Their Flying Machines*, *Chitty, Chitty, Bang, Bang*, et many many others

- Challis as our Lighting Camerman on *The Riddle of the Sands*. (Remember that mountain in Yugoslavia where we almost sang the roof off the tent on those rain-soaked nights? Chris was there too. Yes, he can also add *Force 10 from Navarone* to his credits.)

When 'Riddle' was located in Holland - Enkhuizen to be exact - we all lived on one of those huge, beautiful, converted Rhine barges. Our home was moored alongside the film's production office, which until we arrived had been the Harbourmaster's hut. Breakfast was provided in the ship's galley. Cups of tea/coffee were available throughout the day, and the evening meal could be had at any of the excellent hostelries in the town. Each morning, those of us who were working came ashore and helped the crew to load the cameras, the sound equipment, and the props, et al. into a bus - there were no union rules on this picture - and off we went to that day's location.

Don't misunderstand me. This was a properly run and crewed picture which did bloody well at the box office. It was simply that it was made, perhaps as pictures should be made, without fuss, and without the mighty millions that tend to be spent in the film industry today. My abiding memory of the first half, the Holland half if you like, is of waking up before the crack of dawn and pushing aside the curtain of my cabin window - oh yes we did each have our own room! - and seeing Simon, laden with camera equipment, trundling off with the Second Unit Cameraman, equally weighted down, to take shots of Simon at sunrise walking across the marshes.

We also went on bike rides. Michael, Simon, I, and...oh what's his name - he played a German in the TV series of *Colditz* and now lives in France, bloody good actor too. Hell, it's no good, I'll have to wait until Dearly Beloved comes in, she'll know...There you are, she did know - Hans Meyer. The four of us used to hire bikes and ride off around the Enkhuizen countryside. We'd stop at a pub for lunch, oh at least six miles from base, and then return. And we'd not feel at all knackered. Holland is of course rather flat!

We did all the train sequences in the Dutch half of the schedule - ten days of nights - on a super little puffer which could have come straight from the first years of the century. Which was good, because that is when the film is set!

And now I'm going to blow my own trumpet. Just a little. (Well if I can't toot the thing in my own book, when can I for goodness sake! I'll have a quick trill too for *Colditz*, mentioned above; I was also in that series.) I've played a good few Germans in my time, and when I was talking about *The McKenzie Break* earlier and my spoken German, well, it was the start of the book and I was perhaps a mite modest! The fact is that my German...is not bad at all. And when Tony Maylem, the lovely director on 'Riddle', asked me if I could do my own dialogue translation - one long scene was entirely in German - I said yes without hesitation (silly fool!) Someone had had a go in fact before I received the final script, but it was no good. It was too classroomy, and I re-did it. Everything you hear is mine. Hans, and Wolf Kahler, the two real Germans on the film, were kind enough to say that my German was excellent. My authentic accent, which is always the first thing that is complimented, is nothing to do with me by the way. It just seems to happen, perhaps because I'm a Scot - rolled Rs etc. - and I'm very grateful.

Have you seen *The Riddle of the Sands*? It's a superly damn good film. I play the part of Boehme, the Kaiser's emissary, 'a horrid little man,' Michael's character calls me. It was a gem of a part, which again carried very nice featured billing.

Aren't I lucky! Straight from one great role to another. And to top it all I had a couple of weeks free in the middle of the 'Riddle' schedule and was allowed to pop back to the UK to do an episode of *The Sweeney*, a damn good series I'm sure you'll remember, starring John Thaw and Dennis Waterman.

'Sweeney' was very professional. It was made, as are all filmed tele-series in this country, using 16mm film stock, as opposed to 35mm, which is fine for the smaller TV screen and keeps the cost way dowm. And they had a hell of a turn round. I was going back to a small budget feature film, for cinema release. It would take a quarter of a year to make, probably more like three and a half months, and we'd end up with about ninety minutes screentime. Comparative luxury. Every single episode of *The Sweeney* lasted a full fifty minutes and took just ten days to film!

The book *The Riddle of the Sands*, on which our film script of the same name was based, was written by Erskine Childers, and his main object in writing it, pre-First World War, was to show that Great Britain had virtually no sea defences along it's eastern shore. An enemy could float barges across the channel and attack the UK almost without hindrance. *The Riddle of the Sands* told the - fictitious - story of how two Englishmen, (played in the film by Michael Y. and Simon Mac.), foiled such a plot. And it worked. After publication of the book there was quite an outcry and our eastern defences were greatly strengthened. This helped enormously when Germany started things in 1914.

Good for the book published in 1903 and good for us making the film of the book some eighty-odd years later.

The day before we left Holland for Friesland in Germany, Jenny Agutter gave us all a party. Indeed it was almost like doing two films. The 'Dutch' film was extremely enjoyable and was rounded off with Jenny's super end-of-production party, but the 'German' film was also immensely special.

There was no respite. We finished Holland, Saturday, and travelled to Germany, Sunday. The crew went by road with the gear. I'd like to have gone with them because we flew!

As it was autumn and there were no holidaymakers around, we were able to keep the costs down in Germany by taking over an entire equestrian centre. And it was really great. We each had a whole chalet to ourselves, comprising kitchen, loo and living room downstairs, with bath room/loo and bedroom above.

Again the idea was that we would fend for ourselves in the evenings, with the help of some expenses of course, and we used as often as not to buy the necessaries in the local village and take it in turns to cook. My speciality menu always seemed to be spaghetti bolognese, but it was nevertheless very kindly received, especially with a bottle of vino or three!

It was at about this time that Michael York and I started to talk about doing a little something on our own. In other words, making the films ourselves with our own production company. I've already said that I've always thought this to be a natural extension of an actorbums life. So does Michael. Indeed, have a look at the credits for 'Riddle' and you'll see that he'd already started. He gets a credit as Associate Producer. But there's a hell of a long way to go before you can get anything off the ground - remember Old King Ken? Suffice it to say that for the time being we are still trying to find a suitable property, the time free, and the money!

On went *The Riddle of the Sands*, and on went our very happy time. The interiors of the boats were filmed in the German half of the film. You couldn't of course film inside an actual sailing boat. Well, I suppose you could, just, but it would be virtually impossible because of the lack of space. So the interiors were built in an old barn. And when Tony, the director, wanted to shoot to the left, they simply took the right side of the boat away. And when he wanted to shoot to the right, they took the left side off. It made everything so much easier, and thus speeded things up. Clever!

We had a fancy dress parade. Actually it was a nearly end of the picture mad house. There was a swimming pool at the equestrian centre - every luxury was ours - and we held the party around the pool. At least it started on the surrounds. It ended with almost everyone in the water. The wardrobe department were not best pleased as they had supplied most of the fancy dress from their coffers, which actually meant that we'd borrowed them from the movie. Not a very good idea really, but we were forgiven.

The party in fact actually made a contribution to the success of the film. One of the chippies, a huge man who was always laughing, dressed up as a woman for the fancy dress parade. He looked quite fetching, and I think he won second prize from judges, Michael York and his lovely wife, Pat.

When you're filming away from home there's a problem which can crop up at a moment's notice, namely, lack of extras. You're in the middle of a scene, the director has set up his shot and...he needs a body in the foreground to make it really work. If you're at home there's no problem. If there are no extras already on the lot, you can have some sent out to the studio in no time. But when you are away from base, in the wilds of North Germany for example, it's not so easy.

Came the day then, shortly after the fancy dress party, when Tony wanted a woman to be sitting in the corner of the pub, in a scene involving Michael and Simon. And there were no extras available. So, what to do? When you next see the film, take a closer look at the lady in the pub, all dressed up in her finery. She certainly does look a very well built specimen. That is no lady, that's big Fred the chippie!

(At the end of this remembrance I'm going to pay tribute to some of the greatest bums of all. Namely the Extrabums, the Stand-Inbums and the Stuntmanbums. I've just read the last paragraph and it could be construed that these irreplaceable people are perhaps taken for granted - 'Oh, ring up casting and get me a dozen assorted extras.' Please take it from me that nothing could be further from the truth. Let me round off 'Riddle' first, then I'll come back to this.)

I think I've tended to tell you more about the leisure, off duty, side of the making of 'Riddle', rather than the nuts and bolts of putting pictures on to film. But that's alright. The pictures we put in the can were bloody good, see for yourself. It's just that this time my memories are fuller with the people, the places and the happinesses - the complete enjoyment of being a part of the thing - and I'm going to to record a couple more incidents.

The first one takes us back for a moment to the Dutch half of the film. Enkhuizen is not very far from Amsterdam and we used to pop over sometimes when we had some free time. The day arrived when there was to be a big change of location, from the week of nights on the train I talked about, to daytime sequences in some offices. You get a day off anyway after you've been filming nights, and because of the change, they wouldn't be ready to film again until the following afternoon. So we had a day and a half free, and about twenty of us decided to go to Amsterdam and 'see the sights'!

I'm sure we are not necessarily naive in our business. We've all seen the odd girlie show - yes, alright, some of us have even been in a girlie picture! - but nothing, absolutely nothing could have prepared us for what was in store. We had the ladies from make-up, those from the wardrobe department, and the Producer's secretary with us, so we chaps certainly felt we should protect them, but we thought nothing of it when someone suggested that we went to see a live show. We thought it would be a laugh. By gum, I think we lasted about twenty minutes. I've never seen so many red faces, and big Fred the chippie/lady extrabum was worst of all!

But Amsterdam seems to take it all in its stride, and the local girls, sitting in their windows whilst they waited for customers, looked sweet. They cheerfully gave everyone a wave and a smile. One of the lasses actually had a queue outside her door. The guys were perfectly happy and unembarrassed waiting for their ecstasy.

And for the time being at least, here's the last memory of this super picture. We're back in Germany again, so it's the second half. There was one of those...what do you call them? Clock golf is it? No - crazy, that's it! You know, where you hit a golf ball over or through obstacles, before hopefully getting it in the hole. Well there was one of those courses at the centre. It was great fun and it was used a lot in the evenings and on Sundays. (We worked a six day week.)

Fred, and two of his chippie chums, organised the 'Crazy Golf Olympics' one sunny Sunday morning. Hosted it too, dressed in very fetching plus-twos. It was beautifully done, with singles, twosomes, threesomes and foursomes; two ball, three ball and four ball; and everybody got a prize and a medal, again provided by Fred and the gang. It was their way, I'm sure, of thanking everyone for such an enjoyable engagement. And do you know, every blessed member of the company took part. Our way I'm sure of agreeing with them.

XVII

Right then. Stand-Inbums, Extrabums, and Stuntmenbums.

I'll talk about stuntmen first. You already know in what high regard and affection I hold these crazy, brave, very likeable people. And I'm an honorary member of their organisation, remember. If, as a featured actor, you are cast in a part which will involve some big action sequences, the producer, the director, and the stunt co-ordinator will decide that it's too dangerous for you to do them yourself. Their given reason is usually that the insurance won't allow it, but what they really mean is that they don't want anything to happen to you, at least until the picture is finished. But long live producers who want to keep me alive say I. I could as lief jump out of a fourth storey window as over the moon!

I've had a stunt double a good few times. I've had to fall out of trains, been involved in fights, got buried in Fullers Earth, etc. (remember *The McKenzie Break*), but I'm neither important enough nor macho enough to require one full time. When I need a stuntman he is assigned to me from the pool of stuntmen who are working on the picture. They pick the one who looks as nearly me as possible, and if there isn't one then it's a heavy make-up job. But it's the stuntmanbum boss' job to read the script, look at the cast, and recruit stunt doubles as required. So if you're going to be involved in some action, you can rest assured that one of the stuntmen on the picture will look something like you and will thus be yours.

It's always advisable to get to know your stunt double. Remember that he will be you during that death-defying fall or whatever. You should, for example, tell him that your tie must be tied in a Windsor knot, and that you only pick your nose with the little finger of your left hand!

If you are a very big star, particularly one who plays big butch parts, like Roger Moore, then you'll have your own permanent stunt double. These gentlemen or ladies are the creme de la creme of stuntbums and normally get a featured credit. They usually have some extra special skill to contribute as well. I can remember going to see Roger's man, Martin Grace, doing a fall in *Escape to Athena*. But this was no ordinary fall, no one else would even attempt it. I don't know what the world record is, but this dive entailed coming off an obelisk some 120 feet up in the air. Think of it, the height of four houses! Five times Martin attempted the stunt, on three different days, but the wind was so strong and the top of the obelisk swayed so much, that he could hardly see his 'catching' bag, let alone land on it. Finally, on the fourth day, the wind subsided and he went. The round of applause which greeted his safe arrival on terra firma could be heard for miles - in Crete probably.

Stuntmen always oversee their own stunts. Perhaps the stunt co-ordinator will help them to arrange the landing bags, but it's the stuntman himself who decides if it's safe to 'go', and who negotiates the fee. I'm told that the rate for the above stunt was far greater that any other daily payment on the movie. And so it flippin' well should have been!

Stand-ins. I confess that I have a hell of a lot of time for the guy who will stand in my stead under the blazing studio lights while they are lighting a scene; who will fetch something I may have left in my dressing-room in double quick time; who will find me a chair when none are in sight, and who will conjure up a cup of tea the moment I come off the set; but I do not understand him. I must not feel sorry for him, that would be patronising, but I do not understand how he can be happy in his work. My stand-in on *High Road to China*, which is coming up later, was an extremely affable chap. We used to share a car from the unit hotel to the locations, and as often as not we'd have dinner together in the evenings. I asked him about his job, and Graham put it like this: he'd started as an actor in the provinces, but he had no ambition, and anyway he wasn't very good. So he'd had a go at stand-in work and found it suited him far better. He earned good money, and when I finished my part in the picture and left, he would be kept on the payroll as a general utility stand-in. So provided there were films being made, he only had to find a new job four or so times a year. And the production managers would mostly ask for him, because he was good at his job and took a pride in his work. It was rather like being a dresser in the theatre or a batman in the army.

I certainly know what it means to have pride in your work, and it's great to have your year mapped out. I...think I see what he was getting at. But I've been driven all my life by the thespian ambition that was instilled in me the day I saw *The Wooden Horse*, and you've surely got to be a little curious about what's around the next corner. Perhaps it's a blind spot of mine, it must certainly be my fault. But no - I'm afraid I still don't understand stand-ins.

Extras. I know of no actorbum however who does not totally understand, appreciate, and value the role of the extra. I've seen very, very big stars make sure that the first person they thank at the end of a good take is the extra who opened the door, or handed them some papers, or whatever. There are literally hundreds of jobs which are entrusted to extrabums, any one of which can make or break a scene.

They are incredibly hardworking and immensely professional people. They usually have a foreman - an extra co-ordinator - who is in charge of everything. He will, for example, be responsible for negotiating any supplementary fees which may be due. Although a basic fee is paid, an extra will get additional money if he has to do almost anything other than walk or sit. There is more dosh for: personally opening doors, being featured, handling props, rhubarbing, saying the odd word - that's a very good one - indeed, every extra thing! The pick of these extra curriculas, and therefore the best cash and kudos, always go to the extra co-ordinators. And quite right too, they put in a hell of a lot of work looking after their flock. A little man in glasses called Ian Wilson comes to mind. See if you can spot him in films, mostly circa 1950 to 1970. He's the one who's sitting next to the starbum in the cinema; who says, 'This way I think,' to a lady extra at the start of a scene in the park; is the body at the beginning of the piece which sparks the story; or is in the front of a walking race when Norman Wisdom joins. You know the sort of thing.

Dearly Beloved and I were watching an episode of *Last of the Summer Wine* on television recently. You know, the three old boys with young hearts who live in a small Yorkshire town. (Actually Peter Sallis is not that old and was with me in the Alec Guinness 'Hitler' film I mentioned. Bill Owen is old. He played one of Robin Hood's men, in the Richard Todd version back in the early 1950's, and he looked craggy then. He's in his late seventies now and he's still prancing around as though he was back in Sherwood Forest...Ah, sweet elixir of life I found you on a film set!) Beloved and I were watching 'Summer Wine', and I kept wondering what was wrong. Don't misunderstand me, I think it's a great show and I love the excellent writing and the thesping but...there was something wrong. Then it hit me. In all the scenes in the town, in the cafe and in the countryside, there were no 'other' people. The only thesps in the shots were the principals. Now this may well be a policy of the programme - it couldn't possibly have been accidental - but I think it's bad, and for me anyway, it does the series no favours. The town looks dead and unreal. To give it life it needs those priceless members of our profession, the Extrabums!

XVIII

Les Miserables. Known in our household as 'The Unfortunates'. Having just returned from 'Riddle', I would have been very happy staying at home for a while. I had, after all, been away and out of the country for something like eight months off and on, mostly on. I'd gone straight from 'Athena' to 'Riddle', and it would have been nice to have done a little TV series down the road. But it wasn't to be. Actually I did sort of do two television series - *Lillie*, and a long forgotten comedy thing called *Luverly Couple* - but only one episode of each, and they only took about three weeks to make. Then I was off again - to sunny France. The southern half of the country indeed, the Dordogne region. We worked in and around a lovely little town called...I can't remember its proper name, probably because I don't speak the language, but we christened it Salad.

Just before I continue I really must make one thing abundantly clear. I have never, I would never, and I will never, complain about the work I do. I'll discuss the script, of course; I'll try to understand a difficult director; but I won't moan about the fee or anything like that, and I most certainly won't belly-ache about where the piece is located. I'm delighted to be offered the work, and once I've accepted, that's it, I'm in it up to the hilt. If the film, or whatever, is being made away from my home base, so be it. I've missed home, chickens and Mother Hen, like mad sometimes and they've missed me. But I'm happy to say that the family understand why I've had to be away so much. And you know, there are compensations. When I've been at home reading scripts or waiting for the next engagement to start, I've been there all the time, and you can tend to get under each other's feet on occasion. But the fact that I've been away a lot is perhaps one reason why, in my family, there has been absolutely no friction at all. Never...well, hardly ever!

I love visiting new places, particularly when someone else is picking up the tab. And although I'm not bankable enough to have my family with me all the time (I'm not sure anyway if that's a good idea. My kids of course are grown up now, but it would have played havoc with their schooling), there have been opportunities for them to join me from time to time, and that's been great.

So Salad was lovely. But it was a hell of a place to get to. Because I'd been doing 'Riddle' and the two tellies, and because my part in 'Les Mis' was, well, 'interesting' is how the casting people describe a part which they want you to do but which isn't exactly the largest part in the world, I was the last to arrive at the location and I came out from England on my own. First there was a surprisingly long flight to Bordeaux.

This was followed by a hair-raising two hour car ride with the worst driver I have ever encountered, who insisted on using only his left hand for steering, changing gear, and for making rude signs at other drivers who got in his way. His right hand was always fully occupied in lighting endless cigarettes. I used to smoke then, and whilst on 'Riddle' I'd acquired a lighter which was made from a bullet. You see them all over the place now, but then they were rather less common. Anyway, my one-handed Stirling Moss thought it was unique and decided he must have it. Trouble was that I was sitting in the back of the car, and in order to do business and to encourage me to sell, he had to turn round. Now my chain-smoking, one-handed chauffeur, who didn't speak a word of English by the way, was not even looking where he was going! I gave him the bullet lighter and prayed that the journey would be over as quickly as possible.

At last we did manage to arrive and I met Richard (Jordan) and Anthony (Perkins) - 'Les Mis's' Jean Valjean and Inspector Javert.

Richard Jordan died young, only some ten years after this, and I'm sorry. But it doesn't make him any less of a fart. He was not that good at his job and this seemed to make him very insecure. As well as starring in *Les Miserables*, Mr Jordan also played one of the leading parts in yet another version of Hitler's last days in the bunker called, would you believe, *The Bunker*, with Anthony Hopkins as Hitler. And all the other super supporting parts, of which there were a goodly number, were played by most of the UK character actorbum cream. I was giving my Himmler on this occasion. Came the day we were going to film Hitler's birthday party, and we all foregathered in this huge chandelier-hung and gold-embroidered hall. We were chatting away and waiting for things to get started, when who should arrive but lovely Edward Hardwick. (I have mentioned *Colditz*, haven't I? I mean the television series. I was the first person to say the word 'Colditz' in *Colditz* and I said it to Teddy who was about to be sent there for being a bad lad.)

Everybody likes E. Hardwick, and the cry went up, in a silly high-pitched voice: 'Hello, Teddy!' Immediately the call was echoed from another quarter: 'Hello, Teddy' And then another and another - 'Hello, Teddy!' 'Hello!' Well, Mr Richard Jordan, who had been sitting at the side of the hall listening to this kind-hearted greeting from a bunch of actorbums to a chum, was completely bewildered, and when the last of us had finished Hello Teddying, he looked at us all with what I can only assume was a sort of disgust, said 'Bloody British actors,' turned on his heel and left. We were naturally rather puzzled by his attitude. Not overconcerned you understand, I wasn't the only one who thought the man was a jerk. Anyway, his American makeup artist, who had been party to what had happened, and indeed nicely amused by it, put things like this: 'We know,' he said, 'that the British character actor is the best in the world. But he [Richard Jordan] can't accept it. And he doesn't understand how you all can play the fool, and then come straight on to the set and wipe the floor with him.' Perhaps Jordan should not have been so bloody arrogant, then he might have understood.

So much for Richard Jordan. Anthony Perkins was a very different kettle of thespian fish. He was superb in *On the Beach*, and Hitchcock's *Psycho*, he could have lived off *Psycho* for the rest of his life. Almost did, for he, too, has also gone now.

(Funny, by the way, and credit where it's due, it is odd how often we return to Hitchcock. I know I didn't like him and I think his work is flawed, but he did do a few good things - I saw *Rear Window* the other night. Not bad at all! Mind you, I am reliably informed that the shower scene in *Psycho*, with the delicious Janet Leigh, was not in fact directed by Sir A., but by one of his assistants. Who told me? Well, I'm not saying, but if you recall I did work with Janet's ex-husband!)

I played one of Tony Perkins' bosses in 'Les Mis', and we seemed to do everything in one take. Glenn Jordan, as opposed to Richard Jordan, and no relation, was our bloody good director and everything went like clockwork. Oh yes, and Paul Engelen was doing the make-up, filling a gap before Roger Moore's next movie. It was great to see the Engelens again, and at last, their gorgeous new baby daughter. We'd been waiting for her arrival on 'Athena', if you remember.

What a wonderful life they lead in France, particularly in this part of the country. Did you know that they never drink the water?! Because I arrived late at the location, I was billeted on my own as the hotel was full. At first I was a wee bit sorry, as I very much enjoy the bonhomie, but on this occasion I soon changed my mind. At the end of each day I was driven out of the town into the lovely countryside, to this most gorgeous old farmhouse. I was the only guest, and I was treated like a king. Dinner was served on the terrace. The food was absolutely fantastic, and it was accompanied by a one-and-a-half litre bottle of wine. 'We never drink the water 'ere, only the wine. Also the children, they drink it also. The wine, she is so much better, yes?' Oh yes. But I could never finish the whole bottle. After all, I did have lines to say on the morrow, and I had to be fit to take my evening strolls through the vineyards. Boy, what a super place.

I'd always wanted to meet Anthony Perkins - a nice if somewhat distant man by the way - ever since I was that tiny wee lad back in Aberdeen, going to three films a day at weekends, and during the school holidays. Because I thought Tony and I must be related...That's not good enough is it? I can't leave it there. It's quite simple really. When I was that little starstruck boy, who, when he wasn't at the flicks, used to go fishing the burns around Aberdeen with his dad the minister, my name was Perkins too, of course.

XIX

Dr Who has played a very big part in my life, and as there is still so much interest in my association with the programme - the large amount of fan mail I receive is most gratifying and much appreciated - I'm now going to put the record straight. It's not true! I have not worked with more Doctors than anyone else. That honour goes to the Brigadier, Nicholas Courtney. He worked with all of them, I missed out on Pat Troughton. But that puts me second in line, and mind you, Nick has had it easy compared with me. He played the same recurring character, whereas I played a different role each time. And I played twice with Tom Baker which surely makes up for not doing a story with Pat! So what I can say with complete confidence is that I have worked with more Doctors than anyone else, playing a different character each time.

My appearances cover some twenty years, and, chronologically, they are as follows:

The Ark. This was very early on. All I can remember is that Bill Hartnell was nice, and that we were all dressed in nothing but ribbons. The girls as well!

The Mind of Evil. I don't suppose I should have a favourite Doctor, but if I did, then it would be Jon Pertwee. I'm sure a great number of adults became fans of the show during his reign. He seemed somehow to broaden the concept. I also played a Doctor in this story - Dr Summers. And as it was coming up to Christmas during our rehearsals, Jon led us carol singing round all the other productions which were rehearsing in the BBC's Acton rehearsal rooms.

The Pyramids of Mars was my first with Tom Baker. 'Pyramids' has proved over the years to be one of the most successful 'Whos' outside the Dalek stories.

The Invisible Enemy. In my second story with Tom I played Lowe, a real villain, who's been taken over by a space virus. This was the story in which the tin dog, K9, first made an appearance. What fun and games the radio controllers had getting the thing to work!

Castrovalva. Peter Davison's first. I didn't understand one solitary thing about this story. But it too has turned out to be very popular, perhaps because everyone is intrigued to know what the hell is going on!

Remembrance of the Daleks. My last to date. Finally I got to work with, and be killed by, those evergreen 'Who' baddies, the Daleks.

I seem to have missed one somewhere, but no matter. Lovely stuff, all of it. I wouldn't have missed any of my Dr Whos for anything, and I'm sure it will continue one day - indeed, e'en as I write my old mate S. Spielberg is becoming involved.

I did a great *Minder* about now, directed by James Gatward, just before he left the studio floor and went off to head the now defunct Southern TV.

I already knew both George Cole and Dennis Waterman of course. George and I had worked together with Richard Widmark, and I'd done 'Sweeneys' with Dennis. By heck, they were both highly professional. I've always considered it my job to be line perfect before I start the day's shooting and to have done as much background work on my part as I can. Granted, George and Dennis knew the characters they were playing, but they always had the lion's share of the dialogue and most of the scenes. I used to be known as 'One take Mike' - not a particularly good idea actually, because the day always comes when you cock up a scene tremendously because you've 'fluffed' your lines or somesuch - but I cannot remember either George or Dennis once causing a re-take because of lines. They used to make an episode of *Minder* every ten days - same as was done on *The Sweeney*. And that included all the action sequences. A car chase, for example, can take a hell of a long time to shoot. Think of all the different angles involved for a start.

I am full of admiration for the professionalism shown by George, Dennis and the whole crew, together with Kenneth Griffith, Lee Montague and me, when we joined them for the episode entitled *A Tethered Goat*.

XX

And now for the commercial break! Commercials (both visual and aural) do figure in a bum's life and they deserve a mention. As indeed do training films, documentaries and in-house videos.

It's nice, if you've got a couple of weeks off or four, to take part in a documentary. There's not a lot of pay, but they are usually fun to do. They're films or videos, same as any other, but made with a much smaller crew, and the whole thing has an urgency about it which is somehow stimulating. I can remember making one such film at RAF Coltishall, Douglas Bader's wartime airfield, concerning an investigation into why an aeroplane had simply fallen out of the sky; I made another in a foundry up north, just before I flew out to Rhodes to make *Escape to Athena*; one was made in a glass factory (I hate handling glass); and in a further epic I played a surgeon.

When John Cleese, Peter Robinson, and their co-directors, sold their company, Video Arts, they made so much profit that it was in all the papers. Bloody good luck to them, it wasn't always like that. I worked with them at the beginning, when they were funding the company themselves. John used to star in the little training films they made - one I remember was about the Common Market, another taught shop assistants how to sell things. The films always contained more than a touch of comedy, and because of his profile, his chums and his contacts, John got some great writers to write, and actors to play with him in these excellent pieces. I was continually bumping into the likes of Tim Brooke- Taylor, and I'm sure I also remember June Whitfield and David Jason taking part.

In-house videos are the least important of this quartet. But there's certainly nothing wrong, particularly when you're a young actorbum, eager for experience, in popping along to do a video, probably recorded on the firm's machine, which will explain to new bank employees, for example, how to close the safe at the end of the day, and check for fraud.

Perhaps I haven't done as many of the above three tiddlers as I'd have liked. But then, the reason I've not done them is because I've not been free. I've been doing something even more exciting, big, and lovely - probably abroad!

Commercials are different, particularly money-wise. I don't think there is anyone who doesn't know that quite enormous amounts of money can be made from advertising British Telecom or Oxo for example. The really big money is of course made by the really big stars. They will normally have been approached by the company direct, or rather direct through their agents. Quite often they will be offered a buy-out - a fantastically high fee like 50, 60, 100, 500 grand. Even a million for a series! Sometimes they will be paid, or indeed opt for, a little less, but with repeats. Here of course they take a chance that the commercial will sell the product like mad and that it'll turn into a series.

With lesser bums it works a little differently. Usually a very much scaled-down version of the smaller lump sum, plus repeats, is the only contract offered, but the final pay haul can still be ginormous if you hit the right one. Do you remember an early advert for The Bradford and Bingley Building Society, where two silhouettes were featured? They became the society's trademark and continued to be used long after the commercial had finished. Well those silhouettes were images of the original actors who had done the original commercial, and of course they continued to be paid, and paid, and paid!

But the 'commercials' side of the business is the one area where I have had difficulties. They were of my own making. Even at the beginning, when I was an unknown, I allowed myself just one indulgence. I refused to trot along to what we all call 'cattle auctions' - casting sessions for commercials - where many masses of bums gather in the hope of being cast. Nowadays I'm too far up the slippery slope to be considered an unknown face, suitable for beer commercials for example, but I'm not a big enough name to get the commercial star treatment - a call direct from the company to my agent. So, no big commercial pay days for me.

Except...on a very few occasions! Let me make it quite clear. In no way have I ever earned fifty or a hundred grand for a commercial. But I have accepted the opportunity to: play rugger at Twickenham - Computers; swill wine with dear Frank Middlemass - Blue Nun Wine (Frank is a lovely man. We made 'The Invisible Man' together some time later and I'll tell you a little story he told us in a moment.) I've also swilled wine down in London's dockland - Portuguese Wine; been a runaway bank manager, caught in the jungle with his very shapely secretary - something akin to Tia Maria; and a business bloke in a lift - National Savings. My God though, you do work hard on commercial production days. There are certainly no 'one takes' in this neck of the business. It's well known that if the representatives of the company do not see their money being spent on take after take, after take, after take, sometimes till well into the early morning, then they don't think they've had value for money!

Frank Middlemass is a super trouper of the old school. He's a big soft lovable pussycat; kind, helpful and supportive. Here, then, is the tale he told us one evening, with great gentleness and humour. We were away on location for aunt BBC's version of H.G. Well's masterpiece *The Invisible Man*...

'Well, my dears,' he began, 'it happened a very long time ago now, in my youth. I was playing a season of repertory somewhere or other, Piscis by Sea perhaps. Anyway, there must have been a port because there were lots and lots of lovely sailor boys about the place. Now then...there was this young boy in the company. He was gentle, gentle as a lamb, and never would he do anything that was not encouraged, if you get my drift. Well, one night, after the end of the evening performance, he happened to be walking down by the docks and he got into conversation with a nice sailor lad, who was very obviously looking for somewhere to spend the night. The boy said he could stay with him at his digs and off they toddled.

'The boy's landlady, Mrs Blah, was a truly wonderful person. Her cooking was out of this world and she would always ask the boy what he'd like for his meals. She called him Mr, and she even made his bed and tidied his room. Indeed she had but one fault. She did not appreciate her guests having visitors in their rooms - particularly late at night.

'The boy explained this to his new friend as they tripped along and told him that they would therefore have to be very quiet when they arrived, so as not to disturb Mrs Blah. Mrs Blah lived in the downstairs sitting room, next to the front door, and they would thus have to pass her door before creeping up the stairs.

'They made not a sound as the boy opened the front door and they tiptoed expertly past the sitting room. But they had barely reached the stairs, let alone started to climb, before Mrs Blah's rasping North Country cackle was upon them. "Mr! What do you think you are doing? And at this hour of the night. Show this person from the dockyard out of my house this instant and go to your bed!" There was no arguing and the boy felt ashamed and very, very small. Like a naughty rascal who's been caught at the tuck cupboard after lights out.

'But he was determined to succeed, and he hatched a plan. He was sure that that which had given them away was the fact that Mrs Blah had heard two sets of footsteps crossing the hall, quiet though they had tried to be. So the following night, after the curtain came down in the pleasant little theatre, the boy arranged to meet his new-found friend again and once more they repaired to Mrs Blah's sumptuous boarding house. This time however he made no secret of his arrival, indeed he sang a little song and banged his feet quite loudly. You see, there was only one set of steps to hear. The boy had reasoned that if he carried his friend piggyback, up to the house, in through the door, across the hall and up the stairs, then Mrs Blah would think nothing of it. Why should she? It was surely only Mr returning from the theatre - alone...

'Dear friends, never, never underestimate the theatrical landlady! Oh, they reached the front door without let or hindrance. They even made the bottom of the stairs with no sound to be heard, other than the boy's footsteps, punctuated by the odd bar of "Fill the Cup". But the moment he set foot on the very first stair tread, the aforementioned rasp wrenched the air, just like a North Country Lady Bracknell it was. "Cripples now, is it, Mr?"!'

Dear sweet old Frank. What a lovely chap and thespian.

XXI

Ever since I spoke about Joss Ackland smashing me in the mouth - in the acting line of duty of course, when we were making *England Made Me* - I've been wanting to delve into a part of the business which I've hitherto only mentioned in passing, namely the art of the make-up artist. And in particular the great part these ladies and gentlemen play in those very believable cuts, bumps and bruises which we bums are required to acquire from time to time.

The make-up fraternity are not called artists for nothing. They are simply that - brilliant artists. The vast majority do in fact paint when they have some free time, or they are superb photographers, and once they get to work on you with their brushes, they really can create magic.

Let me tell you about my death at the hands of Helmut Griem in *The McKenzie Break*. If you remember, the only weapon raised against me by Helmut was a rubber spanner.

The sequence starts as the roof of the hut begins to cave in. I rush into shot and see Helmut loosening the extra supports which I've put in place. He sees me. I scream. He raises his spanner and whacks me on the head several times. I spurt blood. What I didn't mention when I first described this sequence was that all filming stopped at this point - after we'd done it twice that is. The bloomin' camera jammed on take one, of course!

The scene still had quite a way to go in fact, and after a fairly lengthy break we continued filming. First, my stunt double got completely buried in my stead. The action continued with him frantically being hunted for amongst the mass of debris. He was finally found, and just as he was about to be pulled clear and would be recognised as not being me, I took over again. I was then placed on a stretcher and carried out to a waiting ambulance. But I was already dead. And my face was hardly recognisable, it was so badly smashed.

And that was why we had had to stop filming. To give Alan Brownie time to get to work on my face and turn it from wonderfully handsome into the mess of blood and bone that can be seen on the screen. First he wiped my face clean of make-up. (Oh yes, we all need a little help. Eyebrows, skin colour, and, particularly in my case, making sure that the balding pate is well powdered so that it doesn't shine in the lights.) Then Alan took his glue and the mortician's wax. A large amount of wax was skilfully stuck to my face, not to change my appearance, but to add an extra thickness of skin. And, for an artist, the rest was easy. Alan simply goudged out bits of wax and filled the holes with blood-like make-up and little bits of white wood and string, which together looked so terribly like bone. All make-up artists have their own methods of course. Alan happened to prefer splinters of wood, and they looked very real. (When we finally come to put this tome together I'll try to get them to include a continuity photo which was taken at the time, to show more clearly what I mean.)

So there you have it. A peep at the wonders that are achieved by the make-up artists. They work damned hard and are always cheerful, even at some very early hours in the morning. They are invariably at their posts first, ready to chat about anything under the sun, if that is what's required to relax those who may be worried about the day's work ahead. They will have cups of tea sent in and cigarettes available for you if you smoke. And all we bums love 'em to death.

XXII

I was about to comment that *Enemy at the Door* was only a telly, but that would be an outrageous thing to say. Film, television, theatre, or radio, it makes no difference. Work is work. I thank God for it and I love it...Do you remember *Enemy at the Door*? Actually, I do only mention it now because we made a film-length episode; we shot it in the Channel Islands, on Sark, it was directed by the super Martyn Friend, and I was terribly seasick!

Sark is one of the smallest Channel Islands, of course, so the actors stayed on Guernsey, and every morning we would go down to the jetty, board a smallish boat, pop over to Herm for costume and make-up (the crew were staying there), and then proceed to Sark to start the day's work. Anyway that was the idea. But the landing stage at Herm is very small and primitive, and for five days the sea was so rough we couldn't land. We'd leave Guernsey, I'd feel sick, and we'd be unable to land on Herm. Work would then be abandoned for the day, and the boat would turn round into the wind and head back to Guernsey. The sea would now be even rougher and I'd feel even more sick. I wouldn't get back to normal till we'd arrived back at the hotel and I'd had a damn good breakfast. Sausage, bacon, fried bread, egg and beans, and a wonderful cup of tea or three! We got so far behind with the schedule through no fault of ours that the show was very nearly cancelled. I'm delighted to say, however, that the elements finally allowed us to proceed further than Herm and a bloody good TV film was made by all.

Especially me! Yep, I know other people have said it on other productions and it's very kind of them so to do, but this time I'm going to say it myself: I was pretty darned excellent as Koener in *Enemy at the Door*, in spite of the seasicknesses!

Funny old business ours. Who would have thought that I'd end up playing the the husband of an Oscar-winning, co-star of Paul Newman's, who was almost old enough to be my mother, and the father of an American mountain boy. But it happened.

You remember The *Waltons*, I'm sure. A very long-running American TV series about a family who lived on a mountain. One of the many children, I think he was the oldest, was called John-Boy, presumably because his dad was also called John. This part was played by an actor called Richard Thomas, and he was damn good. He directed some of the later episodes, and after the series finished he went off in search of new mountains to climb.

One of the more interesting of these was a re-make of *All Quiet on the Western Front*. Richard played Paul Baumer, the leading part, I played his Dad, and Patricia Neal, who of course had won an Oscar for 'Hud' with P. Newman, played his Mum - my wife. For the sake of this nosegay I'll stick with the above-mentioned...No I won't. Ernest Borgnine was also in the film and I must include a big bum like him! His performances have given me untold pleasure over very many years.

Have you ever heard of a film company being given permission to blow up a town? Neither had I, but it happened on the remake of 'All Quiet'. It went like this: There was this really beautiful town in Czechoslovakia, up near the German border. A little like Interlaken in Switzerland, it had all the charm of the region - neat white houses, pretty gardens, window boxes full of flowers, winding streets, the sound of distant cow bells. You could almost see the cuckoo clocks sitting on the wood-carved mantlepieces. The place hadn't changed for...oh, at least 100 years. Which made it absolutely perfect for the film maker who was making a film set in 1914 and looking for a town to demolish.

Now that there is no longer a Warsaw Pact and the threat of Communism has receded, I don't think such a thing would be allowed to happen. But it certainly did then. Coal had been discovered underneath this charming town, and in order that it should not be lost, the - then - government built a cheap concrete monstrosity of a place for people to live in, some five miles down the road, and moved the entire population of the town into it. In one day. Every man, woman, child, baby and animal. And they were about to start digging up the lovely old town when along came our film company and offered them huge dollars if they'd hold off for a few weeks and allow us to film there, and blow the place to kingdom come and back. Of course the Czech government agreed - every Eastern European country wanted dollars then, still do as far as I know.

(I had the most extraordinary time in Poland not long after this as a matter of fact. I was chased down the main street in Warsaw by three different money brokers. They all wanted to change my dollars into their local currency, and if I had no dollars then pounds sterling would have to do! These chaps had a very neat way of folding and then counting the zloty. Even though you thought you were getting a good deal, you ended up with much less than you'd expected. I never got caught, thank goodness, but watch out.)

All Quiet on the Western Front is a very good film and it should not be compared with the Lewis Milestone 1930 version. It can stand, excellently, on its own, and my thoughts of its making are very fond.

I remember how hard Pat Neal had to work to overcome the results of the seven strokes she'd suffered. What a trouper. Even learning a line was immensely difficult, and she worked like stink to negate the limp she'd been left to endure. I was full to the brim with admiration and I love her to death, bless her.

I remember this huge bear of a man called Ernest Borgnine, over sixty-five he was then, grabbing my hand and shaking it almost to a pulp. 'How are you, Michael. Glad to meet you.' And he went on, 'I so much enjoyed your work on *The McKenzie Break* and *Escape to Athena*.' I was delighted and very touched.

I remember how, when we were working, our super director, Delbert Mann, used to wear the uniform he'd worn as a pilot during the last war. Flying jacket, breeches, riding boots, the lot. I don't know why he did it, but I guess it must have been superstition, because E. Borgnine told me that Del had worn the same clobber when he'd directed him in *Marty*. That was the film which won Ernie the Oscar for Best Actor - Del's good luck gear most certainly worked for Mr Borgnine!

I remember how Ernest was a father figure both off and on screen. He was very helpful to the youngsters who played the soldiers in the film, and in the movie itself he played Cat, the older army regular who's seen it all before. Ernie's a nice, kind man.

I remember that I had my rather lovely cord suit and my shoes stolen from my location caravan - but so what, the poor Czech people had nothing then. We had quite a number of the local population working as extras on the film and also playing small parts - the lass who played our daughter was Czech - and when lunchtime came, served from their abundant chuck-wagon by our old friends the location caterers, the locals couldn't believe their eyes. Many of them went round twice and I'm sure it was the only real meal they had on filming days. I trust and hope that things are better now in what used to be Czechoslovakia.

And I remember that twice on this movie I had the offer of a lovely bed companion. But I saved myself for Dearly Beloved. On both occasions!

XXIII

I don't know how many pages ago I said that I'd tell you about going into business for ourselves - Michael York and I were talking about it, if you remember. So, away we go then, now is the time! It is in fact quite a painful episode for me to write about. Not because we've all tried as hard as our other commitments will allow and have not, as yet, got anything off the ground, but because along the way I've lost a goodly number of dear friends.

There was the Production Controller at the old Westward Television, Terry Fleet. He suddenly died of a heart attack. Then we made a very good contact with an independent TV Production House in London, and our chap there died too. And then one of my partners, Peter Grimwade - I'd known Peter for many years, ever since he was a production manager on *Lord Peter Wimsey* to be exact - died of AIDS a couple of years ago. (Yes, it does happen in our business, same as in all others. But it doesn't make the person any different as far as his work is concerned, or indeed as a human being. Peter was a bloody good egg, a very hard worker and a good friend. He was also an excellent writer - see *Dark Treasure* just coming up - and he was reliable and kind, which counts for a hell of lot.)

It was Peter in fact who first suggested that we approach Westward Television in Plymouth. By this time Ken - Old King Coles from *England Made Me* and that naughty film - had been added to our little band. And apart from Michael York, who was very eager and willing to be involved, provided, very understandably, that things did not conflict with his other work commitments - indeed we were all in that boat - we had also acquired two television Directors and two Producers, one of whom went on to become head of drama at Scottish Television.

I won't mention the names of the two Directors. They seemed to think that it was not a good idea to be associated with us after the partnership split up - which in its present form it did. Once they were back to being simply (big) TV directors, their insecurity dictated that it was better for them not to know us. No hard feelings I assure you, fellas. It's your loss...that's the way the cookie crumbles, at times.

I will, however, tell you of the two Producers. The one who went to Scotland and became the Head of Drama, Robert (Bobby) Love, has remained a staunch friend and ally and I've done some super work for him. He produced the two-hander I did for STV - the one which won an award in America. T'other producer, Robert Banks Stewart, has devised and produced such goodies as *Shoestring* and *Bergerac*, and I last worked for him on *The Darling Buds of May*.

I can't go on for much longer talking about something which has not as yet happened! Let me simply say that those of us who are left, plus some new members, Ben Rea from Auntie for example, very much hope that we'll get something up and running soon. Perhaps even before these memoirs have been completed. I'll let you know.

But I did say I'd tell you about Peter's *Dark Treasure*. I hope it will give you a sniff of the pleasure and heartache we have thus far derived from: ArTec Ltd. (Artist's and Technicians), and Torgrade - Film Production Ltd. Yep, we've had two companies thus far.

Dark Treasure is a damn good yarn and centres on the now defunct tin mining industry in Cornwall. Because of its setting, Peter (Grimwade) thought it might be the sort of project that would interest the old Westward TV Company - old because it is now no more, having lost its franchise. And Peter was right. Westward TV had never made anything like a six part drama series, but Terry Fleet in particular was very keen that we should make it, as equal fifty-fifty partners. But there was the rub! Even Terry hadn't realised that it could not be done. Or rather, his bosses wouldn't allow it to be done.

The only thing that stopped us making *Dark Treasure* with Westward was the fact that the Westward board would not give us half the revenue they would be due from the the UK network TV showings, and half the money from the adverts transmitted in their area, whilst the show was on the air. It was therefore not a true fifty-fifty partnership. We had the locations set up, the cast, the money - our half of the money was a hell of a gamble for us - but Westward wanted to play it safe. You see, they would have got back their half of the investment from the money they received from the UK. In other words, they risked nothing. We on the other hand would have to wait for hoped-for sales abroad, which even if you're lucky can take years. Terry Fleet fought tooth and nail to get his people to see that it was grossly unfair to expect us to take all the risk, but he fought a losing battle.

We did not make *Dark Treasure* with Westward. Terry Fleet died suddenly and then Peter...But one of these days we'll make it. Things are becoming more and more interesting for the independent production company. Dear Peter, Terry and the rest, will see us get into production on our own account, I promise them.

But in the meantime, it's back to the main theme. And I'm happy to say that there's *Rough Cut*, *Green Ice*, 'Raiders', and *High Road to China*, etc., etc., still to come!

Rough Cut. Now I'm going to be just a little bit bitchy. It was Noel Coward who described one triple-barrelled named actress I also worked with as the three worst actresses in the world. He was not talking about Lesley-Anne Down. I wonder who on earth he could have meant!

Miss Down was the leading actress in *Rough Cut*. Her leading man was Burt Reynolds, and apart from David Niven leaving that message of best wishes for me, which

I've already mentioned, I don't think there's much more I wish to say about what was a very grotty film. This Miss Triple-Barrelled and Mr Reynolds were extremely aloof, but for different reasons. He because he didn't give a damn about anything or anybody - and his first claim to fame was as a nude model for goodness sake! She because she was trying to be what she thought a big star should be...Wrong, very wrong. Please, Miss Lah-di Dah Dah, please see my earlier paragraphs on Stephanie Powers.

I did have one good bit of fortune on this film. Well sort of. The first call an actorbum has on a movie tends to be very early in the morning, so they can check make-up and wardrobe. This film was no exception. Therefore, imagine the following: I go to bed at 10.30pm, and I set the alarm for 4.30am. The part I have in this picture does not warrant a studio car to collect me, therefore the onus is on me to get myself to the studio. So, I've listened to the weather forecast and I've put in a request for a telephone 'wake-up' call as a back-up. Everything is as ready as it can be. Finally, Dearly Beloved and I settle down and I fall fast asleep. Dead to the world. Bliss. Imagine all this...Then think of the telephone shrilling at the side of the bed at midnight, barely eighty minutes later. I pull myself back into wakefulness and manage to grab the receiver. 'Michael! Sorry to ring you so late, but you will not be needed tomorrow. Or is it today? Ha! Burt has had a bit of a turn and he can't work. I'll ring you when we can continue. OK? You can go back to sleep now. Bye.' Go back to sleep. Ha again. I didn't sleep all the flipping night long. But I have to admit that it was a kind of heaven when 4.30am came round and I didn't have to face the cold black morning!

Poland and the Money Brokers. I've told you about them already. But I've not mentioned why I was in Poland and what I was doing. *Sherlock Holmes*, that's what. The most

British of all things British being made into a television series in Poland. Mind you, I know why it was made there. It was so bad, that they didn't dare make it anywhere closer to home!

Let me make it abundantly clear, the following named thespians are in no way to blame for the shambles. I was at drama college with Geoff Whitehead. Paddy Newall, alas no longer with us, was a very special chum, and I lived not far from Donald Pickering at one time, and he's a smashing chap too. And what is more, without question their talent is excellent. But have you ever heard of a 'Sherlock Holmes' series, with Geoffrey Whitehead as Sherlock, Donald Pickering as Watson and Patrick Newall as Lestrade?

The Poles were very keen. Indeed, when they were told to build Baker Street on the back lot at Warsaw Studios, they built something that would last. I'm sure that the false house fronts they made which depicted old London are still there today as good as ever. I'm certain the cobbled street is. If you build a cobbled street for a film in this country, or America, you use pretend-rubber cobbles. But not in Poland. When I had to fall off the back of a hansom cab, I fell on to real, hard, bottom-bruising stone!

No, the trouble with this series was the scripts. I've not said a lot about scripts thus far, and I know some very clever stuff seems to have been made without a script at all. But for my and almost everyone else's money, you might as well not start making anything unless you have a bloody good script. That is, it has to be, your beginning.

I can't remember his first name, so I won't guess in case I libel someone else, but the producer of this Polish piece had the surname Reynolds - his first name certainly wasn't Burt! Shelly perhaps? And I'm sure I'm remembering correctly when I say that the scripts used were ages old, had possibly been filmed before in America, when television film was in its infancy and very much less demanding, and had been acquired by him (Reynolds) from...God knows where. Probably some very minor tycoon's dustbin!

The actual set-up in fact was quite appealing. The idea being that the three above-mentioned actorbums would spend eighteen months in Poland making the series, and they would be joined, if and when, by the odd bum out from the UK, who would do two episodes back-to-back, playing the guest lead part in each. Polish actors would play everything else. There wasn't much else, actually. These wonderful scripts were cut so close to the bone that they had as few characters in them as possible. However, all actors must be understood, and after a day's work playing my own part, I spent some enjoyable hours re-voicing the Polish actors from previous episodes.

I'm delighted to report that the lads who were playing the three leading parts did not, after all, have to stay in Poland for the full eighteen months, interesting though the country was. The whole thing was cancelled long before then.

But it was nevertheless a fascinating piece to have done, if only because it showed me my third Communist country in a comparatively short time. First there had been *England Made Me* and *Force 10 from Navarone* in Yugoslavia. At that time Yugoslavia, as far as I could see, was simply a Western country which just happened to have a Communist government. Then I did 'All Quiet' in Czechoslovakia. I found this country very sad. One of the locals said to me 'We did try, you know. We had our uprising in 1969. We waited for the West to help us, but they did not come and Russia sent in her tanks.' After that I think they lost heart. They didn't care any more. I hope things are different for them now. I'm certainly sure that they are now different in Poland. Those people would never let themselves be beaten. When we did 'Sherlock', there was only one hotel in Warsaw where you could supposedly live like a Westerner. You know, a restaurant with a goodish menu, room service, well-stocked bar etc., and yes, we were billeted there. The Poles were not readily allowed access to the hotel, even if they could afford the inflated prices - dollars or sterling only. They really did have to queue for hours in the street for the odd cabbage. But they never allowed the finger to drop. I went on a picnic with the Polish film crew and the one finger, and also the Churchillian version, the V sign, could be seen everywhere. 'Fuck the Russians,' they said. 'Just let them try!'

George Pravda's finger was up there with the best of them, but he, nevertheless, almost turned down the chance to go to Poland on this series, because he thought he might not be allowed to return to the UK when he'd finished filming.

Georgie and I first met on that Simon MacCorkindale TV play *Three Weeks*, and he was a super sweet guy and great actor. He, of course, always played the foreigner - the Pole, the Czech, the Yugoslav and the Russian, etc. - and thereby hung his dilemma. I don't think anybody knew where George was actually born, perhaps he didn't know himself. But he spent the whole of the last war dodging, first the Germans, and thereafter the Communists, as part of a travelling - one night stand - theatre group, and he was fearful when he went back to Poland to do 'Sherlock' that the authorities would find from their records that he was still wanted. I can't argue against his fears, because none of us who have not experienced persecution can have any idea what it is really like. What I do know is that Georgie was damn glad to return to good old England, and I feel certain that he knew something that we did not. But drop the digit - never, not Georgie.

When I came home I brought with me a list of banned books, by authors such as James Joyce, which had been requested by the Polish crew. I was asked to send them out one at a time, because this way some of them might get through. And they did. I had a smashing letter from the Polish assistant director. His wife had been allowed to leave Poland some years before to visit a sick relative in America and they'd agreed that she should not return. This guy had not of course seen his wife since, and he'd had his passport revoked so that he could never join her. But he's done so now, thanks to the Cold War's end.

My final memory of a super people: I had an afternoon off and decided to go to the cinema. The only film showing was *Gone With the Wind*. A splendid film certainly, but one which I think we now take a little for granted, seeing that it's over fifty years old and has been on telly several times. But not the Poles. There was a full house and we sat on hard wooden chairs for the whole four hours of this English soundtrack version. No pee-pee break, no ice creams, nothing. And at the end, the whole audience stood up and applauded for fully three minutes. It was really very moving. I'm sure that Clarke Gable, Vivian Leigh, Leslie Howard, and the rest who are no longer around, were delighted, wherever they may be.

XXIV

Dame Peggy Ashcroft is next. And I can already hear her saying 'Now, Michael, I've told you before, none of the Dame stuff. I'm Peggy, or Peg, plain and simple.' Peggy was one of the loveliest, sweetest, kindest, best actors I've ever had the pleasure of meeting, God bless her.

Caught on a Train was filmed for the most part on the Nene Valley Steam Railway outside Peterborough. We all stayed in some Road House on the A1 nearby, of which I have no memories at all. I do however have super memories of Peterborough itself. Peggy and I became good mates and spent a number of afternoons looking round the town. No, the city. We spent a day in the Cathedral and as Peg pointed out, 'no matter how small, a town is a city if it's got a Cathedral!'

You remember in my paragraphs on *England Made Me*, I mentioned that the director, Peter Duffell, was kind enough to ask me to work with him again? Well, although it was quite a while before he had something suitable which he thought I'd like, he remembered. And no, it wasn't 'Caught on a T.', it was before that, a play for television called *Murder Rap*. I played a barrister and it was a very nice piece as I remember. It was the last work that Queenie Watts did - a super character actress. Oh, and speaking of character actresses, it was during the recording of this play at the BBC Television Centre in London that an incident occurred!

Do you recall a little, round, vibrant, red-haired cockney actress called Rita Webb? If you do you'll enjoy this story even more. Now, how can I quickly explain the inside of the BBC Television Centre? Or rather the studio complex...Four reception areas, each serving three studios. But we're concerned with just one of these: three studios, served by one reception area, with a whole lot of dressing rooms attached. These dressing rooms are allocated to whichever of the three studios needs them, but there are only so many which are on the same floor as the studios themselves, and they are always given to the actors who are playing the biggest parts - quite right too. If you are not playing such an important role, or indeed if you are an extra, you are given a dressing room downstairs in the basement. Not only that, although you may have the place to yourself, this room is clearly designed to accommodate at least three other persons (some of them hold as many as fifty), and it doesn't have a loo of its own either, and it's miles from the tea bar. I think you'll understand how some actorbums may feel just a wee bit down graded when they arrive at the studio and find that they've been given a dressing room on this lower berth.

When we came to record *Murder Rap*, one of the other two studios in our complex was doing something which included an appearance by Rita Webb. And as I made my way to my dressing room (on the studio floor) I heard this distinctive voice rasping up from the basement below: 'I'm not 'aving a bleedin' dressin' room dahn 'ere. I'm not a fucking mole!'

Back to *Caught on a Train*. After we had recorded *Murder Rap* successfully and said our goodbyes, I thought I'd done pretty well and that there was a good chance that P. Duffell might ask me to do something else with him in another eight years. But not a bit of it. In less than no time he'd sent me the script for 'C. on a T.', this smashing film for TV, which went on to win a BAFTA. A simple story really but - and we're back to the importance of writing again - Steven Poliakoff had written a cracking script. It concerned a carriage-load of assorted passengers who are crossing Europe by train. That's why, apart from a few bits that were shot in Germany, we made most of the piece on the Nene Valley. Theirs being the only steam railway in this country that has a substantial amount of European rolling stock.

On the first day of the schedule, before a camera even turned over, we were summoned to the station waiting room, which was to serve as our Green Room throughout the production. And when I say we were summoned, I don't only mean we actorbums, I mean the whole flipping crew as well. The only person not there was Peggy, and some of the assembly waited with a deal of trepidation, I'm sure. Peg duly arrived, gave her 'Now none of the Dame stuff' speech and had everybody eating eating out of her hand before the first coffee break!

We did many long nights of days. Nights of days because it was supposed to be night but in reality it was day, and the train was shoved into a tunnel and we pretended. We worked damned hard, and Peggy, who was then in her seventies and had a very painful knee, never complained. Indeed, in addition to her great performance, she was both complimentary and interested.

It was very difficult filming in the cramped carriages and sometimes it was impossible to have the person to whom you were speaking actually sitting opposite you. When it was your close-up, for example, the camera had to be in their seat, so you had to cheat the eyeline. Rather like I did on 'Force 10' when Bob Shaw couldn't be there because he was drunk. So when I was supposed to be speaking to Peggy and it was my close-up, she dutifully crouched as near to my eyeline as she could in order to say her lines, but I told her not to bother. I asked Peg instead to give me her lines from wherever was most comfortable for her, and she was completely fascinated when I got a piece of sticky masking tape from the camera crew, stuck it on the back of the seat where Peg's head would have been, and played my lines to it.

Peggy had spent most of her life in the Theatre, it's true, but we all know that she'd also given some super performances on celluloid - 'The Nun's Story' and 'Sunday Bloody Sunday', for example. I think she was probably taking the piss, or should I say Michael? No piss will do, it's a good word and Peggy would have approved. But on this occasion she said 'Michael, how can you possibly act to a piece of sticking tape? I couldn't do it. I'm sure I couldn't. Let me have a try,' and she did as I had just done on her next close-up. Using this very old film trick to get the eyes to focus on the right place when the person you are speaking to isn't there - she was magic.

What a gal. God Bless you Peggy Ashcroft. You are one hell of a loss to us all.

Peg would have liked this next one too. I've told you about the naughty film I did for Old King Ken, in which I was his, clothes on, guest star, so I might as well relate the story of the naughty voice-overs.

A small sound studio in the West End of London. Two actorbums: one a middle-aged, balding, bespectacled gent, whose Dearly Beloved may think he's the cat's whiskers, but who will never win a Mr Universe contest. The other a lovely, small, round grandmother; cuddly certainly, but never a Miss World. Picture these two intently watching a very, very naughty pornographic movie, far, far worse than that excellent example of the art of soft porn, King Cole's masterpiece, *The Erotic Inferno*. That film was given a certificate. The one these two are watching never will!

And to top everything, the film they are so avidly scrutinising is not even in English, it's in Swedish, or Dutch or something - probably Dutch. And no, we hadn't suddenly become sex maniacs, Jenny and I were re-voicing the film into English.

The re-voicing/voice-over market is huge. Apart from porno films, there are masses of other foreign imports that need to be synched. Damn silly word that, a complete contradiction. Have you ever seen a re-voiced foreign film where the English words actually match the movements of the mouth? We try very hard, but it just can't be done. If a chap is saying 'auf wiedersehen' on the screen, you can't simply take the sound of his voice, throw it away, and substitute the English word 'bye' or even 'good bye'. Try it for yourself in front of a mirror and you'll see. Mind you, there are some actors who can get very close to it. In fact in Germany, where they never use subtitles as far as I know, some bums spend their whole careers re-voicing and they're really expert.

As well as synching, there is also of course a mega industry in voice-overs. Documentaries, bingo halls, travel audios, the list is almost endless...I've already mentioned radio adverts - I've just finished doing some of those for the *Daily Telegraph*. There are simply masses of situations where a voice is needed. And the work is immediate, so you don't usually have to wait very long. Or worse still book yourself up weeks in advance, thus running the risk of not being free when Hollywood calls. But...many years ago, before the onslaught of the mobile phone, I played golf with a lovely guy and bloody good golfer who, oh dear, here we go again, is no longer with us, called William Dexter. We were on the tenth green, I think it was, when suddenly this high-pitched sound emanated from his back pocket. Bleep, bleep, bleep. 'Ah shit,' said Bill. 'It's my bleeper. They want me for a voice-over, I'll have to go. Sorry.' I've done a good few voices in my time, and although I'm very aware that voice-over work can be damn lucrative, I'm not sure if I'd enjoy being tied as closely as that. Apart from anything else it spoilt our game on this occasion. Ah shit!

I don't know. I get started on a little story and it escalates into a novel! I was telling you about Jenny and I in the studio, re-voicing this wonderful film. We actually had a whale of a time. Let me give you a tickle of what went on. The lady in the film starts to take her clothes off, 'Ah...Oh,' from Jenny. 'Oooh...yes...Oooooh,' from me.

The man, having also divested himself of all garments, walks towards the now naked lady, his ding-a-ling standing proud and to the fore, 'Ah...Oh,' from Jenny. 'Oooh...yes...Oooooh,' from me.

The man is now on top of the lady, 'Ah...Oh,' from Jenny. 'Oooh...YEEEES!'

I'm sure you get the idea. Slight problem though. Whenever we got to a particularly 'Ah...Oh,' part, or an 'Oooooooh...Yes,' I'm afraid that Jenny and I tended to collapse into fits of giggles. Corpsing it's called in our business, and a very bad thing it is for an actorbum to do. Shame on us. Thank goodness therefore that the people who were in charge of these re-voicing sessions also corpsed. They said it was the only way to get the job done, and

Jenny and I were asked back to do lots more porno re-voicing on other naughty films, I'm pleased to say. They were really enjoyable days. And I promise that I had never corpsed before, and I've never corpsed since...Well, hardly ever. There was one time back in rep when a whole stageful of us stopped the show because we couldn't stop laughing. It was certainly a dreadful play right enough, but I'm afraid the corpse just happened, and it's very contagious. I'm pleased to report that on this occasion the audience joined in and laughed too!

The Bunker. I've told you already about the daft-voiced 'Hello, Teddy!' (Hardwicke) incident concerning Richard Jordan, star of this epic, so what more can I say about *The Bunker*? Let's see... Anthony Hopkins, in my opinion, was not totally convincing as Hitler. An extremely fine actorbum was having a day off. The Paris film studios are vast - our arrival at Hitler's headquarters was all done in the studios, massive German cars all over the place. The make-up was not good (a very rare occurrence), they almost wrecked my Himmler toupe...Andrew Ray was in the piece. You don't often see him now, but he was great as a child star in *The Mudlark* and *The Yellow Balloon*. The snug unit hotel was in a lovely little Montparnasse back street. Great grub and vino in the restaurant - I particularly enjoyed dipping my croissant in my breakfast coffee! And that's it, I think. On to...

XXV

Ah hah! *Raiders of the Lost Ark*. Now then...!

There are very few people I'm sure, who would disagree with what I am about to say. Namely, that ever since a small budget film called *Duel* appeared on the scene in 1971, there has been no one person who has been anywhere near

The start of it all - as the war raged around us. Mum, Dad, and Wendy at the christening of Equity member 40307.

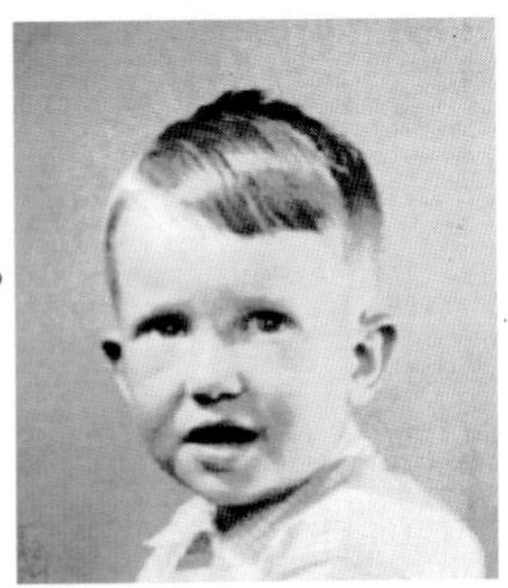

(Above and right). Aged 3 years. An embryo bum actor - rehearsing for **The Invisible Man** *perhaps?*

5th birthday party and my first costume part as a Red Indian.

Thirteen and raring to go - a great hairline and it's all mine!

Sixteen and Ann on my mind.

Aged seventeen. The school production of Victor Rietty's **To Live in Peace**. *Me in the lead, of course!*

RAF Bridgnorth - Passing Out. 5050481 Aircraftsman 2nd class is centre of the first standing row.

Young man about - RADA.

First publicity shot - Perth Repertory, early 1960s.

Mean, moody and magnificent as Mick in the Rep's production of Pinter's **The Caretaker**.

The lady ASM with the shapely calves!

Jane Eyre *at Perth. Going down the stairs: 1st, Donald Sutherland's ex-wife Lois; 3rd, Pamela Craig, who went on to become a stalwart of* **The Archers;** *4th, Dearly B., in front of Christopher Robbie who became a TV announcer. 40307 is bottom right of course and looking particularly handsome!*

The night before the wedding.

Our three: The Chartered Accountant, the Doctor of Medicine, the History and Politics Teacher.

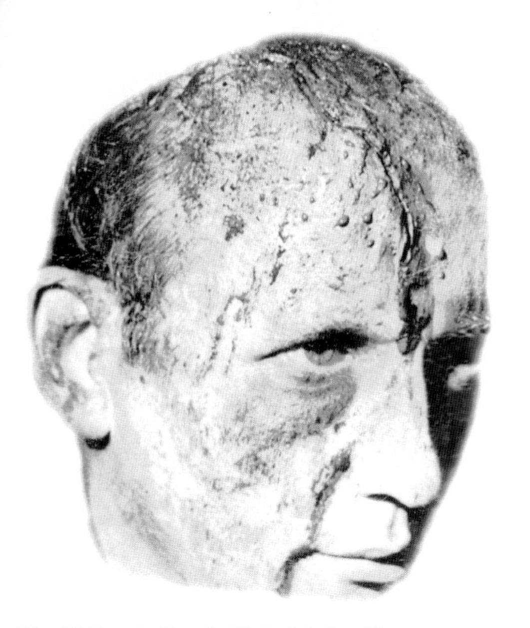

The McKenzie Break *(United Artists/ Levy-Gardner-Laven). As promised, a make-up continuity photograph of the gash.*

Escape to Athena *(ITC/Pimlico). Sergeant Mann...*

And David Niven keeping us enthralled with his stories. Here with Elliott Gould. . .

Roger and I discuss the striptease scene with Director Georgie.

The Riddle of the Sands *(Rank/Worldmark). With Michael York.*

And with Fred, the 'female' extra!

The Dirty Dozen - Next Mission *(MTV). Where did all that blood come from? Wolf Kahler looks on.*

Dr Who - Castrovalva *(BBC). The head-dress hides the sideburns I'd grown for Mr. McKinley in* **Maggie.**

The Invisible Man *(BBC). With dear Gerald James.*

The Outsider *(Yorkshire TV). With Ted (one egg) Morris.*

And with Emily Richard and Peter Egan - the Big P.

My eldest, Simon, then aged 15, did this cartoon of me as The Rev. Mr Bunting, after we heard that I was required to do the nude shot.

The Dark Side of the Sun *(BBC). As Col. Von Reitz. Taken by the producer, (Little) Vere Lorrimer. . .*

High Road to China *(Golden Harvest/Pan Pacific). Trying to keep a straight face with Jack Weston.*

Grange Hill *(BBC). During a break in filming, Mr Bronson discusses a forthcoming 'march' with Danny Kendall (Jonathan Lambeth).*

Star Wars: The Empire Strikes Back *(TCF/Lucasfilm). As Admiral Ozzel, of course.*

Indiana Jones and the Last Crusade *(Paramount/Lucasfilm). As A. Hitler. For once, upstaging Harrison Ford!*

as influential in our business as Steven Spielberg. Everything seems to carry his name. Adventures: The 'Indy' Films, the *Jaws* films, and Dinosaurs. Science Fiction: *Back to the Future* 1, 2, and 3. Cartoons: *An American Tail*. The above of course are only examples, there are endless alternatives.

And on top of it all the man is a very nice guy. I said at the beginning of these pages that no one would ever call Steven a bum, if they wanted to work again. Well in fact I'm sure he'd be flattered. He'd have to be eligible of course. We don't allow just anyone to call themselves a bum. Only those who have appeared in front of a camera, or on a stage, or in a sound studio - performers - are allowed to call themselves bums. I know for certain that when Lord Olivier coined the phrase, this is what he meant. Bums are thespians - actors. Lord Larry was a bum of course, so am I, so was my stand-in, my stuntman, and so was little Ian Wilson the extra. But directors, cameramen, sound, makeup, costume, props, lights, etc., they are all nice people, but they are not bums. Let them find their own collective noun!

So that kind of leaves S. Spielberg out of it doesn't it? He's a director, a producer, an entrepreneur, an angel (one who puts up the money), a writer, an ideas man. He's everything he wants to be, but he's not a thespian, and therefore he's not a bum...Wait a minute though! Dearly Beloved and I have been racking our brains...there was this American film. Made for TV we think it was...some people were looking for someone...It might have been to do with Watergate. They knocked on this door, in a hotel we think, and this man opened it. He was smallish, wearing glasses, designer stubble - and yes, it was he! Dearly B. and I obviously can't remember the name of the piece - if you can, do let me know - and Stephen was, for certain sure, only doing a favour for a director friend, or it may have been an in-joke, but it was definitely him playing that part.

And he was darn good, dammit. Must he be good at everything!

So I am now, ladies and gentlemen, more than happy, I'm extremely honoured to welcome Steven Spielberg Esq., into our privileged circle and to call him a bum. In fact, Steven, you are, without question, a very, very big bum indeed!

Now I'll continue telling you about Indy. I first met Steven in a suite in one of those swanky hotels at the bottom of Park Lane in London, and he had flu. I'd been asked along because the casting director thought that I might be right for the part that my very dear friend Ronald Lacey finally played in this, the first Indiana Jones movie. Steven was in his dressing-gown when I was summoned, a nurse was in attendance and he really looked foul. Put me right off my stroke. I'd been ready to concentrate on my impressive list of film credits and how marvellous I'd be in his movie. But instead I found myself asking if he really felt well enough to see me and could I call a doctor!

I can't remember exactly how long Steven's schedule for 'Raiders' was. But as things turned out, I'd done another movie and had started a television series before he'd finished 'over-shooting' Indy, because of the weather.

I'd no idea I would be doing this other movie when we first met, (more of it later), but I did know that I was booked to do the TV series. My agent thought, though, that the starting date for the series was so far in the future that it couldn't possibly hinder my doing the Ronnie Lacey part in 'Raiders'.

And it didn't. The plain truth is that Steven felt Ronnie was more suited to the part than I. And he was right. Even if I hadn't known Ronald Lacey for many years, and been a mate, I'd still say that he was smashing in the part. I won't go so far as to say that I wouldn't have been pretty good in it myself - we've got to remain competitive! - but Ronnie it was who got the nod this time.

And anyway, what would have happened if I had been offered the 'Raiders' part? I couldn't have done both it and the television series. And I certainly wouldn't have been free to kill Omar Sharif in the movie I've yet to tell you about.

And I wasn't left completely out of 'Raiders'. Steven was very diplomatic and what he actually said to me that day in his bedroom was, 'Michael, you're not going to be free to do a part that goes all the way through my movie, because of your television series. Why don't you come to La Rochelle and Munich with us for the beginning of our shoot and play the German U-Boat Captain?' The fact that I didn't really play that part either is not Steven's fault. It was the flipping weather again. Oh I went to La Rochelle alright and I actually went to sea. But I never got anywhere near saying a line.

The U-Boat was in fact a very empty barge with a U-Boat type mock-up top. The result being that when there was even a puff of wind, the blooming thing lurched from side to side so violently that they could never get a camera to stay steady long enough to do my scenes. I also, of course, got very, very sick again, as my part entailed spending all my days at the top of the conning tower. If there is nothing but an empty hull beneath you, then the top is going to swing even further, from side...to side...to side. I'm getting seasick just writing about it. Imagine what the real thing was like!

The upshot was that we never did my lines and close-ups at sea. And we never got to Munich to do them either, or the interiors of the sub, at least not at the beginning of the shoot. I never said one damn word in *Raiders of the Lost Ark* and my name was taken off the credits by mutual agreement.

And all because of the weather. We were unable to film at sea because of the wind, and then we couldn't go to the tanks in Munich, because we simply ran out of time. The company, because they were due to film in Tunisia, I think it was, and I, because I was due to start the TV series I've mentioned. (The 'Raiders' sequences which required the huge water tank in Munich - it's large enough to take a submarine - were done at the end of the shooting schedule, with another bum saying my lines: 'Dive, dive, dive' and all that heroic stuff.)

Before however I go on to tell you about the series, and the killing of Omar Sharif film, let me say that you can just see me in 'Raiders', I'm in several of the long shots. Look very hard and very carefullly - I think the best opportunity is when the U-Boat comes into the submarine pens. There is Yours Truly standing proudly at the top of his sub. (It wasn't shaking now you see, 'cos we were in the dock, so I wasn't feeling sick and I could be as proud as I liked!)

In spite of all, it is a very happy memory. Steven S. asked me back later to do the third Indy film. And there are masses of fish restaurants in La Rochelle which are second to none. Fish Potage - completely out of this world!

XXVI

The next chapter didn't start too well, actually. I rang Dearly Beloved from France to say that I'd be returning on the following day, to be told that the TV series had been put back. Not something a bum likes to hear, that. 'Put back' can mean postponed, which in turn of course can signal cancelled.

However, I had a nice last evening in France. Dinner with Harrison et al., and I didn't allow myself to think about the possibility that I was coming home to no work. 'No work', 'out of work', 'resting', 'reading scripts' - it all adds up to the same thing, I'm afraid. No lolly coming in to pay the bills, and the drastic feeling that nobody,

NOBODY will EVER again, EVER, EVER, EVER, want you to play ANYTHING!...I must remember to tell you a wee bit about 'No Work'.

But me? Why, I'm the lucky so-and-so who always lands on his feet, aren't I? When I got home the next day - it must have been a Thursday because I know I had a couple of days at home this time - I felt that my family were keeping something from me. They had a little secret. They wouldn't look me straight in the eye and they kept giggling. Finally it all came out and I didn't believe them. Yes, the series had been postponed for two months, but in the meantime I was flying out to Mexico on Monday to do another moving picture!

Can you blame me for doubting? But it was absolutely true. You remember *Escape to Athena* of course. Well the dear producer of that film, Jack Wiener, had gone on to his next production and he'd asked for me. I was one of only two actors in the whole of the blessed UK who were wanted for this movie. I mean, apart from anything else, what an honour, eh?! My agent had taken the enquiry about my availability to go to Mexico several weeks before, just after I'd left for France - La Rochelle - and before my television series had been put back. Of course she'd had to say that I wasn't free. But I don't know, she'd had a feeling, and had decided not to say anything to Dearly Beloved, who as always was there, in my shoes, when I was elsewhere, if you see what I mean.

And my agent was right. Within the space of forty-eight hours the following had happened: the series had been postponed - no question of it being cancelled, it was simply some location problem. My agent had immediately contacted Jack Wiener and told him that I would be free after all. Jack had said great, and had arranged for an American actor from Hollywood to fly to Mexico. Unlike those nights of song on 'Force 10' when we were allowed insurance cover because there was nothing else we could film, this guy had to stand by, pretending to be me, and act as weather-cover until I arrived. If it had rained, they'd have had to change the schedule and film interiors, and this American actorbum would have actually played my part in *Green Ice.* All I had to do, then, was pray that it didn't rain in Mexico before next Wednesday, which was the earliest I could arrive in Vera Cruz. It was Thursday now if you remember, so everyone crossed everything for me and did non-rain dances. It's not easy getting a reliable weather forecast for that part of the world when you're in Surrey, England. In the end however the good old Met office came to the rescue and told us it would definitely not rain in that part of the world for at least three months, when the rainy season was due to start.

Anyway, even if they were wrong, I had to leave Heathrow on the following Monday, so at least I'd have the flight out there. All twenty-three hours of it! Hey, ho. You know that I don't particularly enjoy boats don't you? Well I'm definitely not the best flyer in the world either. But for Jack Wiener, indeed for any movie, I would of course fly to the moon if necessary.

(Somewhere there is a photograph of fellow bum John Abineri and me, taken as we were about to take off and fly to Ireland to resume work on *The McKenzie Break*. John didn't like flying much either, and although he had something like six kids and I had two and a half at the time, the photo shows us, whiskey glasses filled to the brim, holding hands like fiercely ardent lovers!)

What Jack Wiener did for me on *Green Ice* was in fact far, far above and beyond the call of all duty. It was flipping bloody marvellous. He'd liked what I'd done in *Escape to Athena* of course and that helped. But he certainly didn't have to go to such virtually impossible lengths to get me into *Green Ice*. I played Jaap, a supposed life-long friend of Omar Sharif's, and it's a jolly good featured part. But there are certainly lots of actorbums around who could have played it. The American who was weather-cover for me for one. Jack must have thought he could do it. He would have, too, if it had rained. But Jack Wiener wanted me, and I'm forever grateful that he did move a good few mountains to make it possible. So before I continue I want to say a very big THANK YOU to JACK WIENER.

Now where was I? Oh yes, in the air for twenty-three hours. Actually it's such a long time that if you don't decide to lie back and enjoy it you'd probably go nuts. So I had a couple of jars, took my shoes off - I'm told you're supposed to do that on a long flight anyway - watched movies that hadn't yet been released in the UK, had lots of food, and in the end arrived in Mexico City.

It hadn't been so bad after all. There'd now be an overnight stay in a nice hotel, followed by a tiny forty-minute flight to Vera Cruz. I was becoming quite blasé. First thing I must do is phone home. They do worry so...But it wasn't Mexico City at all. We'd only got as far as our re-fuelling stop in Houston, in the good old US of A. Oh, no! I didn't even ask how much longer we still had to go, I could work that out for myself. If we were in Texas, then we still had to go to the end of the United States, over that thin bit that joins the two Americas and then on, and on. A hell of a long way...and I hadn't even seen the script yet!

We were bundled into a bus and trundled down the tarmac to the 'in transit' area. Everywhere there were these huge air-conditioning machines. I should have got an inkling of what was in store, but I didn't. After all, I'd never experienced anything like this before. But I was in America for the first time and that was interesting. I had an American hamburger, with American fries and an American Coke. That was extremely interesting - just like the ones I'd had on London's Waterloo station on my way home last week!

In the end of course I did arrive in Mexico City. On the Tuesday at about seven in the evening, and it wasn't raining. The hotel was very pleasant. I had a bath, a very nice dinner, a good sleep and by nine the following morning I was winging my way towards Vera Cruz - that little forty-minute flight I mentioned.

Forty-minute flight it may have been. But I defy anybody to tell me of a more dramatic climatic change. No, it still wasn't raining. But there certainly was plenty of water, it literally poured off me the moment I stepped from the aircraft. Mexico City had been a very nice 68 degrees fahrenheit (20 celsius) but a wall of heat, such as I'd never experienced before, hit me head on as I staggered towards the airport exit. Vera Cruz, and the Gary Cooper film of the same name which I'd always thought was super, would never be the same again.

I finally emerged from 'Arrivals', dripping wet by this time, and there to meet me was Mick, one of the unit drivers - they who drive everything anywhere for the film unit and are indispensable - who had also worked on 'Athena'. 'Michael,' he said, 'how the hell are you? You must love us one hell of a lot to come to this God-forsaken place. Anyway, nice to see you. I bid you a very warm welcome to Vera's Crotch!!'

It was a hell of a place alright. I don't remember one road that didn't have a little river of piss and pooh running down the side. The beaches were covered with every type of rubbish you can imagine, and smothering the town, hovering over it like some gigantic blanket from which there was no escape, was a dreadful acrid stench, which mingled with the ever-present energy-sapping heat and, osmosis-like, seemed to ooze itself into one's every pore.

Mind you, it was a place where people did exist (lived is too strong a word) and life did go on, sort of. After I'd written some postcards home - the sweat that dripped off me virtually obscured my words - I had a dip in the hotel swimming pool, which was hot. Then I met Omar, Ryan O'Neil, Anne Archer, and of course, Jack, and thanked them all for waiting for me, and I began to feel somewhat better. They were nice people and I didn't really care where we were. I could put up with anything. I was making movies. I was happy.

I went out to a local restaurant with John Wall, the film's accountant, another colleague from 'Athena', who has remained a chum ever since, and Dan, my standby, my other self. Now that I'd arrived and it hadn't rained, Dan was on his way back home to Hollywood of course. But he was not at all bothered that he wouldn't be playing my part. In fact he was perfectly happy. After all, as he pointed out, he'd been drawing my salary for four weeks!

It was a nice eating house, overlooking the town square in Vera Cruz. Tablecloths, napkins, and patient waiters. I bought some great leather belts for the family, from a man who was so laden he almost crawled to our table, and I finally started to relax. Anticipating a sumptuous meal, I picked up the menu. Ah...Fish Soup, that's what I'd have to start with. The fish soup had been great in all those restaurants in La Rochelle. I found I was actually quite hungry, and awaited the arrival of the soup with eager anticipation.

Have you ever had a really good fish soup? I'm sure you have. Well, the bowl that arrived that Wednesday evening was absolutely...the most vile collection of slops I'd ever seen. It made me retch just to look at it, and I couldn't do that for very long. God knows where they'd got the fish from, let alone how long they'd been dead. Huge great fish heads, with large staring fish eyes, looked up at me out of the bowl. Then a stinking tail-fin would emerge. Yuk! Suffice it to say that I'd always loved fish, but after this episode I couldn't even look at a fish for very many months.

However...Thursday morning was spent having costume fittings, reading the script and generally preparing myself to start work. In costume I was particularly fortunate. Yvonne, the Costume Designer, had also worked on 'Athena' (Jack Wiener being loyal to good talent again), so she already had all my measurements. She'd flown back to Mexico City especially and had a selection of suits waiting for my approval.

I'm asked on occasion how we bums come to be wearing what we wear in front of the cameras. I'd like to say that when an outfit is admired it was my choice, and when it is hated, the costume designer forced me to wear it, but it doesn't of course work like that. If he's in uniform there can be no discussion, except how well the thing fits. But as a rule, what an actor wears is the result of a mutual decision between the actor, the costume supervisor, and the director, with the actor usually having the casting vote. It would be no good for him to be dressed in something which made him unhappy, and he should know the part better that anyone. Of course if the actor is playing a character who's supposed to feel uncomfortable, then he'll choose his clothes accordingly, if he's any sense.

There are exceptions to the aforementioned however. Some directors will tell you what they think you should wear, and vehemently argue their case for a particular garment. Silly, but if that's the way they like to work, OK. But there was one guy who went even further than this. He insisted on dictating exactly what the costume must be. In my case - and I'm sure in all others - he even paid me a day's extra wages to come out to the studio before my contract started, get dressed up in what he'd demanded and do a one-man fashion show for him, so that he could make absolutely sure he hadn't been cheated. Although I got more pay, I think this attitude was excessive. It gives no reign to the actor's, or indeed the designer's, creative imagination, and their feeling for the part. Mind you I should have expected it. The director I'm speaking of was renowned for treating his actors like cattle!

Out in good old Mexico it was very different, of course. The director was not Hitchcock, and Yvonne had bought a great selection of suits and shirts and ties and shoes, and we chose three of each. We then sought out the lovely director, Ernest Day, to show him the package and ask for his comments, almost as a matter of courtesy. He loved it.

It is not unknown, by the way, for the costume lady, the director and the actor to decide on a suit, which is perfect for the part of course, but when the film is completed, well, the company don't want it, it's no good to anyone else and it just happens that the actor feels that he could perhaps make use of it, 'if you are quite sure that no one else wants it.' And why not? There's surely no job on earth which doesn't have its perks. However, as far as actorbums are concerned, this particular perk can normally only happen on features. The suit or whatever, shirt, tie, or flannels, will have been bought especially for you, and if the company is due to disband when the film is finished, as most small outfits do, they particularly want to be rid of annoying things like clothes. They may only have been worn half a dozen times, but they take up so much room. On TV, or when you're doing a period piece, your costume has probably been hired, or has come out of stock, so normally there's no sale. But I do have a very nice pair of shoes which were bought for me by BBC Glasgow ten years ago and which I still wear regularly!

So, and in spite of the fish soup, I settled in, and before long I was as much a part of the company as if I'd been there from the start.

One chap I knew from previous productions was the armourer, Karl. It is of paramount importance - indeed you can't get insurance otherwise - that there is a firearms expert in attendance on a movie which has shooting involved. I hate guns, and I'm grateful that there was someone to show me how not to point the thing directly at Omar. It's that lying camera again of course, but you can point at least a foot off target and the camera will make it look as though you've taken deadly aim. OK, I know we're only using blanks, but you never know. And anyway, I'm told you can burn someone with a blank. Never seen it myself mind, but you can't be too careful with firearms. Nasty things.

Another member of the crew was Dave Bickers. More years ago than he or I care to remember, Dave was a daredevil cross-country motorcyclist, side-cars and all. I used to watch him on the box and was full of admiration and very jealous. After hurling himself around dirt tracks all over the world and winning everything in sight, he looked around for something less hair-raising to do when he reached a sensible age!

After he'd worked on a couple of movies, looking after the stuntbums gear, Dave realised that there was a job that needed creating in the film industry, and on his next film he was appointed Stunt Technician, the first of the breed. He's been indispensable to the business ever since. On *Green Ice* for example, stuntmanbum Roy Alon put his trust, and indeed his life, in Dave's hands. In the story, Roy, doubling for the actor, is winched over the top edge of a skysraper. He then free falls, gets stuck half way down, and finally crashes to the ground. A very hairy sequence with no cheating, and the whole thing was the responsibility and the brainchild of Dave Bickers. It's spectacular, see for yourself. Many times since then Dave has suggested new and safer ways of helping the stuntmen to accomplish the impossible.

The director, Ernest Day, was a nice man who had in fact started on *Green Ice* as the lighting cameraman. Something had gone very wrong with the original director. It had happened before I arrived, so I'm not really in a position to comment, but I understand it had a lot to do with going to beautiful and expensive locations in Mexico, and in particular Mexico City, and filming every blessed thing in tight close-up. There was absolutely no production value. The film might as well have been shot on Wimbledon Common, or even in a studio, for all the Mexicaness that was achieved. But once Ernest Day took over, everything changed. He'd been promoted to fill the departing director's shoes, and whether we were in Vera's C., or Mexico City, or the Hinterland, or America, he always let the camera speak first. As an ex-cameraman he let his lenses do the talking. This, certainly in my view and in the opinion of very many others, made him an excellent film director, particularly when it came to visuals. And boy did we have some visuals on this movie. Have a look at the film next time it's around and you'll see. Look out too for some early sequences shot over the roof tops of Mexico City. These should of course have been breathtaking but they're not. They were the responsibility of the first director, before he got the elbow, and in order to make them almost work, a hell of a lot of close stuff has had to be cut.

It's sad to report that Ernest Day did not find it possible to continue as a film director. He did direct a small budget piece, *Waltz Across Texas*, which Anne Archer asked him to do, but he soon had to return to his original career as a lighting cameraman. It's certainly not easy to make a permanent shift from camera to director and I do wish Ernie had managed it. Perhaps in truth, and in the end, he was just too good at his first job.

Wherever Ernest is now I hope he's happy and enjoying his work as a L.C., but at the time we are concerned with he was still very much at the blunt end of things, as director of *Green Ice*. During my, thankfully, fairly short stay in boiling Mexico, before we moved on to more sensible climes to do the studio sequences and the remainder of the film, one of the Mexican crew was almost killed by a black widow spider which fell on him from a tree; nearly all the crew got the squirts within a few days of arriving (by the time I arrived there was enough experience to warn me what not to do thank goodness - I hadn't eaten that fish, remember!); there was a camera lens which kept getting steamed up because of the humidity; and the beach which was, as I've said, covered with muck, had to be cleaned - miles of it every day - because it might be in long-shot and it was supposed to be lovely clean North America.

Now I must tell you about the shooting of Omar Sharif. Sounds like a film title itself, doesn't it? This takes place right at the end of the picture when Omar, who has been warned by me never to set foot in the United States, does so, and is shot by me, supposedly his old and faithful friend. In reality of course I am nothing of the sort. I've been appointed by the Concession to stay at his side and make sure that he doesn't step out of line. We shot this sequence in good old Vera's C. and I'm sure you remember that it was hot. Well it now got even hotter. So scalding in fact that I could only bear filming for a few minutes at a time!

Let me set the scene: Omar wants to marry Anne. She and Ryan escape to somewhere wild on the American coast. Ryan has nicked all Omar's emeralds - his Green Ice. Somewhere along the way Anne's been hit in the arm by a tranquillising dart which has made her very drowsy. They arrive at this isolated empty beach house. Ryan carries her in and lays her gently on a sofa. It is dark inside the house and - cut to outside. A landing jetty threading its way out to sea and, yes, Omar is stepping ashore. On to American soil! Something I've told him he must never ever do because if he does the Concession will be sure to get him. Nevertheless, he takes his gun from its holster, strides up to the house, and pushes open the door. We cut inside. We see Anne and Ryan, with Omar standing in the doorway. And next to the door there is a window with its blind drawn. Omar has just said, 'Where are my emeralds?', when his attention is suddenly switched to something happening outside on the veranda. We can't see what it is because the camera is still in the room looking out. But we can see a shadow, the silhouette of a man on the drawn window blind.

'All these years I thought you were my friend.' - BANG! We cut outside, and there am I - smoking revolver in my hand.

Not bad eh? And it worked damn well. After the bang, Omar died superbly - not an easy thing for an actor to do: pretend to be shot. The only problem with this whole sequence was getting my shadow to show up sharply on that window blind so that the required dramatic effect could be achieved. You'd have thought with all that sun around it would have been easy. A doddle in fact. Not a bit of it. In order to get a really dark image, a huge bank of arc lamps had to be positioned outside the window, and I had to stand between the window and the lights. I could only manage my appearances in this tunnel of a hot house - a matter of a meter wide at most - in very short bursts!

A lot of people have said that *Green Ice* is not in fact very good, and before I tell you if I agree with them, let me say what are, for me, the film's main pluses and minuses.

The pluses:

The robbery by balloon across Mexico at night is superb.

The stuntmen, Roy Alon in particular. I've known Roy for ages and we've worked on several movies together - the second 'Dirty Dozen' for example. Every time we meet I sing a parody of that lovely Sigmund Romberg number from *The Desert Song*, 'One Alone' - 'Roy Alon'! Silly I know but we like it. As I've said, Roy does one of the most spectacular falls I've ever seen down the side of the skyscraper, expertly assisted by Dave Bickers. Did they use a dummy for part of it? Dave isn't saying and certainly neither is Roy.

Omar Sharif's death I've already mentioned, as I have my own exquisite performance!

The locations. The production values achieved by Ernie Day. The music. The...

Alright already! As Dearly Beloved is fond of saying when I'm right and she's wrong. So why doesn't *Green Ice* work? There, I've admitted it, even before I've got to the minuses. As a top feature film I don't think it really does. But why? I don't like being associated with a failure and it really should have been damn good in an adventurous sort of vein.

Let's try the minuses:

The script. Yes, that could certainly have been better. I've already mentioned how important a script is to a project. But this script wasn't that bad, it just wasn't too good. The film couldn't have failed on the script alone.

Ryan O'Neil. Now there's a possibility, I'm afraid. Omar and I did one scene in which Ryan should have appeared but didn't. At least not on the day we were working. He was sick. Omar and I talked to our old friends bits of sticking plaster. (Dame Peg if you remember should have been seated, so I'd used one piece. This time, because Mr O'Neil was supposed to be standing up, there were two bits of plaster, one for his head, the other for his midriff. You can talk quite happily to a mark for one close-up, but it becomes extremely difficult when the other person is not there for the entire scene and the continuity lady is reading their lines.) They did O'Neil's close-ups at another time, and OK, the fact that he didn't appear, on this and several other days, could have been a reason why the film failed. A big one. But even though Ryan O'Neil hadn't worked for quite some time prior to *Green Ice*, and had had to take this part for which, I'm told, he was something like sixth choice, because he owed the taxman, he still had quite a reputation with Joe, or should it be Josephine, Public, and he looked pretty enough. No, I'm convinced that the film could not have failed simply because of R. O'Neil. Robert Shaw wasn't in attendance when we did half his scenes in *Force 10 from Navarone*, but that didn't stop the film from doing damn well, and it was a sequel, a type of film almost guaranteed to fail. You could argue, and I'd certainly agree, that Shaw is a better actor than O'Neil, but I still think that my argument holds good. Ryan O'Neil on his own was not responsible for the failure of *Green Ice*. Apart from anything else the film also featured Omar, and Anne, and Roy Alon and Equity member 40307!

Did *Green Ice* not work because there had been a change of director? No certainly not. Ernie Day saw to that.

So what the hell was the reason then?! The answer...is that there is no one reason. I'll talk later about so-called sure fire hits that failed. There are hundreds of examples, probably thousands. *Green Ice* just happened to be one of these.

A wee thought though. At the end of the day it doesn't matter how hard you've worked on a project, or how good it is, or how much it's cost. The final arbiter, the one person who really decides if a piece is worth paying good money to see and thus making it a hit, or at the very least financially secure is...you. Of course it is. We make these movies and tellies and do theatre productions and radio plays as well as we possibly can, we even make adverts and re-voice foreign girlie films, but it is you, the punters, who determine the ultimate fate of our dreams. (But please see my chapter on *The McKenzie Break* and my dinner chat with Helmut Griem!)

Before I finally leave *Green Ice*, we were doing some of our interiors at Elstree film studios in England, and who should I run into in the restaurant but the 'Raiders' cast. Harrison F., Karen Allen, Ronnie Lacey, John Rhys-Jones - the lot. They were also working indoors, and they were bemoaning the fact that *Raiders of the Lost Ark* was taking so long to make. They were getting bored. 'You're already doing another movie, and you'll be on to your television series long before we've finished.'

'Don't worry,' I said. 'Your film will be the hit of all time.' How right I was!

I did enjoy *Green Ice* though. I really did. Apart from anything else, it was great to work with so many damn good film people, and it was a pleasure to shoot a nice guy like Omar!

XXVII

So now what? Well, I was going to tell you about the bad times, when a poor actorbum is 'resting' or 'reading scripts', but I don't feel like it at the moment. Far too depressing.

No. I shall move straight on to that TV series. The one I'd been offered before I started 'Raiders'.

As soon as we'd finished, or rather wrapped, *Green Ice*, I went back to my home country for two six-month stints, to do one of the most satisfying parts I've ever done, and one of the happiest. I played a Glasgow plumber, Mr McKinley - Dad - in an eighteen part adaptation of a well-known Scottish novel or two called *Maggie*.

Apart from anything else it was great to be working in Scotland again, and I was fortunate enough to find a splendid flat. It was on top of the hill at the far end of Glasgow's Sauchiehall Street, and it was owned by an actress who lived in Carlisle. I paid a nominal rent to live there, because the landlady wanted me to 'show a presence' as the flat was packed full of antiques, and had been preserved just as it would have been in 1922. If you're ever in Glasgow and have an interest in such things, go and have a look at it, 45, Buccleuch Street. The flat was later sold to the National Trust for Scotland as a museum and is open to the public every afternoon.

My heavens I had a grand time on this engagement - and that apart from actually doing the show.

I spent countless wonderful weekends fishing the many tributaries of Loch Lomond. Took me right back to my early childhood that did, when I used to trot up Deeside with my Dad.

I made several trips to see Aberdeen play Glasgow Rangers, and Glasgow Celtic. Something, again, I'd not done since I was too small to see over the barrier and had to be lifted on to our neighbour, Mr Smart's, shoulders. (My Dad didna like the fitba', the dafty!)

In partnership with Mary Riggans (my wife, Mrs McK, in the series), I won the jackpot on the BBC club's fruit machine three times! I'm quite lucky that way. The thing to do of course is wait until some poor twit has put in loads and loads of money and won nothing. Then, hopefully, all you have to do to win the jackpot is pop in a couple of quid. Most important though is to work out beforehand how much you can afford to lose, and stick to it. Then a very happy evening can be had. Particularly if you've spent a good day in the studio, are free on the morrow, and can thus have a dram or three to help things along!

I didn't know that Glasgow and its surrounds is excellent hunting territory for the committed train spotter. It has something to do with the railway depots in that part of the country apparently, and my eldest, Simon, who was a very keen train numberologist at the time, joined me one school half-term and we tramped very happily all over the place.

There was a great cast of Scottish actors in *Maggie*, playing my wife and children. Apart from Mary - a smashing lady and a great friend with whom I worked on *Take the High Road* some eight years later - the children who played our kids and their friends were also super. They came mostly from the Glasgow Children's Theatre, and

Maggie herself, the lynchpin of the McKinley family who organized everything and everybody - particularly her Dad - was played by Kirsty Miller.

The best compliment I can pay Kirsty is this: when they were interviewing for an unknown young lass to play the title role of Maggie, the very first girl they saw was Kirsty. They thought she was absolutely perfect, but they didn't believe it. 'It just never happens,' our director Renny Rye said to me. 'You never find the right unknown for a part in the first person who walks through the door.' But they had this time. They saw dozens of other young hopefuls, but none of them could match sweet, bubbly, natural and professional beyond her years Kirsty. After we finished the series she went on to do other things for a while, propelled by her excellent performance as Maggie, but I've not heard of her for some years...Kirsty, if you happen to read this eulogy and are still in the business, please get in touch. You're far too good a talent to lose and I'm sure I could help you to find a good agent.

Ron Patterson played my brother-in-law. Ron was also in *Take the High Road* later on, but I don't imagine that many people have heard of him outside Scotland. He was very seriously considered for my part in *Maggie*. I'm very glad they thought it was worth the extra expense - and expenses - to bring yours truly up from London to play Mr McKinley! But I'm delighted that they found a part for Ron, because he was damn good.

I was by far the most well-known actorbum in the series, because everyone else was either Glasgow or Edinburgh based. And I think this, above all, vindicates my moving South and going to RADA, instead of to the Glasgow college of acting. Life in our business is hard enough. I certainly didn't want the added burden of trying to earn a living with one arm tied behind my back, as do the Scottish based actors. The majority live and work almost entirely in Scotland, with nothing but a Scottish accent for company

- think of the competition, apart from anything else. And on top of everything, to have these flipping Sassanach Scots coming up from London and taking the best parts! . . I thank the God of bums that the Scots bums like me. At least, I'm always made to feel tremendously welcome whenever I go back.

XXVIII

Tax! I'll be jotting shortly about *High Road to China*, which starred Tom Selleck, Robert Morley and Jack Weston, among others. It was absolutely fabulous, but I very nearly got into trouble with the taxman myself this time, and I must give mention to the woeful tale. Ryan O'Neil is certainly not the only one who's had revenue problems.

Before my present very, very nice tax inspector gets the wrong idea, I'd better explain! 'High Road' was made in the former Yugoslavia, and at the end of my stint on the film I was asked if I'd mind taking my last two weeks pay home with me, in cash. It would mean that I'd get the money more quickly, as it wouldn't have to go through the post and via my agent, and it would also save the film's production office valuable time. Easier all round. Ha! When I got back, I dutifully paid my agent the commission owed and I told my accountant what had happened. I gave him precise details of the sums involved, and he promptly forgot all about the conversation.

Now I dare not mention any names here, but if I tell you that the gentleman concerned was financial adviser to a high powered chap at the BBC, and that, when I was young and green and knew no better, I had been strongly advised to put my affairs in his hands, then I'm sure you'll have a smidge of sympathy for my predicament! Anyway, this 'accountant', who I later learned was completely unqualified, told me that everything was under control when, several years later, the taxman wrote direct to me and asked about this Yugoslav money. They also said that they'd written to my accountant three times but had received no reply. The film company had, quite rightly, included all the money they had paid to me on their accounts, and the revenue people had of course discovered that I therefore appeared to have earned more on 'High Road to C.' than I'd told them I'd received, on my tax return - the tax return which my accountant had completed from his records (minus the Yugo cash), and which I had signed. I should have read the thing more thoroughly, but tax forms are nasty, and I was away at the time and only saw it fleetingly. And anyway, that was what I paid an accountant for, and I trusted him. But, I had signed it and it was thus my fault.

We actorbums, together with musicians, writers, directors and such, are funny when it comes to tax. Although we are freelance, and freelancers are normally classed as self-employed, we are not really self-employed at all. We are 'contracted' by whichever company we happen to be working for, and whilst we are working for that company we are its employees, just like other people, and we pay Class 1 insurance contributions. We change jobs frequently that's all. More frequently than most people have hot dinners!

But tax-wise we are treated as freelancers. Our tax is done once a year, and although there has been a change, and we now pay the tax due at the end of the current earnings year, in the past everything was retrospective. We never paid tax for a given financial year, ended April 6th, until the following year, and it made for huge problems. You might for example have had a very good year, but when the time came to pay the tax you could be broke. However, there is not one bum, I'm sure, who would like their tax to be deducted at source (PAYE). That would make for even greater difficulties, particularly when trying to claim a refund, or expenses.

Back to the money I'd brought into the UK illegally, for as far as Her Majesty's Tax Inspectors were concerned that's just what I'd done. I'd not told them, and I was therefore trying to get away with it. There wasn't that much money involved, only a couple of weeks pay for goodness sake, but I felt like a criminal. I was sure they were going to shove me in Wormwood Parkhurst and throw away the key! I had to act quickly. I changed my accountant of course, or rather, I left him, who was unqualified, and found myself a fully-chartered chappie. He's since retired and I hope I didn't hasten the day, for he worked like stink to get me back on an evenish keel. Finally, I'm very happy and relieved to say, H. M. Tax believed I was innocent - which I truly was - but foolish in my choice of financial adviser. I was most certainly that. I was fined, but not nearly as much as I would have been had they not believed me. Through no real fault of mine, I had come within a fingernail of being investigated by the Tax Inspectorate.

Come to think of it I've not been too lucky, accountant wise, all the way through. I'm told that I must keep this vague! But only a few years ago I employed a certain southern counties company. They have offices in some of the major towns, so you wouldn't have to hunt very far to find them. Not that I can see any reason why you should want to. These people sent the Tax Inspector two differing sets of accounts for me, for the same year, and then charged me a fortune for trying to sort out the mess which they had created. Let it be a lesson to us all. And don't ever, I implore you, employ accountants, qualified or not, until you can be confident in their ability to look after you.

XXIX

Re-voicing girlie pictures can be great fun, but not of course particularly rewarding from a thespian point of view. And dubbing ordinary foreign movies is a pain, certainly as far as I am concerned. However, sometimes needs must. There's a film called *From a Far Country*. It's something to do with Pope John Paul II and his early years I believe, and it's not very good. It's not very good even though Christopher Cazenove is one of a very few Englishmen in the piece, and at least every other part plus one, has been re-voiced by 40307. Actually I did have a little fun finding different English voices for all those Polish, or Hungarian, or whatever, other bums. But at the end of the day it's really just another way the business has of tying your hands behind you. I wouldn't have minded quite so much if the original foreign performances in this movie had been good, but in the vast majority of cases they were not good and it was left to me to try and give them some credibility.

Now, *High Road to China* - the movie! I can remember saying at the start of these writings that I wouldn't recount every flipping engagement I've ever had, because it would happily fill at least six volumes. But when I returned from Scotland and *Maggie*, I hadn't a clue what I was going to do next. I had nothing lined up and not one script to read. Even my woes in Taxland were still to come.

I was wondering what I could do to keep myself out of Dearly Beloved's hair, and had already started to paint the outside of the house when the phone rang. 'Fancy another stint in Yugoslavia? Same town you were in on 'Force 10'. Same hotel too I shouldn't wonder.' And she was right, my agent. It is strange isn't it? In less than no time I was in the same hotel, and in the same bedroom that I'd occupied on the 'Navarone' picture a good few years previously. And this was the second time it had happened - remember

Kirkcudbright? And later on it was almost to happen a third time, back in Greece. Och weel, as we say in Scotland, I think it's certainly more than coincidence. I think it's flipping weird.

And I still couldn't get a proper English breakfast in the hotel dining room! Last time, if you remember, it had been Richard Kiel who had been my amused audience. This time it was, as often as not, a lovely stuntman called Terry Richards. (Terry's the guy with the red beard who signals his man to try to kill me at the start of 'High Road', and among many other stuntbum parts, he also played the vast Arab in 'Raiders 1', who is shot by Harrison.)

Perhaps it's a bit cheeky, but knowing that I was returning to Yugoslavia and the same hotel, and anticipating that there might still be a problem with the breakfast, I'd bought a frying pan before I left home. I asked if I could show the hotel how to cook bacon and eggs - British style. The same chef was on duty in the kitchen as in days of 'Navarone', and I was welcomed. I'm not a cook, but I managed a fair bacon and egg - I have to admit that the bacon was still in fact ham, but it was sliced and properly fried, and at least it looked like the real thing! Terry and I greatly enjoyed our breakfast, and washed it down with a lovely British-style cup of tea, after of course I'd nicked some cold milk from the cereal table. OK, now I'd shown the hotel how to make ye olde Full English Breakfast. At last we could start the day properly.

The next morning was Sunday, as I recall, and Terry and I found that we'd been joined for breakfast by almost the entire British contingent - all the actor, stunt and stand-in bums, and all the crew. Imagine then my dismay and mortification when the meal, accompanied by my friend the chef, arrived with full ceremony. 'Here you be, Mr Sheer-ad. Your breekfest. We have made it better for you also, no?' I looked at what he had brought. Instead of frying, as I had instructed, they had poached the whole flipping thing in milk!

Ages ago I mentioned that I worked with Brian Blessed. He arrived to start work that same evening and we had dinner together. I told him of my breakfast follies and he laughed and laughed and laughed as only Brian can.

We did a lot of night shoots on 'High Road', and for the first and only time ever I missed my call. The very worst night call you can get is one that's for midnight. What do you do? Do you stay up, or doze, or go to bed early? I've never been able to decide. If you stay up or doze, you might not be bright-eyed and bushy tailed on the set. If you go to bed...I went to bed at 6pm on the first night and asked to be called at 10.15pm. But I couldn't sleep. At least I thought I couldn't! When I woke up at three minutes to midnight, it took me fully ten seconds to convince myself that it wasn't three minutes to eleven. The hotel had called me at 10.15pm all right and I'd promptly gone straight back to sleep. It was a ghastly, really horrid realization. I was keeping everyone waiting. It must be costing thousands and thousands and...But of course it wasn't. Luckily we were filming in a large mansion almost next to the hotel, and third assistant directors are not fools. One of their many duties is to make sure that the actorbums are on the set when they are needed, and they always call you at least ninety minutes beforehand. On this occasion the film unit had been working since the early evening, and when I rushed in, at three and a half minutes past twelve, they were all having their midnight meal. 'We'll do your wardrobe and make-up after dinner, Michael. We won't be getting to your scene until two-thirty at the earliest.' Bliss, oh what bliss. Nobody had even realised that I was late. I had time to relax, collect my thoughts and have something to eat. Might even have a doze!

I did too. Filming delays are inevitable. We had one on *England Made Me* which lasted three days. (The Yugoslav singer couldn't get her tonsils round the melody of Sir Noel Coward's song, 'Mad About the Boy'. It's a wonderful piece, but difficult enough for an English lass to sing.) Whatever it was that caused the long delay on this occasion, it meant that we got further behind and, would you believe, we never did get to my super scene with the delightful leading lady, Bess Armstrong, that night. At six in the morning I returned to the hotel and...went back to bed. And slept the day through until the hotel called me again that evening.

Jack Weston is one of nicest, shrewdest, most talented actorbums it has ever been my pleasure to meet and work with. Jack was earning more on 'High Road' than anyone else. He was rightly very proud of the fact that for every second he over-ran his contract stop date, he would earn thousands of extra mega-bucks in penalty payments. Going over your contract nearly always happens on movies because of all those unforseen delays. I went over my contract on 'High Road' by almost seven weeks and did quite nicely, but an agent who can negotiate a contract where the penalty payments will earn you more than double your agreed salary, is certainly worth his or her 15 per cent commission. They sure don't treat bums like that in our country.

Mind you, Jack's many and continuing film and TV performances show that he was worth it, I'm sure you'll agree. And he'd been around for years and had done masses of super work before I'd even started - just think of all those lovely overpayments!

Jack was great company. He had the next room to me in the hotel and was always inviting his neighbours round for tiffin. He had a most gorgeous girlfriend. How he managed that I don't know. He's older than I am, he's round, and he's totally bald!

He was always cracking jokes. I think Jack needed other things to occupy his adrenalin because the acting bit came so easily to him. Have a look at the scene where Jack and I are standing side by side, watching anxiously whilst Tom and Bess fly around the sky in very dilapidated aeroplanes. (In reality, marvellous work by the stuntbum pilots of course.) My suppressed laughter does not show, really it doesn't. But all Jack and I had to do was stand and look, which is not too difficult, and Jack Weston kept up a non-stop, one-man patter of funnies for the whole two days we were shooting that bit of the movie.

The entire sequence in fact took much longer than was hoped, again because of the weather. We were filming, again, high up some mountain, and it was so damn cold that the cameras froze. When they'd been thawed out, it was discovered that the lights were not strong enough for us to shoot. And when we finally did manage to get going we, the actorbums, had to chew on ice cubes before every take, to neutralise our warm breath so that it didn't show. Try it yourself. It works alright but it's not very pleasant.

Tom Selleck. Now there's a darlin' man. Scottish actually. Extremely proud he is of the fact that his Grandad, or it might even have been his Dad, came from the same part of the world as I. On the first day's filming, actually it was a night (yep, we were night filming again), Tom said to me, 'Michael, all I've ever done in movies is play a dead body [he was referring to the film *Coma*], so you're going to have to help me through this.' Silly arse. He'd done more super TV films and series than most of us have had ice cream. But Tom was quite sincere. A very modest, very unpretentious and very unassuming friend. He was also a damn good, hard-working and very conscientious probum. He always wanted everything to be absolutely right, and would spend as long as was necessary to achieve this. On one of the ice cube days, for example, he wasn't happy with his performance in a very long master shot, and having apologised to the assembled company for keeping them out in the cold, Tom told the director, Brian Hutton, that he wanted to go again. And we went again. All good directors will listen to their actors, and if they think a request is valid, from whomever and for whatever reason, they'll concur. (Tom simply felt he could do better, but I've seen a director agree to go again, after a perfectly good take, because he thought the starbum could do with a boost of confidence.)

A wee word about the pecking order. It is always necessary to have some people who have more of a say on a movie than others. Stands to reason really. You can certainly have too many cooks, and somebody has to carry the old can if things go wrong. (Don't they, Helmut? Funny how we keep coming back to my dinner conversation with Helmut Griem, that far-off day in Ireland when we were making *The McKenzie Break*.) Every member of the crew has responsibility for his or her department of course. Thus props can say what they think about props, sound about sound (remember Basil Fenton-Smith?), camera about camera, and so on. And the buck always stops with the director and the producer who have the final say.

With actorbums it tends to be a little different. I've already talked about what goes on before we start filming, regarding costume and make-up, etc. When we finally reach the set and start working, we are your actual creative creatures who must 'feel' if things are right, and it's always a good idea to work out where you come in the pecking order, so that you know how much pecking you can do and how far you can go.

If you are an extra, for instance, you can't go around saying that you want to go again on a scene, but you can suggest to the director that it might be easier for the star if you opened the door, after he's finished his line. See what I mean?

A featured bum like me can certainly talk about doors. He can also make suggestions regarding the shape of a scene, talk about his own dialogue, and suggest, on his close-ups, that he'd like to go again if he's not happy. Very rarely, if a scene is particularly important to his character, he can ask if it would be possible to do the master again.

If you're the star of a movie you can of course say what the hell you like - Peter Finch overruling Basil on *England Made Me*; David Niven getting them to change the schedule for me on *Escape to Athena* - but in spite of the fact that I benefited greatly from the kindness of the above two examples, I'm still bound to say that it's not always for the good when a starbum utters.

With the exception perhaps of Telly Savalas and, because of his drinking, Robert Shaw, I've been very fortunate with my stars. I've worked only with good solid professionals, who know their art and take a pride in doing the job as well as possible. And this certainly does on occasion result in their asking to re-do a scene, or whatever. I'm afraid, though, that it's so very precarious up there at the top of the slippery slope that some stars just can't stand the pressure. They become very insecure and then - even if they are as talented as that wonderful creature Marilyn Monroe - they not only stop takes and ask to go again, as often as not they are very rude, and often don't turn up for work at all.

Phew - I said a wee word about the pecking order! That was a while ago and I've not yet given a mention to my old chums the stuntmanbums. They are always in complete charge of what they do and obviously try to get it right first time!

So, back on that Yugoslavian mountain, with the ice cubes and the cold. Tom Selleck wasn't the only one who wanted to get things right. I used as much clout as my position in the pecking order would allow, Jack Weston used his - more than mine because his name was above the title - Bess Armstrong had still more. In fact her's was second only to Tom's, but she was relatively inexperienced, even though she was playing second lead, and she tended to leave things to us seasoned campaigners. She was a super trouper though, loved her work, and was very conscientious.

That illustrates how the pecking order works, I think, but it makes it look as if we spent the whole of 'High Road' squabbling here and demanding there, according to our position in said order. Nothing could in fact be further from the truth. I honestly cannot remember one harsh word being uttered on *High Road to China*. It was a very, very enjoyable location. If someone wanted to say something about the production off the set - the rushes for example - they said it. If someone wanted to say something whilst we were on the set, they said it there too. The director always listened and acted accordingly, or if he disagreed, he gave his reasons, which were readily accepted.

I've mentioned the director, Brian, already, but only in passing. Brian G. Hutton, you deserve at least a couple of lines all to yourself in my book!

Actually I don't quite know where to start telling you about this excellent poker player, who started out as an actorbum (*Last Train from Gun Hill* especially springs to mind), who is more American than hamburgers, but was born in England's garden county of Kent, in that most English of towns, Royal Tunbridge Wells.

He's a grand film director that's for sure - my favourite, apart from 'High Road' of course, is *Where Eagles Dare*. And he really can play poker. I've already said that I can't play very well, but I know when I see a master at work. Brian cleaned one school out in an hour, and it included our producer, Fred Weintraub, no mean player himself.

The entry in my film reference book only describes Brian as a director now, with *Where Eagles Dare* certainly his most successful film. But if I look up *Last Train from Gun Hill*, I find the actoring performances classed as excellent - Brian tracking Kirk Douglas and Earl Holliman through the shadows is very eerily effective. So how to sum him up? I'll just leave it thus: As a damn good poker-playing film director from Tunbridge Wells in Kent, Brian G. Hutton makes a great American cowboy and is a very nice guy!

Not a great deal more to say about *High Road to China*. Bess Armstrong married the first assistant director - I wish her happiness wherever she is now. I never met my 'boss' in the story, Robert Morley. Robert did all his scenes months later and they were slotted in during editing. To be truly honest I think this made his contribution appear somehow isolated. But he was surely an asset to the film, and certainly worth waiting for and working round.

Terry Richards killed me - lovely death it was, I was terribly brave - and I came back to the UK with my last two weeks' pay in my back pocket!

XXX

And now, I've got to do it. After all, this is warts and all writing. And anyway I promised, so here we go. I will now try to tell you about the dark side of an actorbum's life.

Reading scripts; waiting for the right offer; shuffling dates; turning things down; waiting for the agent to ring; the money wasn't right; they cast the other chap because he was smaller, or fatter, thinner, more hair, less hair, black, brown, green - I could go on and on, but what I'm afraid it all boils down to is that the actor is OOW. Out Of Work. Poor bugger...It's not an easy state to describe. Saturday and Sunday you're the same as everybody else. You watch *Grandstand* or do the garden. Maybe go for a walk. You do all the weekend things, just like the chap next door. But come Monday morning you're back to being a statistic. Along with with millions of others from other professions, you're out of work again. But (selfishly no doubt), you feel it is even worse for you. For you are an artiste, you burn to act and to practise your art. Your soul will die inside you if you are not given a chance, any chance...You have hopes of course - high hopes. You've got to be optimistic for heaven's sake. The phone will ring today, or by tomorrow at the very latest. You go out into town. That'll make it ring. You make very sure of course that the ansaphone is working properly before you leave. Full of hope, you return and nonchalantly pass the machine. You pretend not to look at the red light, but you sneak back and...no, the light is not pulsing, it's steady as a rock. There is no message. Nobody wants you. Nobody cares. Nobody will ever again ask you to be in their production. You will never again enjoy the heady intoxicating feeling of being needed, and above all else...loved.

It's at times like these that you need a Dearly Beloved. They are truly worth their weight in gold. They'll remind you that you've got so much to be grateful for and that you've done lots of wonderful work. They'll tell you not to be silly, that of course the phone will ring. I have to add that when I've been OOW it has luckily lasted for such a short time that I've hardly experienced the gloom. Anyway, I am an optimist, thank heavens, and I wish all my fellow actorbums could be the same. As the child sings in *Annie*, the sun will come out tomorrow. It always does!

But I would like to issue the tiniest wee word of warning to my fellows. When we start out as very young hopefulbums, let us by all means accept whatever is offered, be it Shepperton or shit. But don't, I beg you, take a job later on, when you've worked bloody hard to establish a good track record, just because you think you are never going to work again. If you have to do the job for the money, well OK. But never for any other reason please, I beg you. It really isn't worth it. Go and play golf instead.

I know what I'm talking about because I did it - once. Only once - but oh dear. I've told you about the naughty movies and sexy voice overs. I've shuffled through what some might well call merde and loved it. I've done the lot, and I've always found something that I can enjoy. Except once...

I had been OOW. I was also getting over the flu, so I guess I was feeling a bit low and was thus caught on the hop. But it had been a few weeks. I was just beginning to wonder if this might indeed be the time and that I'd be reading those non-existent scripts for the rest of my life, when the phone rang. Dearly Beloved answered, as she always does if she can. It gives me a split second to collect my thoughts and that can be enormously valuable.

How silly of me to worry that I'd never work again, what a bloody fool I was. Now, where am I going to this time I wonder? What far flung exotic location? There'd been that enquiry from Australia, that would be nice. It was the one continent I'd never been to...

'Allo, 'Allo. No, it wasn't my agent at the other end of the phone, this was the show I had been invited to do. Nothing wrong in that. Course not, it's a good show. And I enjoy comedy, I've guested in masses of comedy series over the years and loved them.

But consider this:

The engagement was due to start next Monday. It was now Thursday. Very short notice.

They couldn't send me a script to look at, there wasn't enough time. And, apparently, there was no machine available, so they couldn't fax me.

They wanted an answer on the spot. Now. Yes or no.

They said that the part was very important. Nearly always a sign that it's tiny. And anyway, the series had so many regulars in it already that there was no room for any additional roles, at least, none that were worth playing.

I knew I was being manoeuvred into a corner. Not by Auntie BBC, she was simply offering the part, take it or leave it. No, I was being coerced by my then agent, who wanted to prove that he could find me work. 'Go on, Michael. I know things have been a bit thin of late, but this could be the start of something big.' It wasn't a good part. In fact it was entirely and completely the opposite. It was the most terrible, stupid, grotty role I have ever - I really do mean this - ever played. By far it was. By this time the show had also long overstayed its usefulness. It was extremely tired, banal, and embarrassing. Terribly embarrassing. No wonder it finished for ever shortly afterwards.

I have always believed that an actorbum should see his celluloid work so that he can build and learn from it. This is the only time that I have not done so. The thing has been repeated, God help us, but although my youngest says that I deliver my five lines as well as ever, I still refuse to watch. I remember too well the agony. I was so ashamed and embarrassed that before the first scene I was completely tongue-tied and had to write the opening line on my hand.

I am not a snob, and I am most certainly not a snob actor. I'd happily play a one-word part in a piece, if I thought it was worth it. So why did I take this part in *'Allo, 'Allo*, which definitely wasn't? Why didn't I play golf instead? Well, apart from the flu, the part in *'Allo, 'Allo* was that of Hermann Goering. I'd played Hitler and Himmler of course, and my agent also said that (wearing padding this time), it would be nice to complete the set. In other words, for the only time ever I allowed my vanity to rule my head. Bloody stupid git that I am. I gave the agent the sack shortly after. End of confession.

Except! Kenneth Connor has since died. He was a great actorbum, particularly in the 'Carry On' films. A really super trouper who was forever telling funny stories, and I'm delighted to have had the opportunity to work with him, even in *'Allo, 'Allo*. So there's my reason for doing that dreadful programme. Thanks, little Ken, I knew I'd find one.

XXXI

And now to show you t'other side of telly. Some rather nice television parts came along after the above and I'm going to spend a few lines on TV series.

Flipping good things, TV series. Apart from anything else they go on and on. Luverly dosh. And I did need the odd extra penny at about this time. My three offspring were of a rather high academic standard - due entirely to Dearly Beloved of course! - and they were about ready to go to university. London, York, Southampton, and then, for number three, a post grad at Cambridge. Not quite all at once, but following each other very closely. And overlapping, which is almost worse financially.

I was very proud. And to make quite sure I could cover the ginormous expenses that were about to descend on me, I started a series of series, and I loved it: *The Outsider*; *The Dark Side of the Sun*; *Auf Wiedersehen Pet*; and *The Invisible Man*.

The Outsider first. Apart from the fact that I played a super part - a master printer called Reuben Flaxman - the series was made for Yorkshire Television, a very faithful employer. I played an equally good role, Superintendent Harrison, in a one-off play for them later on. As well as doing *Emmerdale* and others.

It was very nice too to return to Yorkshire. The train sequences for *The Five Red Herrings* (Lord P. Wimsey), had been shot alongside Lake Windermere. OK, I know. But Cumbria is near enough to Yorkshire for a chap from Aberdeen! Anyway my Mother was born in Menston, which is just outside Leeds, and lived there before she emigrated to Scotland and married my Dad. Hence my dual nationality. (Although I am English but definitely come from Scotland, as my Mum comes from Leeds, I can also have a damned authentic North Country accent if required. Shush!)

As well as me, *The Outsider* boasted a damn good actoring cast. John Duttine, Joanna Dunham, Carol Royale, et al. And Ted Morris, who became a very close friend.

You won't have heard of Ted. But for many of us he is the true actorbum. His kind are the salt of our business. He personifies in one small dear man what I've been trying to tell you about throughout these pages.

Ted is dead now. He died of cancer some years ago, aged only fifty-five. But right up to the end he lived for his work. He was still dedicatedly playing at Oldham Repertory Theatre the week before he died. He never earned much money, indeed he once told me that there were times when he'd had nothing but an egg to eat all day.

He'd decided that he wanted to be an actor quite late in life, in his early thirties, and took the plunge one Friday. Just like that. He finished clerking on a Friday evening and on Monday morning he woke up a professional actor. He'd no idea where to start. He'd done amateur work, but he'd never been anywhere near a professional stage, let alone drama college. So he just went down the road, Manchester accent and all, bought a copy of *The Stage* newspaper, and started from there.

Ted never married. 'Who would have me? Anyway, I couldn't afford another egg!' Never came South either. Yet he was somehow managing to buy, on mortgage, his little flat in Hazel Grove, outside Manchester, and was just able to live from his chosen love - The Business. But by gum it was hard. Oldham was the other side of Manchester, and the rep were fortunate enough to have Ted in their plays quite often. Trouble was, the pay was bad, and in order to make a little profit, he saved on fares by bicycling right around Manchester to get there. Imagine it. Two and a half hours it took him each way. He didn't get home until one in the morning.

Granada and Yorkshire Television were also lucky enough to benefit from his talent from time to time. Great for them. A life-saver for Ted, because the money was so much better. Nevertheless, a good year for Ted was £7,000, and there were many bad ones.

When I first met him he was going through probably the best work patch he'd ever had. He'd been doing a little something for Granada - an episode of 'The Street' I think - and now he was playing my mate in *The Outsider*. He loved it and we loved him. It was a privilege to spend three months with such a talented and likeable guy. He used to keep us in stitches at meal breaks, talking of the times when he'd had only that egg to eat. 'The local butcher took pity on me. He always let me choose the biggest egg.' 'One October I found a specially nice one which was covered with brown speckles. I sat on it for three months in the hope that it might turn into a chicken in time for Christmas.' By no means an easy thing to do, to make merriment out of one's hard times, but I never saw Ted down or despondent. He was a cheeky chappie too. In *The Outsider*, a super lady actor called Pauline Letts (her brother Barry was a producer at the Beeb, *Dr Who* et al.), played the matriachal owner of the newspaper where Ted and I worked. In one scene Pauline visited the printing press and had to be very stern and angry about something.

Nobody knew, but Ted and the director had arranged it betweem them, probably to relax everyone on a cold Monday morning. Came the first take of the master. We were all there, John, Carol, Joanna, Norman Eshley (remember him, once married to Millicent Martin?), Ted and I of course, and the entire crew. The doors are slammed open and Pauline strides in. It really is very tense, and everyone is looking suitably afeard. Everyone that is except Mr Ted Morris who calmly steps forward, tugs his forelock in the best yokel tradition and and says, 'Morning, Miss. Can I fuck you now?'

Thank heavens we kept in touch. Ted did of course come South occasionally, when a programme from the North he was involved with required some southern location work - *Lost Empires* was another nice piece he did for Granada - and he always stayed with us. And when I went up to Manchester to do *Bulman* and *Coronation Street*, etc., I stayed with him.

Ted never got the parts he deserved, and there were times when he really did have it very tough. I asked him on *The Outsider* if he wasn't angry that the business hadn't treated him better and he looked at me aghast. 'Michael, please never even think it. I couldn't be happier. I'm doing this television series with you and all these other grand people, and when it's finished I've got a part coming up at Oldham rep. Why, I can buy two eggs now!'

Hey-ho. I haven't told you much about *The Outsider*, have I? A damn good series in which I too am superb! Indeed, I have a show tape in which two of the scenes are from this series. One is with John, Ted and me, the other is just Ted and me. Notwithstanding blowing my own trumpet, I do not agree with Sir Donald Wolfit. If you are going to give of your best as a bum, on stage, film, television, radio, voice-over (or show tape), you must have the best actors to work with, not the worst as Sir Donald used to have it. I trust these lines show in what high regard I hold Ted Morris, and how darn lucky we all were to have known him. He is greatly missed by many.

The Dark Side of the Sun. Wow, what a gig! I knew none of this whilst we were making *The Outsider*, but 'Dark Side' was being set up even as we were filming in Yorkshire. And no sooner had we finished, than I was asked if I'd like to go to Rhodes (again), and play an ex-Nazi called Col. Dietrich Von Reitz, in a six-parter set in Greece, written by the man who had penned both series, Michael J. Bird. Would I...?!

Michael is one of the best writers I know. He started out as a journalist, but had always wanted to write for the screen, and he made the jump very quickly. After his first play was produced, he was soon inundated with commissions. He's written some marvellously original series for TV, and because he's had a love affair with the country all his life, a number of them have been set in Greece - *Who Pays the Ferryman* and *The Lotus Eaters*, for instance. He is a super guy and very shrewd. Well, apart from doing deals with Olympic Airways and lots of high-powered businessmen, he suggested me for 'Dark Side', didn't he?!

I happen to know how 'Dark Side' came about and it illustrates, I think, how highly Michael is respected. Whilst riding on the top of a bus, or in the bath or something, he had this great idea for a series, about a strange cult in Greece, who had a leader who was possibly a living dead. He scribbled the idea down, literally on the back of an envelope, and took it to the BBC. The Beeb said yes please, here's the money, a producer, and the crew, go and make it! When I accepted Reitz, Michael admitted that he wasn't yet sure how the story would turn out as he'd only written one and a half episodes. But he said not to worry, the Colonel would certainly feature all the way through. And he did of course.

A quick word about the logistics before I transport you once again to Rhodes. We did all the exteriors on Rhodes. Every bit we could possibly film was done there, a good deal of the inside of the castle included. Then we returned to England and the BBC rehearsal rooms in North Acton - the Acton Hilton - to rehearse the interiors. And every fortnight we went to Glasgow to spend two days in their studios putting said interiors on tape. Can you appreciate how this old Scottish bum felt? Ten weeks in Greece, with Dearly Beloved coming out to join me for a holiday, then back to my spiritual home every two weeks. Who could ask for anything more!

The actorbums: Peter Egan - I called him the Big P - played the dead/alive leader I mentioned. A sweet vegetarian called Emily Richards, who'd made a big impression in the Royal Shakespeare Company's superb production of *Nicholas Nickleby*, played the girl, and Patrick Mower played her husband, who was killed in the first episode but kept coming back as a ghost, or as Peter Egan. Equity member 40307 played the Big P's deputy, who took over the organisation when it was thought P had died a second time, and there was lots more actor cream, some from Greece (one lovely lady in particular), playing lots more good parts. For even if it's small, Michael J. has never written a bad part for an actor. He is the ultimate sympatico. He knows how much an actorbum can treasure even a tiny part, if it is well crafted.

I've been unfair to the 'lovely lady in particular', mentioned above. Betty Arvaniti is one of the foremost Greek actors and she played a leading role in 'Dark Side'. One evening later on, a few of us were sitting in a tiny taverna, way up in the hills above Rhodes. Suddenly the owner was upon us with three bottles of his best vintage, a gift he said because we were working with his beloved Betty.

And so I returned to Greece. Clear blue sea, constant sunshine, sandy beaches. At least that was our climate after the end of March. We arrived in early February, and there can be some rather nasty storms at that time of year. Of course I knew Rhodes from my heady days working on *Escape to Athena*, and thus had a distinct advantage over the rest. I knew where the post office was - remember, always post your letters and make your calls home from the post office, not from the hotel - I knew where the best restaurants were to be found, where you could hire bikes, find a cinema, go for walks, swim...everything. I was terribly popular for a while!

The hotel. I must mention the hotel. Yep, the same one. Along the road from Rhodes town, where Stephanie Powers had raced me to humiliation. Not quite the same room. I did ask, but the floor where my 'Athena' room had been was being redecorated for the coming summer and I had to settle for a room on the floor below. Nearly but not quite. But it was a mirror image of my old room - bathroom on the right as you entered, main two-bedded bedroom/sitting room beyond, with balcony overlooking the sea. I think it's close enough to be included in the coincidence of same hotel, same room. Apart from anything else, that makes it three times it happened. Three is lucky, and, by the Colossus, I sure was being lucky about now!

I haven't mentioned the producer and director. Perhaps my getting this wonderful engagement wasn't entirely due to Michael J. If you cast your mind right back to my start in television, both David Askey, the director of 'Dark Side', and Vere Lorrimer our producer, (little Vere), were Directors on dear old *Dixon of Dock Green*, in those not forgotten, but far-off days. I'd worked with them both off and on since then - do you remember a series called *The Expert* with Marius Goring? I gave a super Judge in that, which Vere directed - but our association started in black and white with Jack Warner.

Back to Rhodes. The Greek Air Force made a storm for us with their helicopters. They took it in turns to hover just out of shot, about twenty feet off the ground, and the swishing blades did the rest. Bloody dangerous actually, and of course they didn't have to do it. Above and beyond the call of duty and all that. But the pilots loved it.

We travelled and filmed in Lindos, which for my money anyway is the most picturesque town on Rhodes. It's...so Greek. All white and shiny, with little winding streets which go up and up and...up. Our Costume Designer was named David Beaton. We were filming almost at the top, and when David had staggered the last few yards - it really was a hell of a flipping climb - I asked politely, 'Are you Beaton, David?' He was too out of breath to answer, otherwise I think he'd have given me at least a fourpenny one!

We did some grand work all round, especially in the newly-restored castle in Rhodes town. It must be my addiction to swashbucklers which makes me single out that particular location. I loved doing 'Dark Side', but when we were working in that castle, with its turrets, its long, wide stone corridors, its vast banqueting halls, and its battlements, it was hard not to pretend that I was dressed in Lincoln green and making yet another version of 'Robin Hood and his Merry Men'. 'Have at you, you varlet!' Up and down the huge staircase I went, pretend sword in my hand - when we were not filming of course. The others must have thought I'd gone barmy!

Hey ho. I could go on and on about this one, and our time in Greece. Vere very sweetly arranged the schedule so that we could have a little holiday in the middle: 'because you've all been working so hard'; and Dearly Beloved came out and joined me for a week. My room in the hotel had the two beds and was thus classed as a double, but they didn't charge extra for Dearly B, all we had to pay for was the food. (Mind you, we did only use one bed!) We had a really super time.

Except...We got talking one day to a retired RAF air traffic controller, who had sold up back in the UK, and bought a catamaran. He and his wife were now sailing round the world. Great life. Very nice people. They even invited us to go for a trip - just out into Rhodes harbour and a quick turn round the bay. The harbour was fine, but once we passed through the entrance, which the Colossus used to stride, it was rough. Terribly rough. I became dreadfully sick again and they all laughed at me. Even my missis!

But Dearly Beloved had a lovely break and so did I. When she returned home, we did another five weeks of very enjoyable work before we followed.

We now started recording the interiors in Scotland, and again I was the expert. Nobody else had been to Glasgow before either. ('What a lot of super work the man's done. What a lot of interesting places he's visited'!) I took my fellows to the Ubiquitious Chip Restaurant in Byers Road, which is just down from Auntie (Glasgow) BBC, and of course I introduced them to the fruit machine in the BBC club. And I still won. Just a smidgin embarrassing actually - I won the jackpot again, twice!

It was an excellent engagement with splendidly fine performances from everyone. There is one odd point concerning this production, however. The BBC (London variety, where most of the big decisions are made), never repeated it. Michael J. Bird had even set up the ending to suggest a sequel - P. Egan, having been killed in Greece, suddenly turns up buying an estate in Scotland - but it was never made. Funny that. Internal politics no doubt...

Auf Wiedersehen Pet was quite extraordinary. I have never known anything like it in my life - before or since.

First there was the fact that I nearly didn't do it at all. Dearly Beloved always reads the scripts that are sent to me for consideration before I do. I get an unbiased opinion that way which is second to none; well, most of the time I do! Her reaction to 'Auf Wiedersehen' was that I should definitely turn it down. So I did. I merely flipped through the pages and said that I was grateful for the offer, that there were certainly some amusing set pieces, but that I was hoping for a movie which would clash. (You must never say exactly what you think - always leave the door slightly ajar.)

In all I turned down 'Auf' three times. But they kept coming back and putting up the money. They rolled two parts into one to make my part more attractive, and they even promised to let me have time off to do other things. How long can a chap hold out? It wasn't as if there really was a movie in the offing, and the 'Auf' scripts were by Dick and Ian, (Clement and La Frenais). Many years before I'd been in their very first series, *The Likely Lads*. (It was my second TV part and a very young Wendy Richard was also featured. Long before *EastEnders* of course). Dick and Ian had gone on to write hunks of smashing stuff: *Porridge* and *Going Straight* for TV, and big movies like *Villain*, for instance. I read their *Auf Wiedersehen Pet* scripts again, in detail this time, overruled Dearly B., and accepted the role of Herr Grunwald, the boss of the building site.

Not often I do that - go over Dear's head - because, apart from being Dearly Beloved, she really is nearly always right. But no one can be a hundred per cent, can they? I think it was probably the theme which she didn't care for on this occasion. Anyway, I'm delighted that I did put my toe down for once, for 'Auf W.' turned out to be a tremendous show to do, a ginormous success, exceedingly enjoyable, and it was repeated. It's selling well on video, too.

We did some of the location work on a building site in Hamburg, and some in the city itself. Then we came back to the UK, where a duplicate site - the complete thing, including sleeping quarters and administration huts - had been built on the back lot at Central TV's Elstree studios. The rest of the series, apart from the scene where the lads find me in a porno cinema, was filmed there.

(Incidentally, shortly after we finished *Auf Weidersehen Pet*, Central TV sold Elstree studios to the BBC, and on the back lot, where our building site stood, there is now a rather famous square, Albert by name.)

The 'Auf' lads were great fellas. Great to thesp with and great off the set. It doesn't surprise me one bit that they've all gone on to do such smashing things - except of course the one who died, poor man. It's odd, but I've yet to work with any of them again. Perhaps they're trying to tell me something!

Nah. But there's a little point of interest here, actually. It bears out what I've said before about people keeping to their own departments - sound, camera, costume, etc. The actor is slightly different, I've said that too. As the last point of creativity in front of the cameras, he must discuss things with others, and go as far as the pecking order will allow him to, if he thinks it will help the production. He also has a duty to do this if it will benefit his performance, so long as it's not to the detriment of the whole. But an actorbum very seldom casts other actors, because it's not his job. (If he's a Lord Larry O. and is directing the show as well, or a very big Hollywood starbum with money power, then it's different. They of course can have who they like.) I've been asked many times if I can recommend someone who can speak Arabic or whatever, and I've been very happy to help, if I happen to know someone who speaks Arabic and I can vouch for their work. But I should never say to a fellow actor, 'If you'd like to play this character in this film, or TV series, the part's yours, I'll have a word with the director.' Because it is not my place so to do. The sensible director, producer, and casting director of a show will listen to the suggestions of others, but they make the final choice. They alone.

Course they do, and quite right too. Far too much responsibility for anyone else. Think what could happen if the actor did choose. I did do it once, when I was high in the pecking order and I had a lot of clout, to help a bum I'd known in rep. He was cast, but he lost his bottle on the set because he'd not done any filming before, and I'm afraid the result was disastrous. There are hundreds - thousands -

of bloody fine actors, and it has to be said, there are some who are simply not so good. I'm very happy to leave the choice to the directors and casting directors. So long as they go on asking for me of course!

So, the reason I've not worked with the guys from *Auf Wiedersehen Pet* since the series finished has certainly got nothing to do with them, we all got on famously. It's just the way scripts, parts, availabilities, and all other things, wag. I'll see you soon, lads.

Apart from the fact that I did my own German translations again, and had a real German lass as my secretary, who could put me right if I got it wrong (only needed on one occasion, thank God!), my main memory of the actual filming of 'Auf' is of long takes. I don't mean long masters which are then chopped up in the cutting room and interspersed with close-ups, I don't even mean those lovely Steadycam tracking shots we used on *Escape to Athena*, I mean long takes, using a conventional camera, which appear on the screen in their entirety.

This is a fascinating way to work - à la Orson Welles' opening shot in *Touch of Evil*. He had no Steadycam in those days of course, and he had to improvise the whole of what I believe is the longest take ever. Over roof tops and down dark, lonesome streets. Boy, that takes guts. You've no close-ups to fall back on in editing, and you've dug a big hole for yourself if something's gone wrong. You can't call everybody back on the set to shoot some more, because they've all dispersed and gone off to other things ages ago. Let me try to explain how a long take is worked.

I had this scene with Tim Healy in 'Auf' - episode nine I think it was. He comes in through the door and on into the site office. He wants to talk to me about my sacking of Jimmy Nail. I get rid of my secretary on some feeble excuse, because I'm embarrassed. I know Tim is going to use the fact that I've been seen in a girlie cinema as a weapon against me, and I ask him to come through to my private office.

There is a hatchway connecting my room to the main site office which is well established, having been used many times before in other episodes.

Before we started to shoot the scene, Roger Bamford, the director, came to Tim and me and said that he'd like to try doing the whole thing in one shot. He had no Steadycam. Apart from being terribly expensive and their use has therefore to be justified (a TV production would find this very difficult), I've already written about their scarcity, and the fact that they have thus to be ordered months, nay years almost, in advance. And Roger had had the idea only recently. So, no Steadycam. And therefore quite a task for us as well as Roger. Quite a job, too, for an a ordinary little camera, and quite a job for sound. But we did it. Three - no, four mikes were used. The camera was put on a shortish piece of track, and it zoomed in and out, and cranked around the outer office, whilst Tim and I moved from one given focus point to another. Then we went into my office, and the shot ended with the camera looking at us through the aforementioned hatch. As it was supposed to be a private confrontation, this way of shooting gave the impression that the audience were eavesdropping. Quite marvellous. But Roger only had the one shot when he came to edit. He must have had a mound of faith in the lot of us. And in himself!

Lovely show *Auf Weidersehen Pet*, which went on for a long time, thank goodness. Apart from anything else, twas about now that Susannah, our doctor daughter, started her training.

Now I would like to present for your edification Equity Member 40307 in the nude...Tarrrah!

Who would have thought it. After all these years of not having to do anything in the least bit questionable (naughty voice-overs and 'dressed' guest star excepted), I end up doing my first nude scene, and my first scene in bed with a woman, both in the same TV series.

How could he? What is the man doing? What will Karen, his number one fan, who has been writing to him with such loyalty for so many years...what will she think? What will all his other fans think? Will he have any fans when this news gets out? Oh the disgrace...Now hold on a wee bittie! First let me say that, directed by super Brian Lighthill, the series in question was *The Invisible Man* - no that's not my excuse, I did not play the title role - then let me add that the lovely lady who shared my bed is a super, respectable, character actress of ...well I'm not even going to guess at her age because it's not polite, but I think that Deddie Davies will allow me to say that she hasn't just left school. She's a sweetie, and I've known her husband Paddy for many years. Deddie and I played The Reverend Mr and Mrs Bunting in 'The In. Man', and the bed scene referred to consisted of my waking up, next to Mrs Bunting, but night-capped and very long nightshirted, because I hear a noise downstairs which turns out to be Griffin, the 'Man' himself.

But what about the nude scene? Well yes, there is no denying it, I did appear in the altogether, and Auntie BBC gave me an extra 25 quid for so doing! This is what happened: I, The Rev. Mr Bunting, and another dear friend, Gerald James, who played the doctor, are cornered by the Invisible Man. We can't see him of course, but we can hear him, and we're ordered at poker point, which we can see, to give him our clothes. It's very cold outside and he intends to make a run for it, because the authorities are getting too close. We cut outside to a bitter wind howling and rain slanting. (Actually the cut mostly served as a way of not showing Gerry and me doing a striptease!) When we return to the main scene, the doctor, Gerry, has fared better than I and still has his long-johns. Rev. Mr Bunting has been left with nothing but his dog-collar, and as the camera pans from right to left across the room we get a flash of 40307's bum. And a very nice bum it is too, so I have been told.

So there you are then. The confessions of a Bum!

But before I leave what was a jolly good series, once again full of joyous thespians, I'd like to say a couple of words or twenty about young Gerry James, and to explain how Gerry and I could be menaced by a poker which was all on its own, because the man who was brandishing it couldn't be seen.

Young Gerry James. Sounds like a Western film! Actually, I'm younger than Gerry by almost twenty years. He was one of the oldest ever students at RADA, and I know he won't mind if I tell you why. We're back in fact to the old acting bug again. That driving determination which bit me when I saw *The Wooden Horse*, and made Ted Morris throw in his clerking job. Gerald James had desperately wanted to take the professional acting plunge for years, but had been prevented from doing so because he had no funds. His chance didn't come until he was in his thirties, and by then he had a wife and family - indeed, I believe it was his wife who gave him the final push. He at last came to London, leaving his brood back home in Wales, auditioned for RADA, and was awarded a bursary for his fees. He worked all his spare time in pubs and restaurant kitchens so that he could send money home and keep himself, just, and he finally achieved his ambition. He became a professional actor. Mostly in the theatre, he has since enriched our art with many stupendous performances. If you are really bitten hard, you have to go for it; you will never rest otherwise! Gerry is also a sweet, kind, and loving man.

And now the visible poker and the invisible man! It's a process called Colour Separation Overlay - CSO for short. It's a marvellous device which I've been involved with on a number of occasions - I had a fight with one of Dr Who's assistants, the loinclothed Louise Jamieson, actually inside Dr Who's brain with the aid of CSO.

I hope I can describe it simply. You need two studios - no, two sets in the same large studio would be better. Call them A and B. In one of the sets, A, you have your regular furniture and actorbums, and the scene you are recording - Gerry and I in the striptease scene for example. In the other set, B, everything is blue. Everything, except that which you wish to see in the actual scene A - the menacing poker.

Now I'm no expert, so I can't explain the technicalities involved, but the camera cannot register the particular blue used in set B, so all you then have to do is dress someone in the same blue - hands and face must also be covered - and get them to move the non-blue poker about in set B, and the camera will photograph said poker. But only the poker. Then it's a simple job to 'overlay' that picture of the poker on to the actual scene you are recording in set A, and there you have it, Colour Separation Overlay. You can try it for yourself. Turn on your video, tune into the video channel on your TV, and you should find a blue screen. Now try recording that blue screen and you'll record nothing.

We in the actual scene/set A cannot see the poker of course. The complete scene, actorbums in the actual scene A, and the poker from set B, can only be brought together in the control room by the director and his technicians. We, in set/actual scene A, react to nothing (or bits of sticking plaster again.) But the person dressed in blue in set B has a monitor. He can see both us, and the poker, and he waves the thing around accordingly.

CSO is a marvellous tool of our trade. Just think what it could be used for - virtually anything. Provided you blue out what you don't want to see, you can be overlaid on to a photograph of Mount Everest if you wish and climb to the very top. Or you could explore the ocean depths, drive a racing car (I'd love that!), or take a trip to the moon and back, without ever leaving the cosy, warm studio.

XXXII

Right. Now we have: Two Hits and a Him. This one sounds like a pop group, doesn't it? These three films are just a little out of sequence - there's no way I'd have played two 'Hits' on the trot. But they were not that far apart either, and you'll see why they've fallen together in a couple of pages time. So let's see...I'll take the 'Him' first I think.

This American film series was called *Space*, and it starred my old mate Michael York. The sections of the series made on this side of the Atlantic were directed by Joe Sergeant, and the 'Him' was the part of Himmler!

Space told the story of the space programme, right from the beginning, and ended with America reaching the moon. So it had to start of course in Germany, during the Second World War, when Von Braun was the father of the rocket, and the V1s and V2s very nearly...but they didn't, and anyway that's another story.

The series took for ever to make and seemed to last a lifetime on the screen. But the beginning, the Second World War stuff, which is the only part I'm really qualified to talk about, was damn good. Towards the end of the war, when Germany was getting jittery, Der Fuehrer thought he had the answer with his rockets, and he put Heinrich Himmler (played by 40307 in this dramatisation), in charge of the rocket programme.

The star part was of course Von Braun, but Michael York didn't in fact play him. Apparently the Von Braun family didn't want the name used, so Michael played a fictitious chap called Kolf. But he was Kolf in name only. In all other respects he was Von Braun, and the details of the American rocket programme were as ploddingly authentic as the makers could make them. Shush - perhaps that's why the later episodes were so boring. Sometimes the scriptwriter must 'beef up' what actually happened, or change the sequence of events, in order to make a thing watchable.

The last paragraph has put me in mind of an old adage which is totally untrue. Namely that the camera never lies. Phooey! If you haven't guessed by now from these scribblings of mine, then I'll say it. The camera, certainly in our business, lies all the flipping time. Think of the vast amounts of sticking plaster which are used for eye lines, the moving to focus marks, the pretending to look happy when you're sad, or feel ill, or are tired...my God there are hundreds of examples. But the best illustration of the camera lying has to be little Alan Ladd standing on a box so that he could woo his leading ladies with dignity. Sometimes, if the shot required it, if it was a tracking shot for instance, they'd dig a trench for the girl to walk in. (Ladd in *Shane* is my favourite western of all time by the way. Remember the little boy, Brandon de Wilde, calling at the end, 'Come back. Come back, Shane.' That is absolute magic.)

Where the blazes was I? Ah yes, Michael York was playing Kolf/von Braun, and I was playing H. Himmler, and playing him for the second time. Remember my happy days in Paris working on *The Bunker*, 'Hello, Teddy' et al.?

Dearly Beloved thinks that my performance in *Space* is some of my very best work, so it has to be good. I'd like therefore to use the performance to illustrate a wee point. To show how the editor on a movie can make an actor's creation even better than it is. More lying!

Everyone has heard the actorbum's lament: 'It was a super part darling, but it ended up on the cutting-room floor.' That can be quite true of course, some damn good performances have ended up not being part of the finished film. They've been cut out, not because they were bad, but because the powers that be felt they were surplus to the requirement of the whole. Sometimes, it's true, performances are cut, or reduced as much as possible, because they are no bloody good. Sometimes an insecure starbum will insist that a brilliant newcomer's performance is cut. And sometimes a tiny bit is snipped from a scene which not only makes the scene better, but also improves the already superb performance of the actor concerned...'Some of my very best work,' quoth Dearly B.!

It will be easier to explain if you can visualise the scene in *Space* where Michael York (Kolf/Von Braun) comes to see me (H. Himmler), and I tell him that I am now in charge. Everywhere is chaos. The war is nearing its final stages, and I am moving from my beautiful palace-like headquarters to... 'Tell the Fuehrer I will be with him in the bunker by nightfall,' say I, having answered the phone at one point.

Right then. During the scene I walk the full tength of a vast oblong polished table and sit down in a large chair. Through the long graceful windows behind me can be seen a huge lake, with rolling hills beyond. (They were real too, we filmed in a mansion in the Cotswolds west of Oxford.) I ask Michael to explain why things are not progressing as well as they should be progressing...and we did two versions of his reply. In version one the camera was behind me looking over my shoulder at Michael, for the whole of his explanation. I had a couple of interjections it's true, but the camera stayed where it was. In the second version we stopped half-way through, changed angles, and did a shot of me getting up from my chair and walking round to the back of it. I then paused, whilst the camera feasted its lens further on the lovely scenery outside the window, and said the only bad lines in the scene. I can't remember them now, but they merely repeated the gist of what I'd just been told by Michael. Waste of time.

So, using my position in the old pecking order, I strongly suggested that it would be much better and stronger, for me and the scene, to forget about production value views on this occasion and to use version one. For me to remain quietly in my seat during Michael's reply. But Joe, as director, quite rightly said that he wanted both versions so that he could make up his mind in the editing.

When I came to do the sound dub some four to six months later - rather like re-voicing a porno movie, that's when you return to a sound studio and add, or change, or re-do, any dialogue which needs it - Joe Sergeant, having said that my performance was great, apologised for the fact that he'd cut some of the scene with Michael York. I was a little upset, until I saw the scene on screen. Joe had used version one, and allowed me to remain seated during Michael's reply to my question. Not only that, he had cut those bad lines and in so doing had improved the scene, and my performance, no end.

OK. Now let's go for 'Hit' number one. You must surely have guessed by now that if 'Him' stands for Himmler, then 'Hit' must stand for Hitler. I suppose I can look quite like him, otherwise I wouldn't have played the brute four times during these first thirty years. And that doesn't include the 'Sex Life of A. Hitler', which I was offered, turned down, and which was never made.

The first 'Dirty Dozen' film made a star of my erstwhile repertory theatre house-buddy, Donald Sutherland, of course. There have been several additions to the original film, each more banal than the last, and the one I did was called *The Dirty Dozen - Next Mission*. Would you believe, it was the second in the sequel line! (So it was only a little bad.) And Mr Hitler was the cameo-featured big baddy.

Our director was Andrew V. McLaglen. Andrew is the son of Victor McLaglen, the great film starbum who'd started his long and great career in early silent pictures.

Andrew V. McLaglen was very and rightly proud of his dad, and had added the V. to his name in memory of his father.

My favourite Victor McLaglen film has to be *The Quiet Man*, with Maureen O'Hara, and John Wayne at his best, but there are masses more. I would love to have worked with Victor, but alas he'd been gone (1959) for quite some time when I came on the scene. Nevertheless, it was great to work with his son and I'd like to tell you two, no, three tots of interest concerning this film: the starbum's performance; using the camera to switch locations; and the special effects.

Star performance.

The star of 'Dirty D. 2' was a guy I used to admire one hell of a lot - again dammit he's gone now - and after our meeting on this movie I admired him even more. His name was Lee Marvin. I saw the movie of *Paint Your Wagon* again recently and it's not awfully good to be honest, except for Marvin. I've not seen a better film performance since he made *Cat Ballou*, with Jane Fonda. His singing of 'Wandering Star' is masterful, and it got to the top of the hit parade, of course.

There is this gigantic battle scene in 'Dirty D. 2', in which the twelve find themselves unexpectedly up against the big boss, Hitler, when they thought all they were supposed to get rid of was some silly old colonel or somesuch.

The filmed battle raged. The youngsters playing the dozen fought hard. They were mostly unknowns, and every shot could, might, feature one or other of them. They quite rightly thesped like mad, in the hope that they'd be noticed and given more close-ups in more scenes later on.

Uninvolved in all this mayhem was Lee Marvin. He sat quietly to the side of the camera, looking what he was in fact, an old man who's seen it all before and is obviously quite content.

Then Andrew V. said to him, 'OK, Lee. Can I get some close shots of you for cut-ins?' And suddenly this old man became a menacing fighting machine. It was quite extraordinary, and to be honest I was completely gob-smacked. Lee marched around; he dropped down on one knee; he fired his machine-gun; he shouted orders; he fell to the ground; rolled over; jumped up; yelled and charged. And the camera caught everything. When Andrew called 'cut', Lee Marvin became an old man again. He staggered, slightly bow-legged, back to his chair and sat down, to wait for the next request from his director. Whatever Lee's troubles in his off-screen life, he was a probum on the set, right down to his bootlaces. I admired tremendously what he did that day.

Switching camera angles to change locations.

Now there's a cheeky thing to do. This scene opens on an airfield in Germany - actually it was an airfield not far from Woking in Surrey - where a large aircraft is taxiing to a standstill - actually that's all the poor old thing could do, it couldn't fly to save its life. The aircraft stops, and a waiting group of German Reich clusters round. The Dirty Dozen, who are hiding behind a brick wall, but watching, wonder what is going on. 'What the fuck is going on?!' quoth one of them (great script eh?). Then the centre door of the aircraft opens and out steps Adolf Hitler - alias 40307.

The camera for the master shot of the arrival was strategically positioned to the left of a large hut, which, on screen, is therefore in the right foreground of the picture, and after all the necessary greetings - done in close-up for inclusion later during editing - this master shot takes over again. The group walk towards the camera and turning to their left (right as you view), pass out of shot behind the hut.

The next master shot is really a continuation of the previous one, except that the aforementioned hut is now on the left of the picture. The group are seen to walk from behind the hut (still going right), and the camera follows us into a railway marshalling yard.

In other words, I have arrived in an aeroplane; I've been met by lots of important people; I've walked with these people from the aircraft, past a large hut, and into a railway yard. I suppose the sequence lasted about three or four minutes. But there were at least as many weeks between our doing the first part of the scene and completing the second.

The secret is that hut of course. Because it was impossible to find an airfield and a railway marshalling yard in the same place, we walked towards the hut near Woking in Surrey, and passed out of sight behind it. When we emerged, we were in fact well over a hundred miles to the north, back at the Nene Valley Railway outside Peterborough, where I'd made *Caught on a Train*.

Although we really did do the railway part of this sequence a long while later, the whole looks great, and I defy anyone to see the join - unless of course they know what they're looking for. Ah, the magic of film and the camera that never lies!

Special Effects.

I could write a book about special effects. But for the moment let me tell you what happens once we arrive in that railway marshalling yard. As I've said, the Dirty Dozen are hiding behind a wall. They're still watching and not believing their eyes. (The wall has been transported from Surrey, together with the hut, and they've both been reconstucted in Peterborough. Not that difficult a task really. There are only small sections of each - those bits that will show - and the wall is made of papier mache bricks. More filmic lies.)

The Dozen's mission has been to shoot and obviously kill the Colonel character, and one of their number is not only a crack shot, he's a crack shot from long range when using a telescopic gun sight. That's why he's been sprung from jail and invited to join this suicide raid.

But what is this guy to do? There is his target, the Colonel (Wolf Kahler, by the way), but he's talking to the big man, Herr Hitler. If the sharpshooter kills Adolf instead of the Colonel, well, the war will be over won't it? 'I'm going to shoot Hitler,' says the sharpshooter.

'No,' says Lee Marvin, 'our orders are to kill the Colonel.' (Still great dialogue.)

Whilst all this is going on we keep cutting to said Colonel and Adolf H., who are inspecting a railway truck. The wagon is loaded with something or other which is very interesting, so interesting in fact that it's keeping them in chummy's gun sights long enough for him to make up his mind. Finally, having cut with increasing rapidity between the two groups - Colonel/Adolf and Marksman/Lee Marvin - we end up with Adolf and the Colonel in tight close-up, and we still don't know which of the two the guy will shoot. Then we cut quickly to the Marksman as he pulls the trigger, and BANG. Adolf Hitler is covered in blood...He's killed the Fuehrer after all. Hooray! The war will be over in no time. But wait, it's the Colonel who is dropping to the ground. Hitler seems unharmed. His flunkies are gathering round and shielding him. He's being ushered into a car and being driven off at high speed. No chance for a second shot now.

But where did all that blood come from? Hitler was covered in it. Spattered all over from head to...It wasn't Hitler's blood at all, it was the Colonel's. When the Marksman with the gun had finally decided to obey orders and had killed the Colonel, the bullet had supposedly entered the Colonel's head with such force that blood and bone had burst out of the far side of his cranium and covered Adolf.

Sorry about the gory details. This is how it was done. Do you remember when I had my brains splattered in

Escort Service - that strange multi-national MI5 movie? Well it's our old friend the wide-barrelled airgun again, just out of shot behind the Colonel and pointing at me. Into its barrel have again been pushed stuff that looks like blood, and bone, and brains.

After the the Marksman pulls the trigger, there is a close-up of Hitler (cut to simultaneously as the gun is fired, which makes it almost seem as though we have travelled with the bullet), and at precisely the same moment, the special effects people fire the airgun directly at my face. It had no great impact, only a very soft sort of putt, a bit like being splattered with mud when a car races past you through a puddle. But the effect on film is very realistic. (I was in fact terrified at the time. But like the trouperbum I am, I didn't show it, even when we had to do it again because something went wrong!)

In addition to the above, all hell broke loose once the Colonel had been shot. Four cameras covered the continuous action, and there were something like 150 controlled explosions in the next three minutes. Our special effects boys are wonderful. No one was the tiniest bit scratched, not even the stuntbums. Dear old mate Roy Alone (Alon) included, who told me that since we last met on *Green Ice*, when he'd done that fantastic fall down the side of the skyscaper, he'd been doing a one-man stunting stint in India. The only stuntman on the entire sub-continent, he'd been doing upwards of five big stunts a day. They make a hell of a lot of films in India. Extremely quickly!

'Hit' two came in *Indiana Jones and The Last Crusade*. Stephen Spielberg had kept his promise to find me something else. To be honest, I would really have preferred not to do two Hitlers back-to-back, but my availability was rather restricted at the time and I took what was on offer. (I said some pages ago that I'd explain my non-availability in two pages' time. And I will, in two pages or some from now!) It was great to work with Stephen again and Harrison and Sean Connery. And Ronnie Lacey was playing Himmler to my Hitler which was a big bonus. This was, I'm afraid, one of the last things that Ronnie did before he died. I never saw him again after we finished working on 'Last Crusade', and my memories are thus saddened when I think of this movie, as are those of a hell of a lot of other people.

But I'm pleased to report that when I saw the film in London, the audience laughed heartily when I, as Hitler, gave Harrison (Indiana), my autograph, and I'd like to relate a couple of other snippets regarding this production. They're both concerned with our old friend the lying camera.

We were filming during one of those very hot summers in the late 1980s, the ones which pushed up house insurance premiums because of the subsidence caused. Along came Harrison and Sean to film a scene. Their costumes were beautifully presented - Harrison in his leather jacket, Sean in thick tweeds - and they were immaculately correct. Or rather they were immaculately correct down to their waists. Below the waist they wore nothing but swimming trunks. They'd been told by Stephen that he would not be shooting them below the belt that day, so they'd devised an excellent way to keep cool!

Sean by the way is an extremely nice chap. Professional again of course, but kind and unaffected by his starbum status, as indeed, I've found, are all those who have nothing to prove.

I've just remembered something else. Not long after this I did a little filmed series called *Press Gang*. Actually the producer won't thank me for calling it little, the thing did win a BAFTA award for something or other. Let's just say that my contribution was little. Anyway, I went along to be fitted for my part as a doctor in 'Press Gang', and would you believe it, I ended up in a suit that Sean had worn in 'Last Crusade'. (Re: my lines on costume. Good period costumes in particular, which have been made especially for a big movie production - in this case 'Last Crusade' - will very often be retained by the costumier which made them for use on future, lesser ones.)

OK, that's camera lie number one. Number two shows how a skillful director, Speilberg, can film a huge parade in less time than it takes some others to shoot a chap crossing a street. This is what happened: Ronnie and I, and other big German brass, were standing outside this very important looking German building (actually it was a private school in Berkshire closed for the summer hols), in front of which was a large circular drive. All Stephen did was to position his five or so cameras so that they cut the circular drive in half. Then he had what looked like a straight road which entered on the right of the screen, passed in front of me, and exited on the left.

A (very) goodly crowd of extras, dressed as German soldiers, were lined up four abreast around the whole of the circular drive, both on the part which was in front of the cameras and that which was out of shot. On the command 'action', the chaps just played follow my leader. When they came into shot in front of me, the men 'eyes righted' and we all saluted. Stephen could thus have the guys going round and round for as long as it took him to get the shots he wanted. Far better than making the extrabum/soldiers walk along a straight bit of road, from given point A to point B. Then getting them to reassemble at point A again. It always takes ages. Think of the valuable time S. Spielberg saved by having them go round and round. That's the sort of thinking which separates the rans from the also rans.

I greatly enjoyed working with Stephen again. We both said when we parted, 'let's make it third time lucky very soon.' Pity really that Richard Attenborough agreed to play that part in *Jurassic Park*. I would have done it far better...!

XXXIII

Another film I did around this time was a tiny budgeted affair in which I co-starred with the MP for Highgate, Miss Glenda Jackson. The piece was shot on the south coast, in Swanage, and it was written, photographed, recorded, costumed, and cast, by children. The kids did everything in fact except direct, and the whole thing was completely...great! Glenda had been doing workshops with The Children's Film Unit and had agreed to appear in their film, which was made for TV's Channel 4 and was called *Doombeach*. Glenda was to play one of only two adults in the piece (slightly taller people, I called them), and I was invited to play the other - a headmaster.

Why did they ask me? Well, we'll have to go back nearly five years for the answer. I first said I'd tell you why my availability had become so heavily restricted some pages ago, then I promised to tell all in two pages time.

Those pages are past and I must now come clean. The two Hitlers, the Himmler, the above film with Glenda, and I'm happy to say, lots of other super engagements, were fitted in and around a five year schedule on...

XXXIV

Dear, unforgettable, stimulating, wonderful *Grange Hill*. I love you, 'GH'. Almost all of you. I've been asked many times why I did you at all. Was it money? Was it the steady work? Was it the prestige? Was it the cast? The fact that I could have almost complete control over what I did and sometimes virtually directed scenes? Was it because, for the first time in my career, I really was the top dog - or certainly one of them? Was it therefore my ego?

I don't know. It must surely have been a combination of all the above and many more. What I do know is that I only committed myself to one season to start with - just eighteen episodes. That's no more than *Maggie*, for heavens' sake.

Although a five-year engagement is certainly some sort of landmark for me, 'GH' was in reality simply another job. A long one albeit, but in a continuing career. I don't want to turn it into any sort of pinnacle, although of course in a way it was.

As always I was superb! But this time there were moments which seemed to go further than that. I'm sure you know by now when I'm taking the Michael out of me, so please don't think me anything but modest when I say, in all seriousness, that I was brilliant at times during my five years on 'GH'. Who would have thought it? You spend half a career doing great work and giving super performances, but the really big, transcending all other, tip top, never to be bettered moments, come for you in a small budget television series for Auntie BBC. You just never know where, or when, it will happen.

So how to approach it. How do I tell you about just another engagement which came to mean so much to me and took five years of my life?...I know!

There now follows The Alphabetical History of my time on *Grange Hill*. That should cover it.

A is for: Agent. Actor. Availability. Adaptability. Alertness. Acton Hilton.

Agent...Before I really get started I'd like to make mention of my new lovely agent and what better place to do this than under A. I've had a wee bit of trouble agent-wise since I finished 'GH' and my then agent retired, and it's no easy matter finding someone who has the enthusiasm, the dedication and the craftiness necessary. Someone who is prepared to put in the long hours that are sometimes called for, when waiting for a call from America for example, and, together with the above and many other necessary attributes, has an excellent telephone manner and is also a chum. A person indeed in whom one can have complete confidence. My new agent is the salt of the agent's earth. Knowing exactly what is needed, and having absolute faith, is what it's all about. If I hear that a director is casting my agent will get straight on the blower and jog an elbow if necessary. Likewise, and far, far more frequently, the phone will ring and we'll talk about some casting I've not heard of and work things out together. Communication is what an actorbum needs and that is what I get from my agent.

Let me make things abundantly clear, a thesp's most valuable asset has to be his Dearly Beloved. But his other almost as indispensible ally is his agent. I don't care how lowly, or indeed how high up the slippery slope he may get. Apart from negotiating fees and all the rest, an agent has to put up with the moans and the tears. Not from me of course, I'm far too advanced and established and butch for that sort of thing. But there are times when a good agent has to be a Mummy, or a Daddy to their clients - there will normally be about thirty of those. Who would therefore be an agent? Very certainly not me. But I'm delighted and very grateful that, backed up to the hilt and beyond by the excellent staff, my agent is an agent!

Actor. We were all actors on *Grange Hill* - all of us, the young and the not so young, the professional and the amateur, the experienced and the beginners - but this heading affords me the opportunity to put the record straight. Larry Olivier gave me the word Bum. I have used it extensively throughout these scribblings because I feel it describes us perfectly, particularly when it's coupled with Thesp, Artiste, Journeyman, Character, Stuntman, et al.

But never let it be said that I am unhappy with the simple, dignified name of Actor. That is what I am, that's what it says on my passport.

Availability. I mentioned that the Hitlers, Himmler, and *Doombeach*, etc., were fitted in and around 'GH', and my first consideration on being offered the series had to be, can I afford the time? Can I afford to be out of the main stream and not be free for large chunks of the year? We used to get a three month break on 'GH' in the spring and six weeks in the summer. I decided that had to be enough, and happily I was offered other work during these times. Damn glad in fact, because I ended up doing a five year 'GH' stint.

Adaptability. I had to be very strict with myself and remember that this job was going to last for a long time. I couldn't show the whole of my character in one fell, three-hour swoop, as I would in a movie or even a six-part series. I had to adapt my way of working and allow my performance to develop over a much longer period. A luxury actually, and completely absorbing. A bit like building a house. A brick here, a window there...it was ten episodes before it was established that my character lived with his sister. An absorbing, fascinating way to work.

Alertness. My God you had to be alert. Some children can't act it's true, but the majority are naturals, and if you're not on your toes all the time they'll do something unexpectedly brilliant and wipe the floor with you. There was one scene early on in the first series which was particularly tricky: a traffic jam. I am in my car outside the school gates and these two lads come up and ask me to sign a petition. I'd worked very hard at home the previous evening to get the thing right, and I was therefore somewhat dismayed when the littlest boy said he hadn't had time to learn the lines because he'd had too much school homework. 'What do you suggest?' I asked. 'Oh don't you worry, Michael,' the little lad replied, 'give us a read of your script.' I gave him the script and he took one look at the three and a half page scene. Then we went for a take and he was word and performance perfect!

Acton Hilton. A restaurant at the very top, with six floors, each serving three rehearsal rooms underneath, that's the custom-built BBC rehearsal block, The Acton Hilton. It was named thus by some actorbum long ago, not because it's particularly grand, but because it's opposite Acton tube station and is very tall. We rehearsed the first series of 'GH' there, before we moved to Elstree, but I've happily done hundreds of shows which started at the Hilton. And each time I work there I forgo the lift, once, and try to race up the stairs from ground level to the top. It doesn't get any easier as the years go by, I wonder if the stairs are trying to tell me something!

B is for: Bronson. Ben. Barber. Blue. BBC. Baddy. Budget. BAFTA.

Bronson. Maurice Bronson. Sir! The character I played. Loved and feared by all. I love him dearly, of course I do, he was the main reason I accepted the engagement. What a part to be offered - the chances for invention and development were almost endless. Bronson was a dinosaur, a Latin scholar who was forced to teach French when his grammar school was amalgamated with two others of lower capability to form the new Grange Hill. I used to get letters from university dons sympathising with my lot, and telling me to stick with it, that I was flying the flag and they were behind me. It's some time now since I left the series, but I still get masses of fan mail. And only recently Dearly Beloved and I were in a restaurant and the waitress kept saying how the programme had never been the same since I'd left, and how very much she and her friends missed Mr B. The other day I was passing a bus stop, just as a bus was disgorging its passengers. They were mostly kids - it was that time in the afternoon - and one of the youngsters was not looking where he was going and cannoned into me. He turned round, and without a moment's hesitation said: 'Oh, Mr Bronson. Sir! I'm very sorry, Sir.' Is that not a type of immortality? Whatever, it certainly means that 40307 made some sort of impact in the part, and it don't 'arf make a bum feel proud.

Ben. Ben Rea. Without him there could not have been Mr Bronson, at least probably not as presented by me. I've known Ben since he was an assistant floor manager, which is almost as long as we've both been in television, and he rang me one day and said, 'I've just taken over as producer on this series for BBC TV and I'm looking for a balding actor to play a new teacher. The idea is that he wears this really dreadfully awful toupee...!'

Barber. Albert Barber was one of our Directors. Very nice BBC chap. He made his directorial drama debut on 'GH' and went on to become the producer later.

Blue...Peter! I went on *Blue Peter* with my lovely dog, Haggis, and his sons and daughters. Karen Ford, who played the 'GH' art teacher, Miss Booth, had a spendid lady dog called Topsy. Topsy was a lurcher cross; Haggis was a Labrador, with more than a touch of Alsation. Karen wanted Topsy to have some puppies and suggested that Haggis was handsome enough to be their Dad. (Which he surely was. I say it as shouldn't, but the Hag was the most beautiful chap most people had ever seen.)

Topsy had her pups - there seemed to be simply masses of them - and we all went on *Blue Peter*. (Arranged of course by our production office - great publicity for the programme.) And the puppies messed their dressing room (downstairs in the BBC TV Centre's basement, thank heavens), like no dressing room has been dirtied before. There was dog-doings everywhere, mounds of the stuff. It took us ages to get the place clean.

BBC. Thank you, dear old Auntie BBC for giving me the chance to play Bronson, I really am tremendously grateful. Just dotting the Is and crossing the fingers! As the old thespian said, 'ITV may come and go, but Auntie Beeb goes on for ever!'

Baddy. I've had said to me on occasion, 'Bronson - oh yes, he was the Grange Hill baddy, wasn't he?' They don't mean it of course, it's just their way of identifying him. But it does rile me somewhat, even when they go on to say how good I was in the part! They're using the word 'baddy' quite wrongly. Bronson, as written, and as conceived and played by me, was an extremely prominent and dominant disciplinarian, certainly. He was passionate about his teaching, and was feared by some. But he could also be considerate and kind, and he was very much respected, and, indeed, loved by all in the end...Maurice Bronson a simple downright baddy - never!

Budget. You will have read of the astronomical budgets that are lavished on some of the big movies today - millions of dollars seem about average! I thought you might be interested to know that an episode of little old 'GH' cost no more than a film director's cigars when I worked on it.

BAFTA. The British Academy of Film and Television Arts, in London's Piccadilly, which once a year awards us our Oscars. Not a statue, as in America, these are shimmering golden masks and are highly prized by the recipients. I've mentioned them before, re: Peggy Ashcroft and *Caught on a Train*. I heard recently that another series in which I appeared, *Taking Over the Asylum*, has won an award, and I assure you it is pure coincidence that in my very first season of *Grange Hill*, the programme won the BAFTA mask for best children's drama!

C is for: Classroom. Catering. Colds. Chaperon. Canteen. Camera.

Classroom. We had a set of classrooms and corridors permanently set up in the studio, but we also did an enormous amount of location work. It was masterly how the production team found schools that had just closed down for us to film in. And because the developers were eager to demolish and get their hands on the land occupied by a recently defunct school, it seemed that we had a different one for each series. When the production moved to Elstree studios, we used the front of the building as the entrance and frontage of G.H. This of course gave us some solid continuity. But there were still masses of shots and scenes recorded in empty schools all over north London and beyond. These were then popped in the editor's pot, mixed thoroughly, and poured out as Grange Hill School. And dammit it worked. Nobody ever mentioned that they could see the join, or that the school looked any different.

Catering. How you can produce a midday meal for all those masses of people from the back of a truck I will never know. But we had breakfast, mid-morning coffee and afternoon tea as well. And it was all scrumptious. Our tums were exceedingly well catered for!

Colds. They used to offer flu jabs at the studio and they were very welcome. A child can get a cold and even flu without seemingly noticing it, but when the taller actors catch them it's misery time. Thank heavens for those jabs.

Chaperon. Mostly there were just two incredible ladies in charge of the children. Strictly speaking, all the kids under the age of sixteen were in their charge, although their affection extended even to the adults on occasion. They made certain their young thesps were always on time. They mothered them when things went wrong, and they made sure that any child who did not toe the line was reprimanded accordingly. Salt of the earth those marvellous ladies.

Canteen. You must have heard umpteen various comedians tell sad stories of the BBC canteen cuppa and sandwich. In fact, the food at the TV Centre is actually quite good, getting better, and the grub at the Acton Hilton can sometimes be great. At Elstree it is super all the time, particularly the breakfasts. After a hard, long drive, it was almost heaven to tuck into their delicious fried bread, egg and bacon. (Proper bacon of course, not as served in Yugoslavia!)

Camera. Where would we be without cameras? I understand close-ups, wide angles and such. I know how cameras affect me as a bum, and I can work with them. I know they lie, and I can be their master. I'd like to understand exactly how they work technically, but I don't. One day I'll take lessons.

D is for: Dressing Room. Dreadful. Drugs. Documentary. Discipline.

Dressing Room. I'm not a snob, but a good dressing room is extremely important, particularly when you've a lot to do and need somewhere to hide and relax. I only did one series of the show at the BBC Television Centre, and I was always given either number one dressing room or number two. Remember my story about Rita Webb and the lowly dressing rooms in the basement? Well dressing rooms one and two were not only on the same floor as the studio, they had their own loos, windows and showers, and were truly for Starbums only! When we moved to Elstree Studios, there were again only two Star dressing rooms allocated to our programme, and I had one of these. Elstree of course had been a film studio long ago, the very first in England in fact, and my dressing room was from the early years. A bit faded now perhaps, but I still had my own loo and shower. And sitting at my table, gazing with half-closed eyes around my room, with its high ceiling and glimpses of 1930s decorative splendour, it was easy to imagine that I was back in those far off days. I was waiting for my call to make *Contraband* with Conrad Veidt and Valerie Hobson, or *One of our Aircraft is Missing* with Eric Portman and a very young Peter Ustinov, two of the many films which were made at Elstree British Studios as they were called then. Aye, I'm still a romantic right enough!

Dreadful. I've already said that some children can't act, and I have to say I'm pleased that very few of these slipped through the Producer's net when he was casting - a casting director was never used when I was on the show - but on a couple of occasions, it has to be said, a child was cast who was downright awful. We taller actors knew it, the Directors knew it, and what perhaps is surprising, the other kids knew it too. But unlike what (I imagine) might well have happened in an ordinary school - teasing, chanting 'so and so can't a-a-act', or even bullying - the children on the 'GH' set rallied round any of their number who was in difficulties and tried to help them. We all did. Right from my first day on the programme I insisted that there would never be a them and us - kids and adults - separation as far as I was concerned. We were, all of us, caring actors. It just happened that some of our group were shorter than the others, that's all.

Drugs. One very strong storyline during my stay concerned drugs. It was excellently handled, and Lee MacDonald, as Zammo, the boy who got hooked, was superb. A pop record was made by the cast called 'Just Say No (to drugs)', and Lee, with some of the others, went to America and met the then President's wife, Mrs Nancy Reagan- once an actorbum too, like her husband (Ronald, of course!) It was part of a world-wide attempt to make everyone aware of the dangers, and our modest TV series is to be congratulated for its high profile contribution.

Documentary. I've lost count of the times I arrived at the studios to be told that there would be an extra crew following us that day who would be making a documentary about us for inclusion in some programme or other. One of our Producers even made one such piece himself. (The children were very kind about me and said what a good egg I was!) These efforts didn't exactly bother us, but we older thesps did have to remind some of the youngsters on occasion that we were making a series called *Grange Hill*, not a documentary about the making of a series called *Grange Hill*!

Discipline. In spite of the above and the like, real hard discipline was very rarely required - I've talked already about the young actors' high professionalism. Only once in my whole five years did I have to seem to lose my rag. Seem to - in reality I was acting of course. The production staff knew and agreed with what I was doing (the lad concerned had been late on numerous occasions and had been holding up rehearsals badly). It would have been fatal and completely unforgiveable for me to have genuinely lost control. One of our Directors made a girl cry by shouting at her. I'm certain sure it was out of frustration, but he was off the show before anyone could say, 'don't be a fool, there's no need for that. Talk to the lass, listen to her problems, don't allow yourself to forget that at the very end of the day, you are dealing with a child.' The lad I admonished, by the way, readily accepted his reprimand and was never late again. He was a good egg, too.

E is for: Early Rising. Extras. *EastEnders*. *Eldorado*. Effort.

Early Rising. The times I've set the alarm for five in the morning so that I could be sure to get to the location on time are uncountable. We are talking little TV here remember, not big budget movie. There was no studio unit car waiting to pick me up on this production. I was entirely responsible for getting myself to work.

Extras. I've said somewhere else that I would never have sent my kids to an acting school for children - let them have a formal education first, then if they really want to...and mine of course didn't - but these places do have some good ideas. The London schools who supplied most of the principal child performers for 'GH', also sent the masses of child extras that were required. The schools were acting as agents for these youngsters and were thus raking in their percentage, but the idea was sound because it stopped the child stars of last week from becoming big headed, and kept things in proportion. It didn't matter a jot that a kid had recently been playing the lead in something, if you were free when the Beeb called for extras, you did it.

EastEnders. Let there be no mistake. We were the first programme to move into the newly-acquired BBC Elstree studios. But we were gracious, and allowed another show to follow us a few months later! It was just starting, and it had some teething troubles, so everyone was very kind and understanding. Even when they nicked our studio and we had to move to another one much further away. The *EastEnders* gang were a good lot. I knew most of them already - Wendy Richard, Leonard Fenton, and Anna Wing, had their dressing rooms on the same landing as I, and they used to pretend jealousy when we finished work before them.

Eldorado. *EastEnders* became, and still is, a huge hit of course. The producer who started it, went off in a blaze of glory to set up something else - do you remember *Eldorado*? Oh dear, how the mighty may fall!

Effort. It has to be. I was continually amazed by the effort that the kids put into the show. We taller thesps, well, it was a darned good job we had in 'GH', and anyway we were professional bums, so we worked hard to get things right. But the children were paid very little, certainly until they reached the age of sixteen. At that age they were, in law, deemed to be adult performers and therefore entitled to the Equity minimum professional wage. But out of all the children who passed through the programme whilst I was in it, only a very few would actually make it into adult actorship (mostly via *EastEnders* - Susan Tully, Todd Carty,

Letitia Dean, et al.). Nevertheless, the kids on 'GH' worked like professionals, whatever their age. As hard as we did, harder sometimes. Perhaps it's just that they were full of hope for the future. And why the hell not, I still am!

F is for: Frocks. French. Fog and Frost. First. Flattery.

Frocks. I should have mentioned costume under C of course, but we in this lovely crazy business do call our costumes frocks, so they can come equally well under F. Everything I wore on *Grange Hill* I selected, right down to my shoes and glasses. There was a different Costume Supervisor for each one-year series, but they were happy to leave us taller thespians to costume ourselves. I used to buy my suits in our local town and charge them to the production. They then became the freehold property of the BBC, but for the duration of the show Mr Bronson was the tenant.

Glasses were a wee bit different. The costume ladies and I had a special arrangement with regard to glasses. I think Mr Bronson had three pairs during his five years, and I'm very grateful to say that I was given said glasses when I finished working on the programme. You see, they were of no use to anybody else because they'd been made to my prescription. I'm wearing a pair now.

French. You must all know by now that I count myself very fortunate to have one language at my fingertips. German I speak, but I cannot utter one flipping word of French. Yet here I was playing a French teacher. When I had to speak in that tongue I had to do it phonetically. Dearly Beloved did GCE French at school and was able to help me, but it took absolutely ages to learn. Agony.

Fog and Frost. This is really a part of Early Rising, but even now, when I watch the weather forecast after the early evening news on TV, I cringe with vivid remembrance when the man says jovially, 'I'd watch out for frost, or fog, or both, tomorrow morning, you early risers.' How ever did I manage to get to the studio over 1,500 times without mishap?

First. Because I left extra early and was nearly always the first one to arrive!

Flattery. I'm far too modest to dwell long on flattery. But the saying, 'Flattery will get you nowhere,' is a lie, certainly in our business. I love it!

G is for: Gwyneth. Graft. Grumble. Guest. Guarantee. Gobbledegook. *Going Live*.

Gwyneth. Dear Gwyneth Powell who played the Headmistress, of course. She had the other Starbum dressing room of the two our series was allotted at Elstree. Gwyneth is a very intelligent, lovely lady. She's also a simply marvellous actorbum and in my opinion she certainly spent rather too long in the programme. She needed new challenges. After all, she'd been there quite a time when I joined, and stayed on after I left. But maybe she knew something that I didn't know. 'GH' is being repeated on Sunday mornings. (More dosh!) They started with the very first episode and the response was good, so they continued. They've already got to Gwyneth. Will they get to me?...YES!

Graft (as in Working Hard, so this is really an addition to E for Effort!). My God, though, there was some hard grafting done on the programme, from everyone. I don't want to give the impression that all the kids were wonderful, all of the time. Children can get bored very easily. But my maxim has always been that the actorbum must be worthy of his hire. Once he accepts the job it doesn't matter a monkey's whether he is two or 102. Age is only a state of mind. And I wish I could have even a penny for every time some very small, rather scruffy, person has come up to me in the rehearsal room and said, 'Michael, can we go through that scene again and then run some lines?' They wanted to get it right, and I'd be a very rich man! (Only lads are scruffy of course, the lasses were always beautifully turned out.)

Grumble. Is what I never heard any performer, large or small, do.

Guest. My children, my next-door-neighbours, even my bank manager and my accountant, all visited the location to watch us filming and were made very welcome.

Guarantee. I've mentioned that I only agreed to do one series of 'GH' to start with, but you had to commit yourself to the next one six months before it was due to start, in the summer of the previous year. But having said yes, it was great to have that guarantee. To know that you had work lined up for a whole year and a half. Even I hadn't experienced that kind of security before.

Gobbledegook. It only happened to me once! We were filming a scene in which two of the very smallest actors were being reprimanded by Bronson. We started the take and all went quite nicely according to plan - until we finished. It was then pointed out that we had been playing the lines from another episode, albeit a very similar scene. It wasn't really our fault - well yes, of course it was. But it was the end of a particularly tiring week, we were doing scenes from three different episodes that day, and something from a previous block of episodes which had been left in abeyance until we had the set. But I'm ashamed all the same and it never happened again. But even once is too many.

Going Live. Twice. Do you remember the BBC Saturday morning show for kids? The first time I appeared on it we had great fun. I took part in a quiz. If I got a question wrong I had to perform strange tasks, like catching floppy jellies in a net, or jumping, blindfold, over a tub of yellowish green gunk. My second visit to the show was rather sad. I'd just finished recording my very last episode of *Grange Hill* and I was invited to take part in the chat part of *Going Live*, to tell everybody how I felt. Although

I was excitedly looking to the future, and my agent already had a film and two tellies lined up, at that precise moment I felt completely gutted.

H is for: High Road. Hotel. Haversack. Homework. Headmaster.

'High Road'. Not 'to China', but *Take the High Road*. I have to tell you about this one because I don't know how I managed it! On 'GH' we used to work from April to December, with a six-week turn around. In other words, we'd take six weeks to rehearse, film, and do the studio work for a block of four episodes. Such a six-week, four-episode period would be used thus: We'd rehearse in a rehearsal room, with bits of tape on the floor to indicate the edge of a room, or the side of a car even, for the first two weeks, then we'd go out to one of the closed-down schools, or the studio, or wherever, and film and video the four episodes for the remaining four weeks.

Now, I've mentioned that as often as not I was fortunate enough to be offered other work during our breaks, particularly during our free time at the start of the year, during January, February and March - one of the Hitler films and the Himmler were done then - but this time we're concerned with the 'GH' six week summer break. A very dear, and long-lasted director friend of mine offered me an eleven week stint on the series *Take the High Road*. Trouble was that the engagement started three weeks before our summer break on 'GH' began (in the middle of our filming schedule for the previous set of four episodes), and ended two weeks after our summer break finished (after the end of the rehearsal period for the next set of four episodes). What could I do? I very much wanted to do *Take the High Road*, but I couldn't ask for that amount of time off, even as a very great favour. But I reckoned without the help of my very old and dear director chum Fiona Cumming, who was now the producer of *Take the High Road*. (Not old in years you understand, just old in acquaintance and affection.) Fiona rang the producer of *Grange Hill* and together they worked out a schedule whereby I could do both.

Take the High Road was made in Scotland, by Scottish Television of course, and they worked things differently there. They still recorded their episodes in blocks, but they'd film all their outside stuff first. After that they'd go into the rehearsal room, rehearse the interiors, and then videotape them in the studio. So for the first three weeks of my dual engagement I travelled up to Glasgow - by train because I hate flying - on a Sunday, and I filmed *Take the High Road* on Monday, Tuesday, and Wednesday. Then I trained it back to London on the Wednesday evening, and recorded *Grange Hill* on Thursday and Friday. I'd have Saturday at home, then the whole thing would start again on Sunday. When the 'GH' summer break started I moved up to stay in Glasgow, and we rehearsed and did the studio stuff for *Take the High Road*. But this period didn't finish of course until the next block of 'GH' had begun, indeed until the end of the rehearsal time, so I missed all the 'GH' rehearsal, and returned only just in time to begin filming. Although I had detailed plans of what the 'GH' director intended and had studied them and my lines on those long train journeys, and although everything went very smoothly, I would not recommend doing two shows at the same time. Even if you're lucky enough to find a Fiona who can make it work. My fellow actors on 'GH', both large and small, were very kind, and happy that I was doing *Take the High Road*, but it must have been tremendously difficult for them not having me there for rehearsals.

Perhaps, though, I had shown that I was conscientious. Apart from the time off to do *Take the High Road*, I never missed a call, or was even late for rehearsal, during the whole time I worked on *Grange Hill*. Even when the snow was so thick that there was only one slippery lane open on the motorway, I made it, one of only two who did. Perhaps that was why they bent over backwards to enable me do *Take the High Road*. A sort of thank-you for setting a good example. I certainly didn't see it like that at the time, it was simply my job and I loved doing it. I was over the moon that I had somewhere exciting to go each morning. But I very much appreciate that I was appreciated...

I've just remembered another one! Dear Fiona had worked a similar miracle when I was about to return, again to Glasgow, to do the the second half of the lovely *Maggie* series.

It was summer then and, prior to my return, the Sheards were on holiday. Again we were under canvas, on the dear old Isle of Wight. This time we'd chosen a pitch near Brook, on the South West side of the Island, the side which has a habit of falling into the sea - the Back of the Wight, the Wild West Wight! It was miles from anywhere. The only public phone box was in Chale, way down the Military Road, not far from Blackgang.

But thank God for it. I'd known of course that there was a possibility of fitting in a 'Dr Who', (*Castrovalva*), before I returned to Glasgow, but we'd had to start our holiday before everything had been finalised. Every day I rang my agent from that phone box in Chale and in the end, bingo, Fiona worked that first miracle. She even got the 'Dr Who' office to pay for my flight to the Highlands so that I'd be in time for the *Maggie* filming. What a gal.

Hotel. In addition to the BBC studios, Elstree village also has a vast film studio complex just across the road from Auntie, and MGM used to have a studio on the other side of the roundabout (a huge white building it was; now, alas, I believe it's a cold meat store). But why anyone should want to build studios in such an out of the way backwater as Elstree in the first place, beats me. Well, no, I suppose it doesn't really!

When ours was built - the first film studio in the country, remember - the railway line had not long been laid to that part of Hertfordshire. I guess it was also cost, and the fact that everywhere would have been so quiet. And with all the lovely open coutryside providing excellent locations, it must have seemed ideal. And it probably was, then. Nowadays, the traffic alone, either speeding north, or back into London, or simply clogging the now heavily built-up neighborhood, is frightful. That's another reason why I used to arrive very early. The distance between my home in Surrey and the studio was certainly my main concern - time had to be allowed for a puncture, or whatever - but the hold-ups due to traffic jams could be horrendous. So sometimes, when we'd worked a very long day, and when I had a particularly heavy schedule on the morrow, I used to escape the traffic torrent and stay in a very nice hotel, two minutes from the studio. (Thirty quid B&B en suite.)

Haversack. In one of my later episodes, Bronson gave a lecture, entirely in French. That was pretty hairy, to be sure. But to illustrate my subject - 'A Walk in the Alps from Yesteryear', or something similar - I used lantern slides. This meant that the hall had to be in semi-darkness, and I could refer to my notes if I needed to, without being seen! It's the only time that I had anything written down in case I fluffed. But be fair, the whole thing was in a language that was completely foreign to me. The lantern slides featured Mr Bronson on a walking holiday some twenty years previously, complete with old fashioned baggy shorts and stout boots; safari jacket, walking-stick and haversack. I greatly enjoyed being rejuvenated by the make-up department for those slides.

Homework. How the younger actors could possibly manage to: travel miles from their homes to the studio and back each day; learn their lines; think about the next day's work; eat; relax and watch a bit of telly, perhaps; play; sleep; AND do their schoolwork, particularly their homework, beats me. But they did. Those who wanted to found the time somehow. Off the top of my head, both John Holmes (Gonch), and Jonathan Lambeth (Danny), went up to University and obtained very good degrees, and several others continued into further education. I'm utterly gob-smacked by the energy and application they showed.

Headmaster. I'm often asked if Mr B. would have liked to be Grange Hill's Headmaster. Mr B. would have loved it. Indeed, when he was appointed to the deputy headship, he allowed himself to believe that it was only a matter of time. Actorbum 40307, however, would most certainly not have been delighted if a promotion to head had been envisaged. I built a lot of the character around the fact that Bronson was continually hoping, yearning almost. If he'd been asked, he'd have said that, unquestionably, he was the very best man for the job. That he deserved it, that it was his due. And yes, if it had happened (against my wishes), Bronson would have been a great headmaster. I'd have seen to that!

I is for: Income. Isle of Wight. Ideas. Improvement. Infatuation.

Income. Some other actor - George Cole as Arthur Daley in *Minder* to be exact - used to describe his work as 'a nice little earner'. *Grange Hill* was nice. Although the fee per episode was no different from that paid on any other series of similar length, we were also paid a retainer during the six week summer break, and the really big bonus was that the series, shown for the first time at the start of a year, was repeated at the same year's end. We received a little something for that too. I've already mentioned that the children, certainly before they were sixteen, did not get very much. In the eyes of the law at least - see under L for law - they were considered to be minors, and were paid what amounted to pocket money. I suppose I understand, although I feel bound to add that I think the labourer should be worth his hire. Whatever his size.

Isle of Wight. In my last series, Grange Hill school went on a field trip to my lovely Island of Wight, supposedly during half term. Now, it is just possible that I'd told someone, sometime, that the Isle of Wight would make a smashing location, and it's also just within the realms of possibility that I had mentioned to our producer that I had a little holiday place in Sandown and that if he was on a location recce, well, he might like to save his hotel bill and rest his head with us. But I'd forgotten all about it - honestly! When I received the scripts and saw that Bronson was to be in charge of this school trip to the IOW, it came as a complete surprise.

We all had a super time, both those of us who were involved with the show, and my family. Bronson took his dress cue from that 'Walk in the Alps' lecture and sported floppy shorts and safari jacket again. We filmed in Bonchurch, a delightfully tiny village near Ventnor, and on the seashore midway between Sandown and Bembridge.

At our IW home Dearly B. has three cacti called Watson, Bull and Porter. She and I bought our Island homes (holiday flat and wee house) from the Island estate agent of that name and I filmed a couple of scenes in their Bembridge office. (Bronson was thinking about the future and wondered if the Island might be a worthy place for his retirement.)

I filmed during the day with the crew and in the evenings, instead of joining everyone in the location hotel (the Cliff Tops in Shanklin), which I normally greatly enjoy, I enjoyed myself even more by returning to my own little nest in Sandown and Dearly B. and our youngest. The subsistence, which you are given when you're working away from home to pay for your hotel and other expenses, paid for us to have a cost free holiday on this occasion. Quite legitimately I assure you. I wasn't required to give the money back - as long as I presented myself for work each morning. And I did, and I worked extra hard!

Ideas. We older thesps were expected to suggest ways in which a scene might be improved, but when we reached an impasse during rehearsal and couldn't seem to find a way round the problem, I used to be particularly delighted when one of the younger professionals would pipe up, 'I've been thinking, and I've got an idea which might help us with our problem.' It often did, too.

Improvement. I talked earlier about the few kids who were not that hot, and how we all rallied round to help. Very often the improvement was quite marked, as it also was with the odd tiny one who was just starting and was a bit of a dud. This acting wasn't instinctive. The improvers just worked damn hard.

Infatuation. Oh yes, as they grew towards the top of the school, love's young dream blossomed, and many a friendship developed. It was nice to see a lad, who last year had been a scruffy thespian, turn up for the next series looking all clean and neat and, forgetting his mates entirely, anxious only to do his lady's bidding. 'Please, can I carry your script for you?' At least one such couple are still together, and the last I heard, wedding bells were about to chime. Super.

J is for: Jonathan. Jonathan's March. Janitor. Jitters.

Jonathan. Jonathan Lambeth. I couldn't let him get away without a mention. Those of you who remember the life and times of Maurice Bronson, will know that Bronson had an on-going duel with a loner called Danny. Jon played Danny and played him exceedingly well. I'm full almost to bursting with memories of all the hundreds of great scenes I had during my five years in the series, and one horrendous row Bronson had with Danny comes to mind. It was in fact near the end for both of us, as shortly thereafter, Danny was found dead in Bronson's car, and

Bronson announced his early retirement. Don't misunderstand me, by the way, Maurice hadn't killed him. But it was the last straw. He'd simply had enough. There was never even a suggestion that Mr Bronson was anything but upright, honest and manly. Indeed, another facet of his persona was that, in spite of his personality, his presence and his commanding voice, he had never even touched, let alone smacked, a pupil, in all his years of teaching.

Jonathan's March. I know that Rupert, my youngest, won't let J pass without I tell you about The March. After one of our summer breaks, Jon mentioned that he'd had a great time walking the South Downs Way with one of his school chums. (Proper school that is, not GH. Jon was one of the very few who still went to his old school and was not tutored at the studio; he used to bring his school work in with him.) I showed polite interest in his South Downs walk, said that I'd always had an ambition to do the Pennine Way, and thought no more about it. Then just before Christmas of that year, Jon came bounding up to me. 'OK, Michael, it's all arranged for next Summer!'

I'd like to say that I walked the whole of the Pennine Way, but this is an honest book. Rupert and I joined Jon and his school friend for a week of trekking. Up hill and down dale, from Cumbria into Scotland, eighteen flipping miles a day. I didn't know I had it in me. Jon of course did the whole thing, he walked all the Way! All those hundreds of boggy, soggy, craggy miles. Well, nearly all. He was quite honest about it, he admitted that, before we joined them, they did get a lift for about two and two-tenths miles at one point. Mind you the rain was pelting down, they were completely bushed, it was very late, and they only had a short time to get to the Youth Hostel and book in. So there was every justification for accepting a lift. It most certainly didn't count against them. But when we returned to civilisation, I had a tee shirt printed which said very proudly on the front, in big red letters, 'I Walked Part of the Pennine Way'. On the back it proclaimed, in letters that were only slightly smaller, 'And So Did Jon!' I wore it to rehearsals when we started up again after the summer break. Rotten thing for me to do wasn't it?

I'm pleased to say that Jon has kept in touch, and he swears that one day he will go back to that two and two-tenths miles and walk it. Rupert and I say that when he does we'll eat the shirt!

Janitor. The Grange Hill janitor or caretaker. Played by George A. Cooper, whom I'd known for years in many a great film and TV part. (As I write I remember him in a red wig being super in *Tom Jones*.) George had further to travel to the studios than any of us, but said he loved the drive.

Jitters. Somewhere in the previous pages, I've talked about butterflies, and how essential I think they are for a tip top performance. I must now amend the statement a little. Controlled jitters are very necessary for taller thespians, but smaller ones don't seem to need them at all. They don't require them in order to turn in a great performance. It's that natural instinct of course. I'm still trying to decide when the change to butterflies takes place. For the lads I suspect it's when they start to worry about other things, like how best to impress the girls. And the lasses, well, perhaps it's when they just can't think what to wear on that special first date!

K is for: Karen.

Karen. Karen Gillett, my number one fan. I've already mentioned her briefly. I think every actor should be lucky enough to have a number one fan like Karen. We've never met, but I can always count on Karen's continued letters of interest, support, and delight at my achievements. Karen was very appreciative and encouraging regarding *Grange Hill*, and we corresponded many times concerning it. She always sends me a birthday card - how she found out when my birthday is I'll never know, I think she did once ask me my birth sign and she must have worked it out from that - and every Christmas, without fail, I receive a most wonderful calendar from her, which stays throughout the year on my desk.

Fans of course come and go, but I'm very lucky in that I have one constant pen pal. It really does give one a sense of continuity, and even more important, the knowledge that there is at least one member of the public who cares is invaluable. And I'm not joking. I'm not the only thesp I know who is fortunate enough to have a special fan. (My Headmistress at 'GH', for example. Gwyneth used to receive much appreciated large parcels.) It gives you hope on a wet and rainy day, when you've no wood for the fire, the phone's not ringing, and you're OOW, to know that at least there's one person 'who luvs ya baby - thinks you're great!'

Karen must have been a baby when she first wrote to me, for she's still only a young lass. She's married now and seems to have suddenly inherited a ginormously huge family. But I'm delighted and grateful to say that she still finds time to write to 40307.

L is for: Law. Lights. Leadership. Linesman. Limitation.

Law. 'The Law Regarding Children in the Entertainment Business' I believe the book is called, and a very excellent and necessary document it is. It lays down how many hours a child may work in a given day, and indeed how many days in a year. That's why a show like *Oliver* will have more than one children's cast during a long run, three sometimes, and why on 'GH', the production office, having got their sums wrong on one occasion, had to stop one of the little lads from working for a while and give his lines to another. We never used to start rehearsals with the kids until after lunch, and filming days were very strictly monitored, for this (hours worked) reason. In fact the children were only allowed to film for fairly short periods, before being whisked back to their Green Room for lessons or play. Their employer, in this case of course Auntie BBC, had to obtain a licence from the local authority for every child, and these were never granted until said child had had a medical. The law also says that a child must have a tutor during term time, unless special arrangements have been made with their school, and a chaperon all the time.

The only occasion when the law falls short in my opinion, (apart from pay), is when the child reaches the age of sixteen. Suddenly he or she is an adult in the eyes of the law. No more lifts to the studios, no restrictions at all. There has to be a cut off point of course, but I wonder if it couldn't be more gradual. That's why the chaperons on *Grange Hill* were so good. They gave their support wherever it was needed, regardless of age.

Lights. Very hot. Particularly when the daylight is fading and has to be boosted. Bright lights in the studio too, and making sure that my glasses don't reflect them into the camera lens. That's one of the reasons why you always have a run-through in front of the cameras before you film. It's not only so the director can check on his shots and the performances of the actors, it's also for the crew, who will all be looking at their various areas of responsibility. The camera operator - he, or she, who actually has their eye to the viewfinder - is the person who will make sure that anything, like a pair of glasses, that could glint or glisten, doesn't.

Leadership. In an ordinary school, if a child is particularly brainy, and therefore good at their studies, they will more than likely be teased, or at the very least they'll be isolated and have to spend a lot of time on their own. Their classmates tend not to understand one of their number who has an over abundance of grey matter. In our school it was totally different. Those Grange Hillites who were the best were looked up to by the rest. Their leadership and inspiration was thus of great value to the production.

Linesman. There was a football match between Grange Hill and some deadly rival school. They needed a linesman, but the part was so minor that the producer and director decided to cut it. I pointed out that I was not due to work on the day scheduled for filming the match, it would be a shame not to have a linesman, and that Bronson would be very pleased to offer his services. I felt it was just the sort of supportive thing Mr B. would do, particularly as he'd already shown an interest in sport. Some people, perhaps, thought I was taking things a bit far by giving up my day off to run up and down a football pitch, but it afforded me a chance to show yet another facet of Maurice's character. My youngest, who is very knowledgeable on the subject, provided me with some great footballish lines to complete the picture.

Limitation. No child can be expected to have learnt technique. Why should they? They were naturals. They didn't need to know how to surmount an acting problem. But even the most gifted of our smaller instinctively natural thesps had their limitations. And a problem could come out of the blue very suddenly.

One of the best 'GH' child actors had what was a perfectly simple line in a scene with me one day. It went: 'I know you do, Sir.' Try it youself, it's not difficult. But the director on this occasion wanted the the word 'you' emphasised, and the poor lad couldn't get it. He hit 'know' and 'do' and it wasn't right, and when he stressed 'Sir', he began to sound so like the very occasional dud child we'd experienced, that we all felt it was better for him to say the line as he felt it. But now the boy was thinking about the darn line, so even that proved almost impossible. This excellent child actor was at the natural/thinking cross roads. He was never the excellent instinctive performer again. He had to go away and learn how to do what was required with technique, and then make it look and sound natural. And he had to tame a new blessed annoyance - butterflies!

M is for: Make-up. Magazine. Megaphone. Marathon. Music.

Make-up. Particularly toupee in my case. A lot of my first series of 'GH' revolved around the fact that Mr Bronson wore a wig. Or did he? In the end Gonch and Hollo grabbed it and all was revealed.

But how do you get a toupee to look like a toupee on the screen? How do you let the viewer see that it is a bad match with your own hair? Believe me, it is definitely no easy thing to do. The Make-up Supervisor and I spent a day trying different toups until we found one that we hoped would work. The problem was that in the camera tests we'd done thus far, the camera which never lies had lied even more than usual and made the toups look good. I'm sure you've found that even holiday snaps have come out making a place look far better than you remember. And how many times, when you're watching a cricket match, or golf tournament on TV, have you heard the commentator say, 'I'm afraid it's really getting very dark here now,' when the picture on the screen looks fine. It's that lying camera again. When we looked at the final choice of toup, we could hardly believe it. It was ghastly, like a bit of old doormat. But on screen it looked what it was supposed to be, a faintly-obvious ill-fitting carpet!

Magazine. I've given masses of interviews throughout my career and during my time on 'GH' the number must have more than doubled. There was even a Grange Hill magazine for a while and I appeared on the cover of one issue, and in the comic strip (as Mr B., not 40307!). And there's the 'GH' annual of course. Sixth sense warns you to think before you speak at an interview, but it mostly makes no difference. At the end of the day, they'll print what the hell they like!

Megaphone. 'Stand by...and ACTION!' Nowadays, if you are due to drive you car into a scene and you're way round the corner out of sight, then you'll have a walkie-talkie beside you and the order to start will come through that. Or there'll be a director's assistant in your eye-line who will wave you forward. But when there are a hundred of you, on a football pitch for instance, the dear old megaphone still comes into its own. It was in use long before the w-ts came on the scene and it never fails.

Marathon. I was challenged to do the London Marathon one year. A group of the kids wanted to raise money for Children In Need. Thank heavens we did something else instead! As part of my contribution, I entered a contest with the then children's programmes linkman, Andy Crane, to see which of us was the nastiest and should be dunked in the gunk tank. I joined Andy in his broom cupboard - one fixed camera in a minute table-sized room - and, live on air, we mockingly insulted each other. I commanded the viewers to vote for Andy, he implored them to vote for me. I won, Crane was dunked. Quite right too, he was far nastier than I!

Music. The theme music for *Grange Hill*, and the incidental music based on that theme, is splendid. I have to admit, however, to a preference for the arrangement used during my time. For me, anyway, it was more in keeping with the spirit of the programme.

N is for: Never.

Never. Never again will I do a job which ties me up for such a long time. I would not have missed *Grange Hill* for all the tea bags in China, I'm sure you appreciate that, but it has to be said that it did take five years out of my life and career. And although I was lucky enough to do some other good work during our breaks, there was a hell of a lot that

I was offered which I could not do. I don't regret anything because I loved 'GH', but...only once!

O is for: Outside Broadcast. Over-expose. Overstay. Organisation.

Outside Broadcast. Now I must come clean. I have used words like 'filmed' when I've been talking about 'GH', and phrases such as 'in the studio'. But the fact is that *Grange Hill* was an OB, there was almost no filming done at all. And from the moment we entered Elstree Studios, Borehamwood, Herts, for my second series, everything, every blessed thing, was videoed outside of studio control. 'GH' ceased to be a studio show at all and became an Outside Broadcast, just like a football match. This meant that the director and his assistant, and the producer and the vision mixer, had to squeeze into a scanner - a tiny room in the back of a lorry.

All our sound men and the camera crew were OB, and were normally to be found at the football, or tennis, or the London Marathon, and they tremendously enjoyed doing our show. Indeed 'GH', mainly I guess because it was so different from their norm, was so popular that the guys even had a roster to make sure they didn't miss their turn. That's certainly a reason why their work was so good. And perhaps it was also partly because, as OB people, they were used to doing stuff where they got no second chance. I can't remember one single occasion when we'd done a scene and had to 'go again' just because the camera, or sound, had fouled up.

Why did we have to do 'GH' as an OB? Well, when Auntie Beeb bought Elstree Studios, the whole place had to be refurbished, and that took a long time. We could use the studios, but only the floor space, we couldn't use the studio gallery - a sort of large observation room upstairs which looks out over the studio floor. This room is normally full of recording equipment and monitors and the like, and it's from here that studio-based programmes are run. But everything at Elstree had passed its sell-by date many years before and it all had to be renewed. I wonder if that's why Auntie was able to buy the place for a reported song!

Over-expose. This is a difficult one. Once you've committed yourself to a long-running series and the money starts rolling in, it is very hard to throw that security away and give it all up. Some of the adult thesps had a heck of a time when they left 'GH', because they had been over-exposed in their part. I was lucky, I had an established career to come back to, but I still found it easier to find good work in Germany for a while, and do voice-overs. I reckon that I probably...

Overstay. Overstayed my time in *Grange Hill* by two years, if truth be told. But, as I said under N for Never, I don't regret it one tiny bit, but I'll not do its like again. Indeed, that's why I didn't stay longer in *Coronation Street*, which, if you recall, I did very soon after I left 'GH'.

Organisation. It still amazes me how any production, let alone an on-going, multi-episodic series, ever reaches the screen. The logistics alone are enormous. It's all done by delegating of course. The BBC delegates to its Children's Department. Children's delegates to its chosen producer, who then hires the directors. They will mostly come from the department, but he still appoints them. (Each series of 'GH' comprised about twenty episodes, and there were usually three directors - one would do three blocks of four episodes, the others, one block each. On a few occasions the producer would bring in a fledgling director and make the number up to four - one director would still direct three blocks, two would still do one block each, but the newcomer would direct any odd episodes over the usual twenty - perhaps two singles). The producer will also hire the make-up and costume supervisors, and line up camera crews and sound et al., all from inside the Beeb. Then the floor managers and the production assistants will be brought on board, and the directors will delegate to the floor managers, who will delegate to the production assistants. The make-up and costume supervisiors will hire assistants of their own and delegate, and...onwards and onward, everyone will go.

Almost the last essential ingredient to be contracted will be the actors, large and small. The actors, that is, who will be appearing in the odd episode - the so called non-regulars. Ah well, always save the best till last, eh!

P is for: Pool. Parrot. Parties. Photographs. Personal Management. Parents.

Pool. The kids had a pool table in their Green Room and I was very honoured when they invited me to take part in their Pool Tournament. I came third and it was great fun.

Parrot. In one sequence Bronson appeared with a plaster on his neck and it transpired that he'd been pecked by his sister's parrot. Sometime later we were rehearsing a scene in the OB studio which simply entailed my walking down one of the corridors and turning right. On the final rehearsal, I walked down the corridor, and just as I was about to turn right, this enormous parrot suddenly lunged around the corner at me. Someone had found it in a long-forgotten prop room, and Ed Pugh, our director, had arranged said lunge. Everybody laughed heartily, including me, when I'd recovered my composure. But I got my own back on Ed - now head of Children's Programmes at BBC Scotland - I found a rubber parrot's head in a novelty shop, and a few days later I walked on to the set wearing it, to give a very Bronson-type rebuff to some small actor!

Parties. At the end of each series we had a super party which was paid for by our Auntie Beeb. I enjoyed every one except my last. We always gave a gift to anyone who was leaving, and a cast member made a speech. At my leaving it was tears all round. (But I loved my gift. It was *The Hollywood Story*. A complete and detailed history.)

Photographs. At the beginning of each series there was a photo session. We all dressed up in our character finery, and the resuting photographs, with our names and that of the character we played displayed underneath, were produced by the truckload. Thank heavens, the cost would have been prohibitive otherwise. These snaps were for our use when replying to the ginormous number of fans who wrote to us via the programme - and still do! I'm flattered to say that only last month I had to ask the production office for a new supply.

Personal Management. Better even than A for Agent, is P for Personal Manager. A PM is a super first class, top-of-the-range agent. Someone who does everything for you concerning the business side of the business, and leaves you to concentrate totally on the artistic side. My agent is a Personal Manager.

Parents. I'm a parent, and parents are OK people. But God preserve us from the theatrical parent who comes on to the set and pushes their Johnny or Jenny to the front of the group, when the director has already placed them at the back. 'Don't you bother, Johnny/Jenny, what that geezer says, this is your big chance. Go on, get a lovely close-up.' We most certainly didn't need them, and I cannot remember ever seeing a parent on the *Grange Hill* set. They'd been banned years before I arrived, thank heavens. But I've encountered these creatures many times elsewhere. Their favourite ploy is to get themselves appointed as their child's chaperon. They really are a particularly horrid breed of professional hanger-on. Their offspring can become anxious and extremely embarrassed, which distracts them, and detracts from their work.

Q is for: Questions, Questions, and Questions!

Questions. Probably the most difficult part of my role as a senior actor on *Grange Hill.* All through my time on the programme I was having tellies repeated on the box, together with new shows I'd done during our breaks and old feature films I'd appeared in, and it was quite natural therefore for any child who was due to leave the show - because he or she had got to the top of the school - to ask me what they should do next: 'Michael, how do I get an agent? How do I meet other directors? How do I join Equity (the actor's union)? How do I get into rep; radio; films; commercials? How do I get more work in television?...How do I make it?' These and many, many other questions relating to the business I found very difficult. Not because I didn't know the answers, but because I don't think one should be too discouraging. If I'd bluntly told them that it's almost impossible, they'd have been very hurt and come back at me with: 'But you did it.' Anyway, I believe very definitely that if you really want to have a go, then you must. So I always tried to be as helpful and encouraging as I could.

You don't have to join Equity now because there's no longer a closed shop (but if you do get the chance, then you certainly must; they'll look out for you re: fees, the law, etc), but back then, if a child had been invited to stay on and do the sixth form at *Grange Hill*, they were lucky. They'd be eighteen or so by the time they left and would probably get their full Equity card straight away. If there was to be no sixth form, then it meant they would have to do a required number of engagements before they could apply to join the union, and that wasn't easy, because you couldn't get a job unless you had a card. Sort of a Catch 22 situation. But those children who really wanted to make the transition managed it. One way was to get other child parts, another to do circus work, or fringe theatre, and so on. I used to suggest too, that they went along and talked about the business in general and agents in particular to the people at the *Spotlight*. The *Spotlight* publishes, among other useful books about the business, the actorbum's register, in which we all have our photograph and our agent's name and telephone number. I also recommended that they have some good photographs done (definitely none of your holiday snapshot stuff), and write to the repertory companies. Indeed I stressed that they should write to everyone; to write and write and write...!

R is for: Redmond. Responsibility. Reappear. Regular. Retainer. Room. Radio. Research.

Redmond. Phil. I've never met him. I'd like to have done. Because, without him, there would never have been a 'GH'. It was his brain child and I thank him for it.

Responsibility. I certainly don't mean that one had to be over-protective of the smaller actors, but there had to be a degree of unobtrusive watchfulness, if only because we taller thesps had been around a bit longer. If we were filming in a street for example, and the assistants and the chaperons were occupied elsewhere, the director was in the scanner, and you were the only - OK, I'll use the word just once - adult around, then it was quite rightly expected that you would do your best to make sure that someone littler than you didn't do anything daft, like run into the road. It goes without saying, too, that a taller actor will try to set an example - if one should ever be needed - by knowing his lines and his moves, and how the scene should be played. But of course he should always do that wherever he's working. Be it 'GH', or a big feature filled with starbums, like *Escape to Athena* or *Green Ice*, it makes absolutely no difference.

Reappear.

There once was a actor in *Grange Hill*,
Who said, 'I've been offered a Playbill.
I'll come back when it's finished,
My fame won't have diminished'.

So he went - and they wouldn't have him back!

Let it be a warning. There shall be no reappearances. I'll be talking under U about understudies, but it won't hurt to emphasise it here as well. No one, nobody, is indispensable in our business. The chap in the above rhyme, (not me, by the way), went off to do his play, a tour actually, happily thinking that he could return to 'GH', almost whenever he was ready. And it was well meant when he'd been told by the production that he could. But came the grey reality of dawn, some eighteen months later, when he'd finished his play, and he said, 'Here I am, I'm ready. When do I come back?', and he was told, politely, that he couldn't. The Production staff had changed, new storylines had been agreed which didn't include him, and he was surplus to requirement. He wasn't needed any more. Everybody was very nice, but time had simply, I'm afraid, marched on in his absence.

Another lass, who played a young teacher in my first series and was great, decided she didn't want to do any more. She was sadly missed at the time. About three months into the next series she realised what a fool she'd been and started ringing the production office, 'Just to see how you are.' Then she showed up at lunchtime and joined us in the canteen. It took quite a while before she realised that she was no longer being thought of by anyone connected with the production of the programme. Hell hath no fury like a show scorned, eh? In fact no, not a fair criticism. There were no sour grapes as far as I know. It was logistics, that's all. They had to know who they could rely on. Apart from any other consideration, storylines and scripts depended on it.

There are exceptions to the above, of course there are. Off the top of my head, I was asked to go back into *Emmerdale*, and there's a lass who returned to *EastEnders*, but in both those cases, they asked us, we didn't ask them. They needed the characters we played. Also, I've not been talking about time off during actual production - me and *Take the High Road* for instance. That's totally different. It's a favour, granted for loyalty rendered. Perhaps even a carrot! The hope being that if they work things so that you're free to do another something, you will want to stay with your first show for longer.

But when you finally decide to leave, be trebly sure, because it will be final. It won't be possible for you to change your mind later. And quite right, say I. Long-running series are not benevolent societies. They are most certainly not there waiting on our whim, to provide us with a pension. These shows are damn good TV, giving excellent acting opportunities, and must be treated with the same respect and dedication as a tip-topper from Hollywood.

Regular. Think of it. What an opportunity for an actorbum to be offered, the chance to be a regular in a series or serial. If you don't want to do it, fine - I loved this one, but I said I'd never do another. But I know masses of OOW thespians who would give their eye teeth to be a regulars forever. Sometimes, when we were joined by a fellow (tall) bum who had been contracted for one or two episodes of 'GH' to play a parent, or a one-off teacher, you could almost see them thinking, 'Perhaps, if I do really well and they like me, there's a possibility that I'll be asked back to do more.'

It's not jealousy, not of us anyway. Perhaps there's just a touch of envy because of the position we are in, but mainly it's because the true, hard grown, down to his boots actorbum, never loses his yearning to practice his art - to ACT. The money does help too of course!

Retainer. Not to be confused with expenses which were paid to us when working and living away from base, retainers were paid during the summer break. At least they were paid unless we happened to be working on something else, like *Take the High Road*, then we would lose the retainer. And whenever we were offered other work, we had to inform Auntie, even if fitted in with seemingly no problem. We were under contract to the Beeb first of course. But the BBC was very kind, certainly to me, and I really was able to fit lots of other engagements in and around my schedule on 'GH'. And they only overlapped that once, on *Take the High Road*. (There was one time, though, when I finished filming at Elstree at 5.00pm on a Friday and then dashed up to Manchester to appear in an episode of *The Young Ones*, on the Saturday and Sunday - I played a judge who sent Jennifer Saunders to jail - but I was back with Bronson again on Monday morning.)

Room. Green Room, in fact. As mentioned, the younger members of the cast had one, where they let off the odd bit of steam, and where we played that pool competition. We taller people also had a Green Room, until they took it away from us to make a coffee bar. Far better, we hardly used the room anyway.

Radio. There was talk of a radio version of *Grange Hill* - mind you, there was also a feature film in the offing at one time. They did do a 'GH' stage play at some near London rep after I'd left the series. I was asked to take part, but didn't and I wasn't free, anyway!

Research. Ben Rea asked me to play Maurice Bronson at the beginning of February, I thus had about two months to research the part before I started rehearsals. Barry Purchase (see: W for writers), had already helped enormously with the scripts he'd written, which introduced Bronson. I'm usually quick to find empathy with a character, but this time Maurice virtually jumped off the page at me. I had the exquisite job of adding flesh to the already hefty bones, and to this end I read books on teaching, and observed lessons at my kid's school. I soon realised that there are of course as many types of teacher as there are actors, so I decided to build the man first and then make him a teacher. I knew a fair amount about

Bronson's background from Barry's scripts, which he'd based on original storyline ideas and suggestions given to him by Phil Redmond and the production department. The rest came from my own feelings, imagination and instinct and I anchored the whole lot on Mr Porter! Mr Porter was a teacher at my children's middle school. He was strict; very, very strict. He used to throw bits of chalk at any child who was not paying attention. He demanded the best and received it. All the children said that they hated Mr Porter. But the moment they left their middle school, to progress to the secondary school where they would prepare for their GCSE exams, they realised what a debt of gratitude they owed him. Nowadays Mr Porter is remembered with a deal of affection. I'm sure by all, certainly by my three.

S is for: Smith. Sullivan. School. Stunt. Security. Scenery.

Smith. John Smith. One of the 'GH' directors. John started his directorial career on the programme. He was also the guy in charge when I was in Scotland doing *Take the High Road*, and thus had to manage without me for the rehearsal period. I hope his talent has propelled him further, it certainly should have done.

Sullivan. One of our two white cats. Dearly B. and I have a Gilbert to go with him. There was this little scene in one of the episodes. It was simply a shot of Bronson walking along a corridor and having a quick word with someone. It was frankly naff, a filler scene which had no connection with anything else in the episode. So I suggested that dear old Bronson should be on his way to a 'How they Used to Live' class. I had two of the tiniest first years with me, and we were carrying lots of things that you would have found in a house in 1900, including of course a pudditat. And Sullivan gave the best performance that day. He was smashing.

School. Three cheers for it!

Stunt. I was involved in only two sequences which could remotely be termed stunts during my whole time on the programme. The first was when Bronson cannoned into a couple of girls and lost his toupee, and in the second, another girl, riding her moped for the first time, knocked Mr B. off his bike. I choreographed both of these mammoth and intricate displays. I'm sure that I was asked to do them because of my honorary membership of the Stuntmanbums union, acquired on Rhodes whilst we were making *Escape to Athena*!

The first was very easy, simply a question of making sure that the two lasses lightly bumped my arms as they rushed passed, and allowed me to do the rest - fall and sprawl over. And land with my head down, so that the hair piece, which for this one shot had not been securely battened down with glue, was able to pop off my balding pate.

The second stunt was similar in fact to the first, except that this time of course we were on wheels. It therefore required a bit more rehearsal and precision. I arranged that Mr B. would be about to turn right - his right hand would thus be outstretched - just as the girl on her moped came up behind him. As she reached me, peeping her pathetic little horn the while, her helmeted head hit (touched!) my extended hand. I then did the rest. I wobbled forward and fell off with realistic Bronson aplomb. No one was hurt in either exercise. My adopted union would have been proud of me.

Security. Security at the BBC Television Centre is of course very strict. Most of the men on the gate are great, however, and understand that when you're coming in to record a show, you must be passed through with speed and no fuss. But one or two have had a 'more than my job's worth' attitude on occasion, and this has made things very difficult. Some years ago, before the new News wing was built at the Centre and parking was still possible within the complex, I arrived to record a show to find a colleague arguing heatedly with the gateman. 'If that's your attitude and you won't let me in, here are the keys to my car. Telephone my production office and tell them that you have refused me entry. I'm going to the pub.' And he didn't return until the man finally agreed to apologise. There was quite a furore. The gateman had merely pushed the car to the side somewhere and done no more. Nobody knew where my thesping colleague was. Studio time was lost, and production was held up for a very expensive half hour.

Only a few were as daft as that of course, but even one is too many. The chaps on the gate at Elstree were smashing, and once they recognised you, or your car, simply waved you on.

When we were working away from base, not living away, but filming in one of the recently-abandoned real schools for example, all the equipment, including expensive cameras and the like, used to be left each night. And at the end of our day, just as we were off home, a contingent or two of burly security officers would arrive, with their flasks and sandwiches, to see the night through. One of them said it reminded him of fire watching during the war. It reminded me of the time I guarded Halfpenny Green airfield from the Martians, during my RAFing days.

Scenery. I've explained that we had a permanent classroom complex set up in an otherwise useless studio, and thus had to do everything as an Outside Broadcast. Well one room, the scene dock, which led off the studio, could still be functional. Scenery would arrive by truck in 'flat' form, having been constructed and roughly painted to order elsewhere, and would be off-loaded into the scene dock. It would then be 'built' on the studio floor - a three walled classroom let's say - the fourth wall being left open for cameras and sound etc., of course. The painters would paint out the joins and put in other finishing touches, under the direction of the d esigner, who would also supervise the dressing of the set, with desks and chairs and pictures and blackboards and fixtures and fittings. Then we'd move in and really start working!

T is for: Transmission. Timekeeping. Traffic and Tiredness.

Transmission. Transmission times were important in a number of ways. The time the programme went out had abolutely nothing to do with us, directors and crew included. That was the sole responsibility of the department, with perhaps the odd word from our producer. But if 'GH' was transmitted too early - say 3.30 in the afternoon - its main audience would not have returned from school. 5.30pm would be too late, because the main audience would by then be into their homework, or any number of other diverting distractions.

The actual, 4.30ish, transmission time was better for the taller actors. Indeed there are a goodly number (I am one who certainly took it into consideration), who stayed in the show for longer than they might have done because of it. The exposure is much greater at 8.00pm for example (the *EastEnders* time), and the work opportunities, after leaving the programme, are therefore less. That's the theory anyway, born out by many instances. There are the exceptions, too. Dirty Den from *EastEnders* never stops, and then there's that Yorkshire copper played by Mr Nick Berry!

Timekeeping. The timekeeping was exceptional. I don't mean the regularity with which we all arrived, I'm talking now about the six-week schedule for each block of four episodes. We had the two weeks to rehearse, and we then had to get those four episodes in the can during the four weeks allotted for the OB. There were no exceptions. If a director, as did happen on occasion, got behind with the day's work, he or she was allowed perhaps two extended days to catch up, but that was all. (An extended day is one when you go on filming after the normal wrap time. It's hellish expensive, with extra money being dished out almost like confetti. That's why each hour, and the confetti paid, is divided into quarters.) One *Grange Hill* director, who was in fact very creative, but who couldn't get back on schedule and overran the four weeks OB time, was not seen on the next series.

Don't misunderstand me, Auntie B. was not being ruthless just for the sake of it. There was enough time in those four weeks to record four episodes, and if someone said it couldn't be done, then they should perhaps be working elsewhere, where the pressure was nil and they didn't have to organise anything. For that's what it was all about, there was ample time if, secondly, the director organised his team properly, and, first and foremost, her or himself!

Traffic and Tiredness. Doing the series at Elstree was fine once you arrived. But it's not an easy place to get to, and if you live in the wilds, as I do, it's even more difficult. No complaints mind, absolutely none. If I choose to live in the glorious countryside, then it's up to me to get myself to wherever I'm required. But over 500 miles a week up and down the M25 can, I admit, be just a smidgin on the tiring side. Particularly at the end of a long day in the studio in December, when it's pitch black even before you start for home.

U is for: Understudy. Uniform. Unscripted. Upstage.

Understudy. In fact, of course, we had none. This wasn't the theatre. But (as I told you happened) when one of the lads was found to be over his permitted number of licence days and his lines were given to another, there was also the very rare occasion when one of the children was sick on a recording day. If possible the scene was re-scheduled, but if this couldn't be done for some reason, then the sick one's lines were given to someone else. Only once, in the whole time I was there, did one of the tall actorbums miss a recording day. He had had an altercation with a burglar, and his cheek was split from ear to mouth. But even he was back in a couple of days. (He recorded his scenes with only the unmarked side of his face on view.) Nobody in this business is indispensable and I do mean nobody. There are many cases of even big name starbums being replaced, by other big names. Thank God for health.

Uniform. I've talked of frocks and costume in general, but I've just received a fan letter which quite correctly refers to Mr Bronson's uniform. For that indeed is what evolved over the years: Crisp, stiff-collared shirt; cuffs, with cuff links depicting one's Alma Mater; bow tie; immaculately pressed suit, with waistcoat where possible; shoes, brightly polished; and of course, blue pencil, protuding no more that two inches from the breast pocket. SIR!

Unscripted. We all got to know our characters extremely well. When we were OBing the show, and the director needed some unscripted lines to cover a car's arrival or whatever, he only had to ask any of us to say something in character and it happened: 'Follow me'; 'You Boy'; 'That Girl'; 'Detention'; 'Walk'; 'Report to me'; 'Come here' - just a few of the Bronsonisms which filled the odd hole in the action.

Upstage. A very naughty thing to do. Never hold back during a tracking shot so that you are in full shot and your companion has to turn his or her head sideways. Never distract the attention away from the speaker, either by coughing, or sneezing, or rustling paper, or, indeed, doing anything which will detract from their performance. Never deliberately sneak into the back of someone else's shot. Never pause too long between your lines, particularly when you are in close-up and the pause will be almost impossible to edit out. Never embrace someone so that their head is off camera. Never wait just too long before making an entrance. Never do anything at all which will, even ever so slightly, pull the audience's attention on to you and detract from the whole. Never, never, never. Unless of course it will help the show, and you are required to do so!

V is for: Voice. Volume. Vacation. Vanity. Vagabond. Viewer.

Voice. As you know, I attended RADA dramabum college and my voice was professionally trained. I've always been good and loud, so there was no need for me to learn how to resonate, but I did need to learn the technique of voice production. I needed to know how to control my voice, and how to make sure that every word I said could still be heard even if I spoke in a whisper. I also needed to learn how to say lines. And this all takes time.

The lion's share of 'GH' kids attended children's acting schools of course so they'd had some voice training. But although this might class me as a dinosaur along with Bronson, I have to say that if anything on our show divided the bigger actors from the smaller, it was the voice. I'm not talking about accents, cockney, as most of the 'GH' lot were, or otherwise, I'm talking about being understood, not speaking too quickly, and what is of paramount importantance, saying the lines naturally. Most of the kids on 'GH' either had a gift for doing this - that's one of the main reasons why they'd been chosen - or they worked hard to achieve it, but some, a very few thank Thespis, didn't. And my heart still sinks when I hear one of them say, 'No I DON'T wanner do TH-AAT. MISS said I COULD go to the OTHER classROOM in THE other builDING.'Oh dear. As old man Shakespeare himself said, 'Speak the speech I pray you as I pronouced it to you, trippingly on the tongue', and naturally!

Volume. And make very sure you have a metaphorical hold on the volume control. Shout when the situation calls for it, by all means, but when you turn the sound down for that whispered scene in the playground, let us hear what you say. The microphones are ultra sensitive, so you can speak very quietly. Don't worry, you'll be heard - provided you don't mumble.

Vacation. I've talked of holidays in the summer and I've talked of free time at the start of the year. But there was a tiddler vacation for most of us, too.

Only a couple of teachers were required to go on the GH school outings, à la the trip to the Isle of Wight. These two episode forays happened every year (one year it was canal boats, another an outward bound course), and although we taller actors greatly enjoyed being included when it was our turn, it was also rather nice to have an extra two week vacation when it was not.

Vanity. It's simply not true that an actor can't bear to pass a mirror without making sure he's still there. Of course it isn't! If you are appearing in front of an audience, and if it gives you confidence to have a quick peek before you start, then fine, quite right, why the hell not? But I did have to smile when, just before we were due to record, the make-up room would be inundated with scruffy little urchins, who would all grab mirrors to make sure that the hair quiff was in place, the acne didn't show, and their scruffy clothes were in order. But vanity? Nah, they were just as scruffy off the set, when the script didn't require it!

Vagabond. Another name used by the first Elizabethans (and Lord Larry), to describe my noble profession. Strolling Players, Rogues, and Vagabonds. I like vagabond. Perhaps I should have used it more throughout these pages. (Insurance companies still think of us as vagabonds and bums. It's hell trying to get a competitive quote, particularly for the car. Indeed, if anyone can suggest where we might enquire, we'd be delighted!)

Viewer. See my notes on you, the viewer, in the Epilogue.

W is for: Writers. Waiting. Weather. Waistline. Walking-stick.

Writers. Of the many writers who worked on the series whilst I was there, Barry Purchase and David Angus deserve special mention. Some of the writers were good, some were very good, a few were not so good, and Barry and David were the best. It's no easy thing writing for a series like 'GH'. Storylines are decided in the summer, almost a year in advance of the actual series which begins shooting the following April. But the writers need that amount of time and more, for these storylines will be in outline form only. It is the writer's job to develop them further and turn them into scripts. As I've said, Barry wrote a great deal of my stuff at the beginning, and when I arrived and made Bronson mine, he seemed to know instinctively the man I was building. David too. David took over later, and he and I are still in partnership today (I came up with an idea for a TV series which David is e'en now developing).

Waiting. Although a very tight ship was run by all concerned, there was still a hell of a lot of waiting around. Always is. It starts with your first call of the day. The production assistants must get you there early, and we understand that. But...I was watching the Badminton horse trials on the box the other day: one horse and rider combination were about to start the cross country section - four and a half miles of gruelling jumps and rough terrain. They were rightly all keyed up and ready for the off, when suddenly, another horse and rider came a cropper out on the course. The two who had been about to start had to wait...and wait, and wait. The rider dismounted, the horse visibly lost its alertness. And when, some twenty minutes later, they were finally given the all clear to start, they had both completely lost their edge, and it took them at least three jumps before they were anything like back to their former competitiveness.

Children in particular can suffer if they're kept waiting too long, and like the horse and its rider, they can lose their sharpness. We all can. The secret is to realise that this will happen as like as not, and to find a way of snapping back. I always tell myself that I might forget my lines. That soon sets me straight!

Weather. *Grange Hill* was no big movie like *Force 10 from Navarone*. It did not have the resources to take out insurance against the weather. 'GH' was a big hearted little television series, and I can never remember our stopping for anything that came out of the skies, or howled across the cold school plains.

Waistline. When I gave up smoking, just before I started my Glasgow commuting to do *Take the High Road*, I weighed twelve and a half stone (around 78 kilos). About right for a chap who's five foot ten inches and a bit tall. But in next to no time I'd started to put on the pounds, and then the stones. I didn't notice it at first. But after a wee while, Bronson's waistcoats started to feel tight, my taste buds came back into their own, food became even more interesting than it had in the past, and I became aware alright! In my last episodes of 'Grange Hill' I took to holding my briefcase, or papers, or anything, in front of my tum. I told myself that it was all in character. Bronson had handed in his resignation and was already allowing himself to relax. That was all perfectly in order. But as soon as I'd finished the show, I gave myself a slap on the wrist, told Dearly Beloved not to give me quite so much pasta, and in no time I was back to my old, slim self.

But take warning. It undoubtedly makes masses of health sense to forsake the weed, but make sure that in doing so you don't substitute another problem. End of lecture!

Walking-stick. George A. Cooper (the 'GH' caretaker), had a special walking-stick which was also a seat. He'd bought it at one of the National Trust's country mansions. In one of my last episodes of 'GH', when my extra poundage was at its height, I sat on the thing and it broke clean in two. I had a heck of a job finding a replacement.

X is for: Xanthippe.

Xanthippe. Well I had to have an X, and this was the only one that remotely fitted. And it does in fact give me an opportunity to pay a wee tribute to Dearly Beloved. With her patience, her understanding, her support, and her love, my wife Rosalind - Ros Sheard the artist - has been an absolute marvel, not only during 'GH', but all the way through my career. Xanthippe was the wife of Socrates and she was a shrewish wife. Ros is absolutely and utterly the complete opposite. And on top of everything, she's a super Mum as well. Our three are a credit to themselves, certainly, but it's their Mother who got them there.

Y is for: Young.

The Young...and the not quite so young actors who worked together so happily on the series. And with such...

Z is for: Zest.

Zest. And if I may borrow a line from *A Christmas Carol* by Charles Dickens, 'God Bless Us, Every One.' There really is No Business Like Show Business. Lord Larry Olivier was right, we may be bums, rogues and vagabonds - but what a simply wonderful, lovely, marvellous, happy thing to be!

I used to say in my curtain speech in rep, 'Ladies, Gentlemen and Children. Thank you for your very kind appreciation of our play tonight. Next week we have a spendid piece for you...'

The second installment of my Memoirs will cover the next thirty years. I'll see you then.

But just before I leave to start my next movie...!

EPILOGUE I

I promised to let you know if our little group gets a production up and running before this book ends. Well, we have one and two bits. I'm already directing Christopher Fry's *A Sleep of Prisoners* for the Edinburgh Festival and video. And I advise anyone who has not read the 'Maxwell' novels by M.J. Trow, to hurry up and do so!

Oh, and Roger, you asked me in your Foreword for THE NOVEL. Well, on top of everything else, the *Day for Death* series of novels has been simmering away for some time, and the first three, *The Piccadilly Run*, *The Promenade Run*, and *The Picture Run*, are now finished. I shall be talking to my publisher about them shortly!

EPILOGUE II

I said during the *Green Ice* pages that I'd say some words about sure fire hits which have failed...

A couple of brothers called Medved wrote an interesting book - *The Fifty Worst Movies of All Time* - in which they suggested that a film called *At Long Last Love* (1975-TCF/ Copa de Oro Peter Bogdanovich), was one of the best things that could have happened to the backers and distributors, (Twentieth Century Fox), because it afforded the company a gigantic tax write-off. The inference being that that was the reason the movie had been made in the first place.

I don't believe it. I cannot accept that anybody actually sets out to make a movie in the hope that it will bomb. *At Long Last Love* had Burt Reynolds, Cybill Shepherd, and songs by Cole Porter, and I'm sure Burt and Cybill didn't expect it would be one of the biggest flops of all time. I'm certain that everyone expected this film would follow on from director Peter Bogdanovich's hugely successful, multi-Oscar-nominated movie, *The Last Picture Show* (1971-Columbia/LPS/BBS), which had been made a couple of years before.

When the studio realised the inevitable, then perhaps they decided to make 'At Long Last' a tax loss. But not before they started shooting for heaven's sake.

And here's another one. *Heaven's Gate* (1980-UA/Michael Cimino) cost between 35 and 50 million dollars and never made back a fraction of its costs at the box office. But those in charge, and supposedly in the know, had given the director, Michael Cimino, a blank cheque and said, 'make what you like, where you like, and take as long as you like. We know it will be a success.' And all because Mr Cimino had recently directed a gigantic hit of a film called *The Deer Hunter* (1978- Universal/EMI).

Daft really isn't it? But there are masses of examples. Before Irwin Allen made those terrific blockbusters, *The Poseiden Adventure* (1972-TCF/Kent), and *The Towering Inferno* (1974-TCF/Warner), the studio had been equally hopeful of a dreadful calamity called *The Story of Mankind* (1957-Warner/ Cambridge). Thank goodness they gave Mr Allen another chance on this occasion. My family and I, along with millions of others, think 'Inferno' and 'Poseiden' are great.

Sequels: *The Magnificent Seven* (1960-UA/Mirisch), *Airport* (1970-Universal/Ross Hunter), and *Planet of the Apes* (1968- TCF/Apjac), are just a sniff of the hundreds of good movies which have spawned indifferent, and in many cases, downright bad sequels. The people at the top seem to think that because they've had a hit with an original, they're bound to make millions with follow-ons. But these nearly always make less and less money, and they certainly get worse and worse, as they go on down the line: 2, 3, 4. Even Irwin Allen couldn't resist making *Beyond the Poseiden Adventure* (1979-Warner/ Irwin Allen). Oh dear, oh dear! The first Navarone picture, *The Guns of Navarone* (1961-Columbia/Carl Foreman), was far better, and has made much more money than the second. (In spite of the fact that *Force 10 from Navarone* (1978-Columbia/AIP/Guy Hamilton) isn't at all bad, and had the added attraction of me!) But the producers, the ones supposedly in the know, thought that all these sequels would be sure-fire resounding hits.

Prequels: *Butch Cassidy and the Sundance Kid* (1969-TCF/ Campanile), was stupendous, but why did they have to make *Butch and Sundance: The Early Years* (1979-TCF)? Easy, because they wanted to capitalise on the phenomenal success of the original.

Remakes: I'm a fan, and I enjoyed Audie Murphy's *Destry* (1954-Universal International), but it wasn't a patch on Jimmy Stewart's original, *Destry Rides Again* (1939-Universal). There are hundreds of remake examples.

But I must be fair. Sometimes, very seldom it has to be said, remakes, sequels, and the others are indeed very superior products, but, somehow dammit, they still mis-hit. The remake *All Quiet on the Western Front* (1979-MTV) is an excellent example. I've already said that it can stand very well on its own. It's a damn good picture, but it hasn't taken that much money. I believe it has just about made back its costs, and it should have made millions in most people's opinion, mine very much included. But it hasn't, and the original *All Quiet on the Western Front* (1930-Universal) still stands majestically supreme. At the end of the day, it has to be said, perhaps one version was enough.

I said earlier that the list of sure-fire-hit flops is endless. I also said that it is you, the cinema-going public, you, the viewer, who decide what will and will not suffice. I must now add that you do it brilliantly ('All Quiet' excepted!) You do not allow the film chiefs to pull the wool over your eyes, and get away with a half-baked 'The Magnificent Poseiden Planet - Number Two Hundred and Two', or whatever. You would rather, by your patronage, turn a very low budgeter like *Four Weddings and a Funeral* (1994-Working Title) into a huge hit. And that's wonderful, just as it should be.

I must mention two more films which I think really explain why every film maker should take very great care. Today's sure-fire hit can so easily shoot you in the foot tomorrow.

Shortly after I made the great *England Made Me* (1972-Hemdale/Atlantic), with dear Peter Finch, and my old chum Michael York, and not long before I made *The Riddle of the Sands* (1978-Rank/Worldmark) with Michael, Peter and Michael had made a new version of *Lost Horizon* (1973-Columbia/Ross Hunter) together. It cost the earth and lost over half its budget. And songs had been added this time round!

And not long before I shot Omar Sharif in *Green Ice* (1981-ITC/Lew Grade), a film which I've admitted did not really succeed, even as an original, Omar had made a moderately expensive movie called *Che!* (1969-TCF), with the lovely Jack Palance as Fidel Castro. This movie lost very heavily indeed and has never made back even its modest costs. (*Green Ice*, incidentally, continues to claw back its budget, and is now about into profit. Please do see it, it's far more than half good!)

What power you lot do have. I've given examples of the many hundreds of hugely over-financed movies to which you gave the thumbs down, and there are equally as many examples of films which you have voted hits, in spite of the fact that they were made on a shoestring budget and you've never heard of the cast or the director. It was even you who discovered Stephen Spielberg. When Stephen came up with his first offering, *Duel* (1971-MTV), which cost next to nothing, you, the audience, thought it was great and quite rightly demanded more.

We lot would be most grateful if someone, somewhere, could tell us how you lot decide what makes a film a hit, or even a moderate success. And what category of film will be next in vogue. Swashbuckler, Comedy, Drama, or Musical; Epic, Western, War, or whatever, it makes no difference. Just let us know.

No, wait a bitty, I've got a much better idea. Rather, let me know. Then I'll go out into this palace of dreams where I work, and make a thumping ginourmous fortune!

EPILOGUE III

In an interview a short time ago I was asked to name my twelve favourite feature films and I found that I couldn't. I couldn't manage fewer than thirteen.

I'm delighted to say that I can still view movies with the same degree of innocent excitement as did that little boy in Aberdeen, all those years ago. I don't have to look for the technical things, and I don't need to be critical. I have a library of over 400 films at home, and when I go to the pictures, either out to a cinema, or sitting in my armchair, I am still as gob-smacked now by the wonder of it all as I was then...Ah! Anyway, it has been suggested, by a certain Dearly B., that you might just be interested to see my baker's dozen. It's a very personal list of course and all the films won't be to everyone's taste. But I can certainly assure you of one thing, each and every one is jam-packed full of entertainment.

So, in no particular order, here goes:

The Wooden Horse (1950-British Lion/Wessex/London Films). This just had to be included. But apart from the fact that it started me off, it is a wonderfully exciting story in its own right. And it doesn't stop when they get out of the prison camp, so we don't feel cheated. We follow our heroes all the way to freedom.

Shane (1953-Paramount). I've also talked about this one already. It really has all the ingredients, and is everything a Western should be. The Stranger, the Homesteaders, the Goodies, and the Baddies. It all works perfectly. And what an impact Walter (Jack) Palance makes in only his third film role.

Reach for the Sky (1956-Rank/Pinnacle). Douglas Bader's life story was an extraordinary one, and this film certainly does justice to it. I've said previously that we should all thank Richard Burton for turning the part down, and giving Kenneth More the opportunity of a lifetime. The film is also jam-packed with some of the very best British character actors. And one-liner performances like, 'What's your name, mate - Death?' add hugely to the enjoyment. Dearly B. and I keep seeing this particular actorbum giving super cameos in other films of the period, but he never seems to get a credit. Can anybody help? At present he's affectionately called 'What's your name, mate' in our household.

The Third Man (1949-British Lion/London Films/David O. Selznick/Alexander Korda). The moment that zither starts playing over the opening credits, I snuggle down in my armchair knowing that I am going to enjoy, for the umpteenth time, one of the finest, most atmospheric films of its kind ever made. Everything is perfect. Including the dog which is carried by the man who is explaining how Harry Lime died. That little dog is under the man's left arm in one shot, and under his right arm in the next. But this bit of glaringly duff continuity is actually quite sweet, because it's so obvious. It certainly doesn't detract one jot from the rest of the film's sheer brilliance.

Singin' in the Rain (1952-MGM). What can I say about a film that was made very quickly, by 1950's Hollywood standards, and became the classic musical of all time? Perhaps I could put in a word of praise for the lady who is often forgotten, but who gives a performance at least the equal of Kelly, Reynolds, and O'Connor. Jean Hagen plays the silent film star excellently. Milk of course was used for the big Kelly number, 'Singin' in the Rain', because the camera couldn't register water.

The Adventures of Robin Hood (1938-Warner Brothers). This one was made before the last war, and before even I was born, but it still shines as brightly today as it did when it was first released. It has everything, and a cast of bums the like of which we'll never see again. A young and dashing Errol Flynn; a young and extremely beautiful Olivia de Haviland; and a superb Basil Rathbone. With Alan Hale as Little John, and Claude Rains almost stealing the whole blooming thing as the Prince...Magic. The magnificent sword fight between Errol Flynn and Rathbone is one of the longest ever.

The Story of Robin Hood and His Merry Men (1952-Walt Disney). Gentler than the above, and has some lovely music. Richard Todd makes a great Robin, and he's backed by a splendid cast of British grown actorbums, including Peter Finch (yes I do know! Peter was born in England, and only went to Australia as a lad and spent his childhood there), James Hayter, James R. Justice, Bill Owen, and Hubert Gregg as Prince John this time, again almost stealing the piece - it's a good part is John! There's also a sweet performance of Maid Marion, given by an ex-waitress called Joan Rice. Joan never did anything else of note, but her inclusion here is sublime. Made by Disney in England, this film is perhaps not as well thought of as the Errol Flynn version, but if I had to choose between Todd and Flynn it would be very difficult. But, perhaps because it was playing at the Swiss Cottage Odeon when I was at RADA, and it meant a lot to me and my maid of that time, I would stay with Richard Todd.

The Jolson Story (1946-Columbia). 'Let me sing a happy song, with crazy words that roll along.' Complete and utter bliss. I'd like to have cheated and also included *Jolson Sings*

Again (1949-Columbia), but although great, the sequel is not a patch on the original. (Sequels again!) No, I'll settle for 'The Jolson Story'. And how! Everything, from Larry Parks down is completely fantastic. Larry was a second feature player who was tugged into the big time to play this part, and his miming to the Al Jolson recordings, and his whole darn performance, is so wonderfully full of vitality. This is a movie which is absolutely out of this world.

The Story of Gilbert and Sullivan (1953-British Lion/London Films). Probably the most flawed of my choices. But Robert Morley et al. are in great form, and if, like me, you are a lover of G & S, then this film is a must. There is masses of music, and the super D'Oyly Carte company sing and perform it beautifully.

The Quiet Man (1952-Republic/Argosy). Even a director with the reputation of John Ford found it difficult to get the money to turn Maurice Walsh's short story, about a boxer coming home to Ireland, into a film. But in the end the studio relented, more in recognition of Ford's past triumphs than with any real hope of seeing their money back. He went to Ireland, taking John Wayne, Maureen O'Hara, Victor McLaglen and Barry Fitzgerald with him, cast the rest of the movie from the Abbey Players in Dublin, and made a masterpiece which is still making money today. And he picked up his third Oscar as Best Director in the process.

The Black Shield of Falworth (1954-Universal International). In days of old, when knights were bold, and good always triumphed over evil. Or if the baddie was not quite all bad, then he was allowed to slink away, never to be heard of again. This is a wonderful film from that era. Universal had a knack of discovering new talent and this time they were in the process of consolidating a new gold mine they'd found - Tony Curtis. Playing opposite him was his wife of the time, the scrumptious

Janet Leigh. The whole cast give wonderfully vibrant performances and quite obviously enjoyed themselves tremendously. (I've been trying for ages to obtain a copy of another Tony Curtis actioner. It was made a little earlier than the above, co-starred the lovely Piper Laurie, and was called *The Prince who was a Thief* (1951-Universal International). Any help very gratefully received.)

Genevieve (1953-GFD/Sirius). A nice, cosy, homespun, very British comedy. As with the zither at the opening of 'The Third Man', the moment Larry Adler starts playing: 'Da, da. Di - da, da. Di - da, da. Di - da. Da...DA - dada da da da diddli di da', I know I'm in for a film the like of which cannot be made anywhere else in the world. It's deliciously full of cream, with a good spoon and a half of sugar. All the performances - John Gregson and Dinah Sheriden; Kenny More and Kay Kendall; Geoffrey Keen; Joyce Grenfell; Reginald Beckwith; Arthur Wontner - are spot on. I still shout with joy when the tyre on Kenny's vintage car gets stuck in the tram line and he loses the race.

Side by Side (A/K Productions/Jon Avnet/Jordan Kerner). This is not even the (awful) film of the same name made in 1982, so why have I chosen to include in my thirteen a long-forgotten TV film, made only a few years ago, about three old men who start their own clothing business? Because I consider it to be unique and perfect. The three oldies are played by septuagenarians, Milton Berle, Sid Caesar, and Danny Thomas, all very big stars in their day. Which also goes to prove the point that, like old soldiers, actorbums never die - I'm delighted to say!

Sorry! I know that's my thirteen, but I've just got to sneak in a couple of others:

Come Next Spring (1955-Republic), a very small budget western with two ex-starbums, Ann Sheridan and Steve Cochran, in the leading roles. I think in fact it was the last movie either of them made. It's a nice, kind film, full of gentle charm.

A Chorus Line (1985-Embassy/Polygram), which, though somewhat house-bound, is nevertheless full of everything my business is about.

And Dearly Beloved has commanded that I include one film in which I appear, making my list a baker's dozen plus three! The choice is virtually impossible, but...I have to plump for *Escape to Athena* (1979-ITC/Pimlico).

I'd like to go straight on to the next reel, but that must wait because it hasn't happened yet.

(I already have the cover of my next book in mind. It will be a mirror photo - my back to the camera, my face in the glass - and the book will be titled *Bronson's Back*!)

This is THE END

Except...for a POSTSCRIPT!

It is now March 1997. Anthony Mingella - who was born on the Isle of Wight, by the way, and who was in fact the script editor on 'GH' when I first started - has just won Oscars galore for his excellent film *The English Patient*, I'm very delighted to say; there's going to be a general election soon; and I have just been to a very special premiere!

And my publishers have allowed me to add a few lines about that night, even at this eleventh hour. I simply had to. I want to try and encapsulate in a nutshell what a wonderful, lovely business I'm in, and how it is truly you who can make those tip-top, never-to-be-forgotten moments for a bum like me.

A couple of months ago I had a phone call from 20th Century Fox. 'Mr Sheard? George Lucas would like to invite you to the Royal Charity Premiere of the new Special

Edition *Star Wars*, and to the party afterwards. Would you be free?' Would I!

'If necessary, I'll fly back from wherever I am.'

'Splendid. I'll send off the invitation then.'

So it was that last week, Thursday 20th of March to be exact, Dearly Beloved and I arrived at Leicester Square, on our way to the Odeon Cinema. And we couldn't even get into the flippin' square, let alone the cinema! At least we couldn't until an extremely burly security guard spotted me and said,

'Hey, it's you, isn't it?'

And I thought it best simply to say yes, so I did.

'Yes, course it is,' he said, 'I'd know Mr Bronson anywhere. You can come in. Down the shoot. You're an Honoured, you're on the List. We've got to be awful careful, what with His Royal Highness The Prince of Wales coming, an' all.'

I've been to premieres and private screenings many times before, but this was different. There were literally thousands and thousands and thousands in the crowd. And they weren't only there to see the Bonnie Prince; he wasn't due for nearly an hour. The thousands and thousands were also there because of a phenomenon that was twenty years old - *Star Wars*.

I couldn't believe it to be perfectly honest. I tried to be nonchalant of course, but it wasn't easy. Particularly when Dearly B. and I had started to walk down between the police barriers, 'down the shoot', towards the cinema. This is how it went.

First there was a murmur. 'Who's that?', 'Is he somebody?' Then there was a shout. 'Hey, it's Admiral Ozzel!', 'It's Michael Sheard', 'MR BRONSON!' Then all hell - in the very nicest possible way - broke loose. The chant that burst forth was all but deafening, 'Mr Bronson, Mr Bronson, Mr Bronson, MR BRONSON!'

Dearly Beloved, who was still at my side, metaphorically supporting me as she always has, said in my ear, 'Now do you believe that you're a star?' I said something like, 'I'm still only a bum. But I do have to admit that this is kind of wonderful,' and outside the entrance to the Odeon Cinema, Leicester Square, I turned and thanked them in the only way I could because of the noise; I bowed and waved and clasped my hands together above my head.

I was completely and utterly gobsmacked. It was quite the most stupendously spontaneous thing that has ever happened to me. And, I'm perfectly happy to admit, there was a (butch) tear in my eye.

Then we went inside. We'd all been requested to take our seats promptly in order not to cause congestion in the foyer, so Dearly B. and I went straight upstairs to the dress circle, which had been reserved for us by George, and before long we were sat, some ten rows from the front, and I was saying 'hello' to friends made twenty years ago.

After no time at all - about fifty minutes in fact - we all stood, and the Heir to the Throne came up the stairs and made his way to his seat at the front. We're not quite sure, but we think he had his eldest son with him. And why not! Our eldest son would have loved to have been there. But in spite of the fact that this premiere was in aid of the Prince's Trust, and our eldest (Simon, of course) is the Prince's Youth Business Trust's Chief Accountant, he was too late. He couldn't get a ticket...ah!

The lights dimmed, there was a small scuffle at the side of the stage, and a nice looking man with a beard came on.

Private Screenings, for us bums and the crew, are always, and very justifiably, vocal. We cheer everything. Every actor on the screen, every credit, and certainly everyone who appears on stage. And quite right too. We've done the work, now is our chance to congratulate our chums, and ourselves. But the roar that greeted George Lucas was so enormous that I'm sure he was just a wee bit dumbstruck, and for a moment found it hard to collect his thoughts and make his welcoming speech to the Prince and us. George has done so much for so many in the business. It was a super, wonderful moment and I'm delighted I was there to be part of it.

Finally the lights went down, the curtains opened and those immortal words appeared on the screen: *A long time ago in a galaxy far, far away...*

Apart from reporting that every time an actor made his or her first entrance, we who were upstairs cheered, shouted and whistled our appreciation, I'm not going to say anything about the wonderful, new re-vamped *Star Wars*. Except that it is...out of this world! Go and see it for yourselves. And see the sequels. I'm in *The Empire Strikes Back* and I die beautifully!

I would like, though, to take you on to the party afterwards. That was even more gobsmacking for this gobsmacked bum.

We left the Odeon at about 10.30pm and walked, those of us who were fortunate enough to be going, to the other side of the square. Or rather shunted, the crowds were as huge as ever, but this time there was the crush of the emptying cinema to contend with as well. No one was concerned, it just took a little longer. We all happily made our way to Panton Street, where relays of coaches bussed us round to Olympia.

We arrived at something like 11.10pm, but it was a further forty minutes before Dearly B. and I actually got inside. This time the crowd barriers were much closer, and the moment I left the coach the cry 'Michael - can I have your autograph?' threatened almost to send Olympia into orbit! How they knew I was going to be there I don't know, perhaps they come prepared for anything, but they all seemed to have pictures of me to sign, and as before in Leicester Square, as often as not I was thanked personally, by name, which was particularly super.

This was Thursday of course, almost Friday. Two short days previously I had attended the London International Book Fair as a guest of my publishers, to promote a little something I'd written about myself which was on the point of being published! The Book Fair had also been held at Olympia and had been crammed with hundreds of cubicles, all over the place, and thousands of people. In the very few hours since the Fair had closed, on the Tuesday evening, the vastness of the Grand Hall had been transformed into the most stupendous party venue. It had a stage at one end with a huge cycloramic backdrop depicting a moon-type mountain range, and in front, a gigantic balloon was suspended from the ceiling with the *Star Wars* logo emblazoned across it. There was a large dance area, several circular bars and an endless stream of lasses and chaps, who continuously circulated with trays of eating goodies of every shape and description, courtesy of *Planet Hollywood*. One of the barmen, who did an excellent impression of Tom Cruise in the movie *Cocktail*, juggling bottles and ice and pouring lashings of drink from a great height, recognised me the moment I approached.

'Ah, Mr Bronson. What can I get for you, Sir?' From then on, until we left, all I had to do was catch his eye, raise a finger, and no matter how crowded the bar was, a new tipple of my choice - Scotch of course, well I am an Aberdonian! - would appear.

Ah me, I could fill another book describing that night. The people who just wanted 'to shake your hand and thank you.' George; Ken Colley; Irene Lamb, remember her? Mark Hamill was there too. All the old friends. And the fans who were still waiting when we left at something like 2.45am, one in particular, Nick Mattocks, who said he knew my postman, Pete! Even the taxi driver who took us home.

I'm particularly delighted, I'm sure we all are, that the evening made over £180,000 for The Prince's Trust. I know this because the Youth Business Trust's Chief Accountant, my son Simon, asked his PR department.

I'm proud of my sons and my daughter and my Dearly B. And I'm proud to bursting, and also very humbled, that I was given such a warm welcome by you all on Thursday March 20th. It really does make it all worthwhile.

Thank you very, very much.

And that definitely is The End...for now!